I0810554

The Campus History Series

BALL STATE UNIVERSITY

On the Cover: On February 8, 1965, with the signing of House Bill 1014, Ball State Teachers College became Ball State University. Here, a group of students celebrates this momentous day in the institution's history, changing the lettering on the Ball State sign on the Administration Building lawn to reflect the institution's new university status. (Courtesy of Ball State University.)

Cover Background: Ball State University Summer Commencement on the Arts Terrace, August 1968. (Courtesy of Ball State University.)

The Campus History Series

BALL STATE UNIVERSITY

E. BRUCE GEELHOED, MICHAEL G. SZAJEWSKI,
AND BRANDON T. PIECZKO
FOREWORD BY GEOFFREY S. MEARNS

ARCADIA
PUBLISHING

ISBN 978-978-1-4671-2790-5

Published by Arcadia Publishing
Charleston, South Carolina

Printed in the United States of America

Library of Congress Control Number: 2017945932

For all general information, please contact Arcadia Publishing:
Telephone 843-853-2070
Fax 843-853-0044
E-mail sales@arcadiapublishing.com
For customer service and orders:
Toll-Free 1-888-313-2665

Visit us on the Internet at www.arcadiapublishing.com

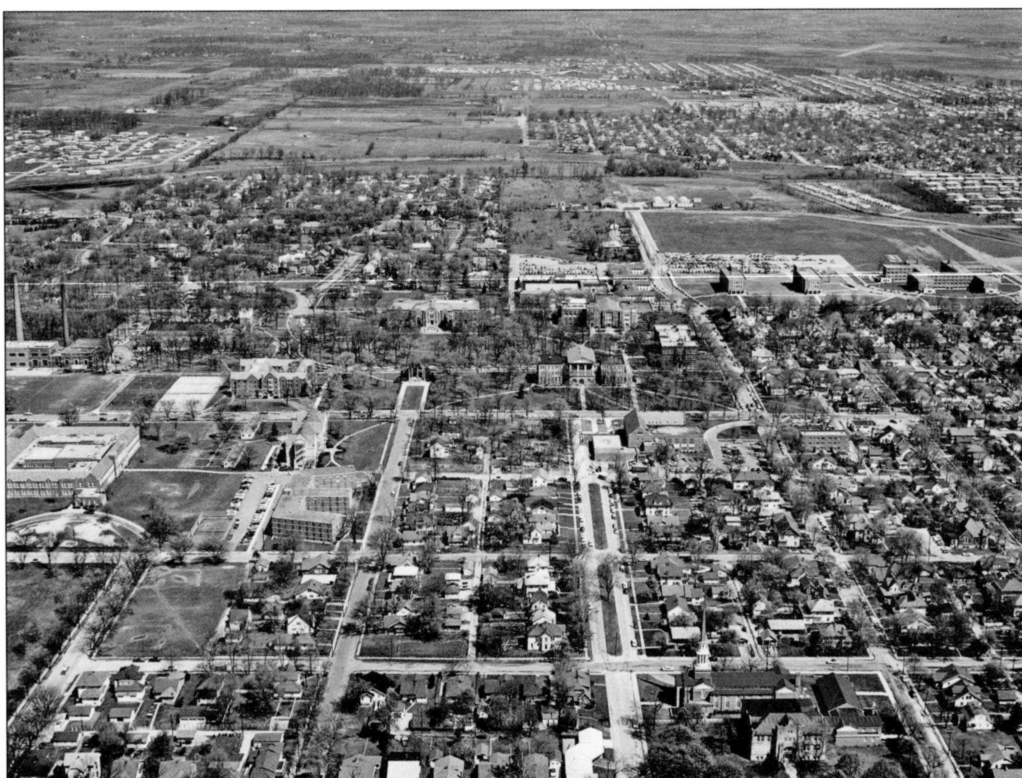

This c. 1958–1959 aerial view shows the Ball State campus and surrounding areas. (Courtesy of Ball State University.)

Contents

FOREWORD

Beneficence is a fitting symbol for Ball State University. The iconic statue's name signifies the importance of performing acts of kindness and charity. She symbolizes sharing the treasure of knowledge and the value of service.

In 1899, community leaders recognized the need for more and better teachers, but four attempts to start a teachers college in Muncie failed. Undaunted, the Ball brothers had the vision to buy the property in 1917, and they gave it to the State of Indiana. The first class started here in the fall of 1918.

In the ensuing decades, our name has changed, and we have grown and adapted to the needs of society. In 1965, the General Assembly recognized our successes and increasing role in the state, so legislators renamed our institution Ball State University.

We have and will continue to meet the needs of the state, the nation, and the world. Two examples include our new College of Health and the Health Professions Building, which is under construction, and a new science building to meet the demands in the STEM fields.

Technology and society will evolve. But two aspects of our university will remain constant. Our values, as articulated in the Beneficence Pledge, will endure. We are committed to academic excellence, honesty and integrity, social responsibility, and inclusion. And at Ball State, education is still about the partnership between experienced teachers and bright, inquisitive students.

The Ball brothers' beneficence transformed two campus buildings into a successful college that grew into a comprehensive university. Over our history, faculty and staff have transformed the lives of about 200,000 women and men. Our accomplished alumni are leaders in their professions and their communities.

As you will see in these pages, we have a proud past. As we enter our second century, we are well positioned to thrive. The best is yet to come.

—Geoffrey S. Mearns
President

ACKNOWLEDGMENTS

The authors wish to acknowledge the invaluable contributions of numerous persons whose work and support were critical to the completion of this book. Much gratitude is owed to Ball State University's administration, including Pres. Geoffrey Mearns, the Office of the President, and the President's Centennial Committee; University Libraries' Dean's Office; Office of the Provost; and the Department of History, whose support was essential in the publication of this work. Special thanks must be given as well to University Marketing and Communications, who supplied photographic content for Chapter 6 and whose leadership and input were critical to the successful design and planning of the book.

Many thanks are also owed to the staff of Ball State University Libraries, including Archives and Special Collections, Metadata and Digital Initiatives, and Library Information Technology Services, whose tireless work in digitizing, describing, and publishing a digital archive of historic Ball State University Archives photographs provided an immense wealth of source material for Chapters 1 through 5. Great credit is also owed to the many photographers who captured these critical moments in Ball State's history with creativity, vigilance, and dedication.

Lastly, a sincere thanks to all members of the Ball State University community—students, faculty, staff, alumni, donors, and friends—for enjoying this book, for contributing to Ball State's vast and diverse successes, and for building a foundation for greater achievements to come in Ball State's next 100 years.

All images featured in the work are courtesy of Ball State University.

Introduction

Ball State University, in Muncie, Indiana, celebrates its centennial anniversary in the 2018–2019 academic year. As an institution of higher education, Ball State has a unique and even unusual history. It opened its doors as a public, state-assisted teachers college in 1918, not as a separate, independent public institution but rather as the Eastern Division of the Indiana State Normal School in Terre Haute. It was the first such branch campus in Indiana and perhaps one of the first of its kind anywhere in the United States. In 1922, in recognition of the major role played by members of the Ball family, primarily three brothers—Frank C. Ball, Edmund B. Ball, and George A. Ball—in the establishment and early financial support of the school, the Indiana General Assembly renamed the Eastern Division "Ball Teachers College" even as it still remained a branch of Indiana State. In 1929, one decade after its founding, Ball Teachers College obtained its independence from Indiana State and became Ball State Teachers College. In 1965, Ball State achieved university status to become Ball State University. To this day, Ball State remains one of the few public universities in the United States that carries the name of a private family as its primary identity.

Higher education in Muncie began well before 1918–1919. The effort to establish a college in Muncie was initially the project of three local entrepreneurs: George N. Higman, the president of the Mutual Home and Savings Association; George McCulloch, the editor of the *Muncie Morning Star* and a man with a host of local business ventures; and Frank Haimbaugh, the editor of the *Muncie Herald* and one of the city's most enthusiastic boosters and promoters. Higman, McCulloch, and Haimbaugh wanted to create what was, in effect, a "new" Muncie, built across the White River to the north and west in an area that was to become known as Normal City. In their view, the residents of Normal City were to be part of what the sociologists Robert and Helen Lynd later described in their best-seller, *Middletown: A Study in Modern American Culture* (1929), as the "business class," to differentiate it from the homes and neighborhoods of Muncie's "working class" on the city's industrialized south side. Higman, McCulloch, Haimbaugh, and other local investors purchased large tracts of land and formed the Eastern Indiana Normal University Association (EINUA) to be divided into plots for sale to potential home owners. In the midst of Normal City was to be a proprietary normal school, or teacher training school, that was to provide a gracious setting for the neighborhoods that the businessmen expected to develop in the vicinity.

Between 1899 and 1917, the investors attempted on four separate occasions to establish a normal college in Muncie. All of these attempts failed: Eastern Indiana Normal University (1899–1901), Palmer University (1902–1904), Indiana Normal School and College of Applied

Science (1905–1907), and finally the Muncie National Institute (1912–1917). When the assets of the Muncie National Institute went up for sale at a bankruptcy hearing in 1917, Frank C. Ball, his wife, Elizabeth (Bessie), Edmund B. Ball, and his wife, Bertha, purchased the property.

The members of the Ball family had been involved in higher education for a number of years before 1917. They, too, supported the establishment of a thriving college in Muncie but wished it to be state-assisted on the order of Indiana University in Bloomington, Purdue University in West Lafayette, and Indiana State in Terre Haute. In their effort to establish a state-assisted college in Muncie, the members of the Ball family found an ally in James P. Goodrich, Indiana's governor between 1917 and 1921. Goodrich's hometown was Winchester in nearby Randolph County, and he also supported the creation of a public college in central Indiana. As a matter of expediency, Goodrich was willing to accept the donation of the Ball family's property to the State of Indiana for the purpose of establishing a branch campus of Indiana State. In that rather unique and even unprecedented fashion, state-assisted higher education came to Muncie in 1918.

Looking back from the perspective of a century, it is easy to dismiss the failures of the four private normal schools from 1899 to 1917 as inconsequential to Ball State's larger story. But enduring examples of the importance of these failures do exist. For example, Ball State's longtime Administration Building (now the Frank A. Bracken Administration Building), the oldest structure on campus, was originally constructed in 1899 and continues to be a focal point of the campus, easily recognizable by its iconic yellow-brick exterior. Student life at the normal schools revolved around social clubs, organizations, and even athletic teams that were typical of other colleges. And one must not forget that the initial goal of the normal schools was the training of future teachers, a priority that has long since been eclipsed at Ball State. But the importance of the student-faculty relationship, a hallmark of the teaching training enterprise, has lived on at Ball State well into the 21st century.

Nevertheless, teacher education was a double-edged sword for Ball State University throughout its history. On the one hand, this emphasis gave Ball State a distinctiveness in student-faculty relations that was unique for an institution of its size. On the other hand, it left Ball State in provincial isolation from other regional universities in the Midwest. Ball State Teachers College did not become Ball State University until 1965, well after such institutions as Miami University of Ohio, Bowling Green, Kent State, Akron, Toledo, Ohio University, Northern Illinois, Western Michigan, Central Michigan, and Eastern Michigan had shed their single-purpose emphases and became comprehensive regional universities.

To their credit, Ball State's senior leadership and members of its board of trustees recognized this problem of isolation from the academic mainstream that presented itself once the school reached university status. In 1973, Ball State took a momentous and bold step forward when it gained admission to the Mid-American Conference (MAC), an athletic conference comprised of the universities previously mentioned. Admission to the MAC did not simply fulfill athletics purposes but also provided Ball State with a place within a collection of comprehensive regional universities, each with a varied menu of curricular offerings and degree programs. Ball State had finally acquired a distinctive identity.

Sensing how the environment was changing, Ball State moved ahead with a vigorous process of academic diversification in the post-1973 period, de-emphasizing teacher education and developing new programs in different areas of the curriculum. In the 1970s came the development of a strong program in the field of management studies in the College of Business (later the Miller College of Business); in the 1980s, a new initiative in information, communication, and computer science; and in the 1990s, new programs in the fields of allied health. After 2000, the university developed new programs in emerging media and revitalized traditional programs in the liberal arts, such as criminal justice and creative writing. Ball State's physical landscape also changed dramatically as new buildings were constructed to accommodate these academic initiatives.

Throughout all of this rather dizzying set of changes, however, Ball State never abandoned its emphasis on the importance of the student-faculty relationship. With this in mind, the purpose of this study is to highlight the student-faculty experience at Ball State University as it has unfolded over the years. Largely in visual form, we will show how students and faculty came to thrive at Ball State and helped to form the distinctive identity that has prevailed on campus for more than a century.

One

The Founding of the Normal School 1899–1917

Ball State University traces its origins to the normal school movement, which was especially prevalent in Indiana between 1875 and 1900. A normal school was a privately supported teacher training school that prepared its graduates for careers in Indiana's rapidly growing public schools. By 1900, there were 8,200 students enrolled in 11 proprietary normal schools throughout the state, including in Valparaiso, Angola, Danville, Indianapolis, and Marion. In Muncie, three entrepreneurs—George N. Higman, George McCulloch, and Frank Haimbaugh—saw the normal school movement as a means of growing the city. Along with other investors, they formed the Eastern Indiana Normal University Association in the early 1890s and raised sufficient funds to buy property north and west of Muncie, constructed a main campus building, and then opened the Eastern Indiana Normal University (EINU) in September 1899.

The EINU failed within two years due to a lack of students and funding, as did its three successors: Palmer University (1902–1904), Indiana Normal School and College of Applied Science (1905–1907), and the Muncie Normal Institute, later renamed the Muncie National Institute (1912–1917).

In 1917, two brothers, Frank C. Ball and Edmund B. Ball, and their wives, Elizabeth and Bertha, respectively, came to the rescue of higher education in Muncie. Known primarily for the success of their glass-making business, the Ball family nevertheless had a lengthy history of involvement in higher education, including in New York, Pennsylvania, Michigan, and Indiana. They believed that higher education had a future in Muncie.

In 1917, the Ball family members agreed to purchase the assets of the soon-to-be defunct Muncie National Institute. After lengthy negotiations that involved Gov. James P. Goodrich and other political leaders, the Ball family agreed to donate their property to the State of Indiana for the purpose of stablishing a branch campus in Muncie of the Indiana State Normal School (ISNS) at Terre Haute. In that unorthodox fashion, state-assisted higher education began in 1918 in Muncie, where it has now continued, uninterrupted, for a century.

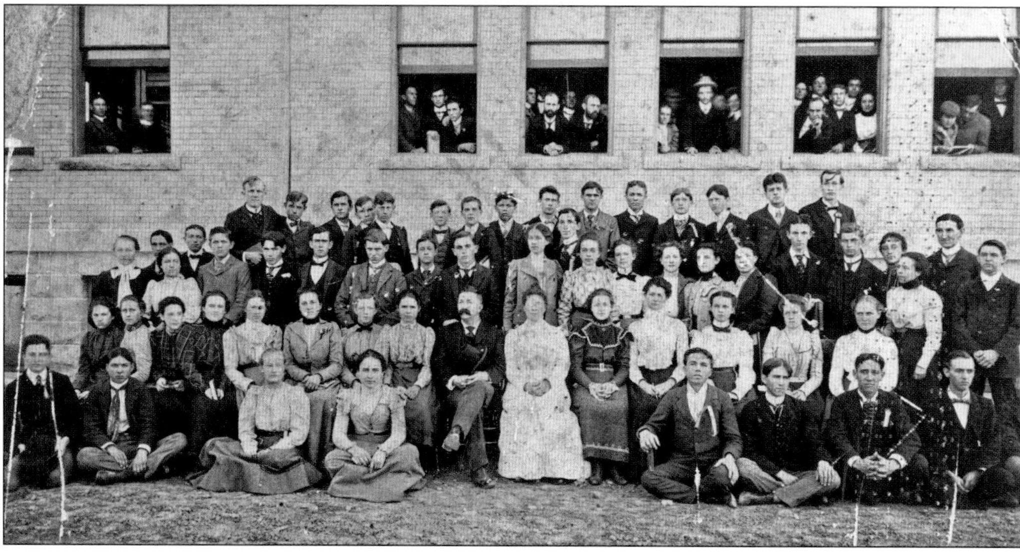

This 1899 photograph shows the first group of students (seated) and members of the faculty (standing near the open windows) in front of the Administration Building of the Eastern Indiana Normal University. Pres. Franklin Abiah Zeller Kumler, wife Mattie B. Kumler, and daughter Margaret Anne Kumler are seated in the second row, ninth through eleventh from the left.

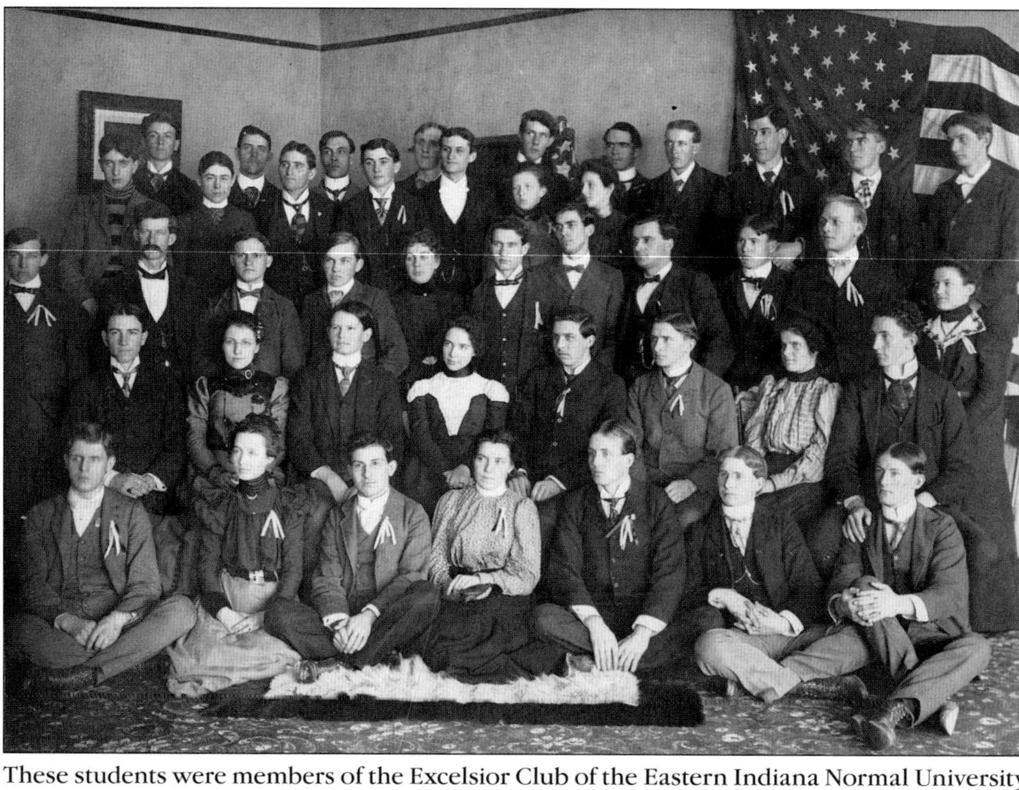

These students were members of the Excelsior Club of the Eastern Indiana Normal University around 1899–1902. Judging by the size of the membership, the Excelsior Club was a thriving student organization on campus.

The Eastern Indiana Normal University fielded a football team in 1899 that included A.E. Deardorff (left) and R.G. Funkhouser (right).

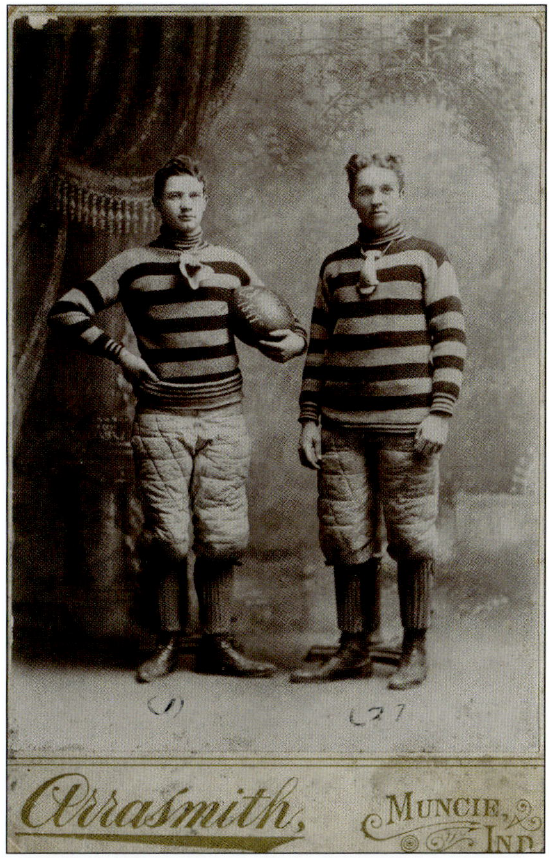

This photograph features the first graduating class of the Eastern Indiana Normal University with President Kumler and his wife, Mattie B. Kumler, in 1900. From left to right are (first row) George W. Hayden, J. Samuel Collier, Joseph W. Gaunt, and M.A. Garrett; (second row) Laura G. Craig, Katie Swain, Ira McKinney, and Ethyl Bowman; (third row) Pres. Franklin Abiah Zeller Kumler, Mattie B. Kumler, and A.E. Deardorff.

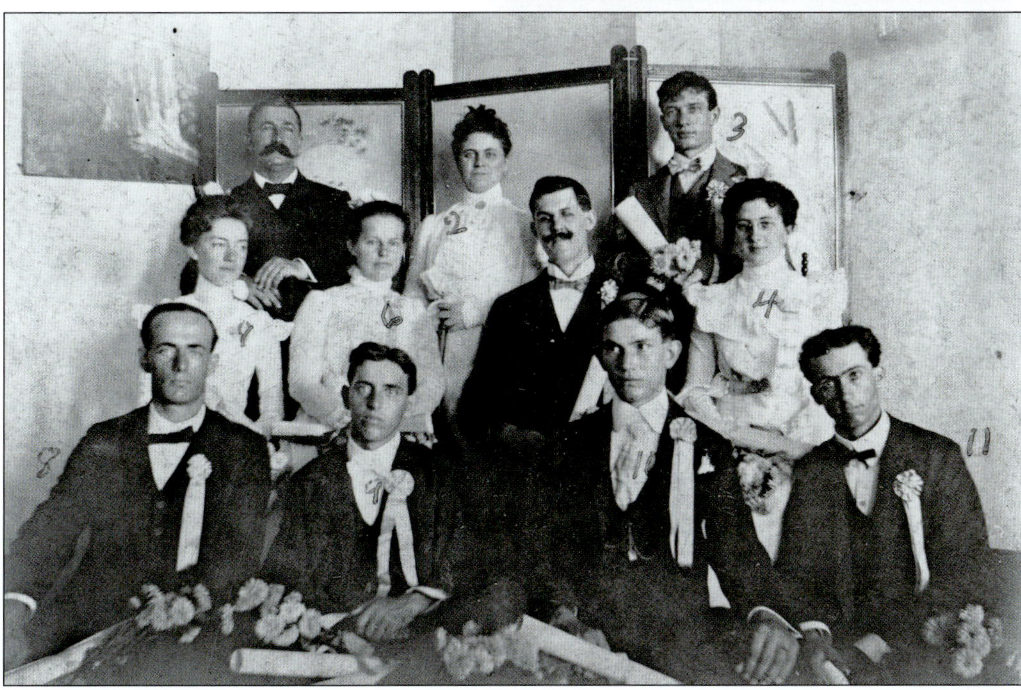

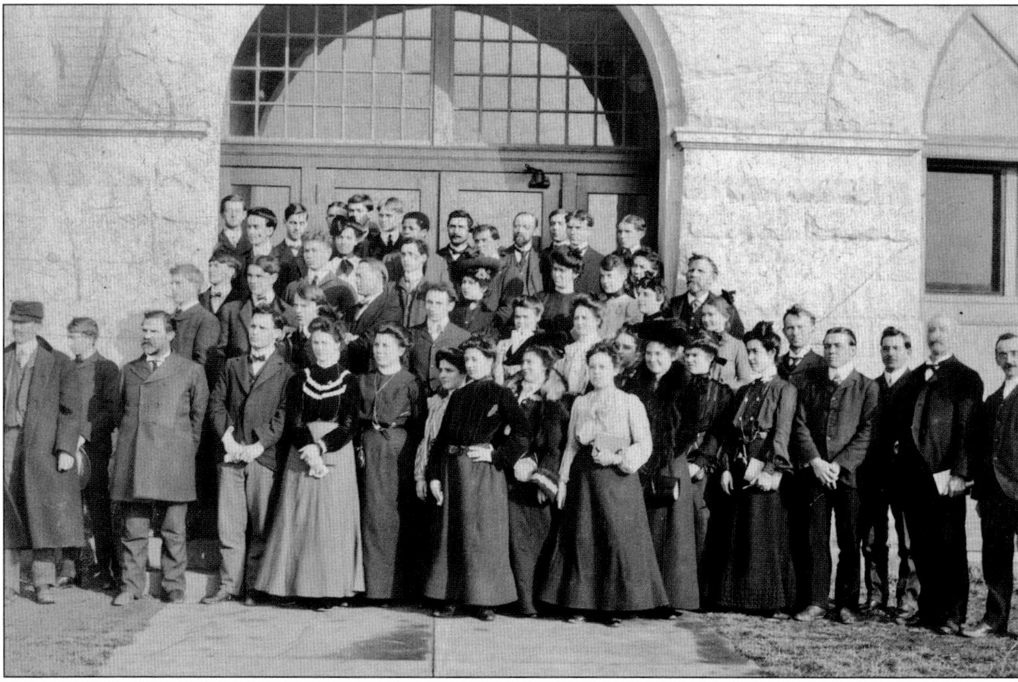

Palmer University was established in 1902 by educators John Latchaw and Thomas McWhinney with financial support from New York philanthropist Francis Asbury Palmer. The university closed in 1904 after Latchaw and McWhinney failed to raise the necessary funds to match Palmer's original $100,000 endowment donation. This 1902 photograph features Palmer University students and faculty assembled in front of the Administration Building.

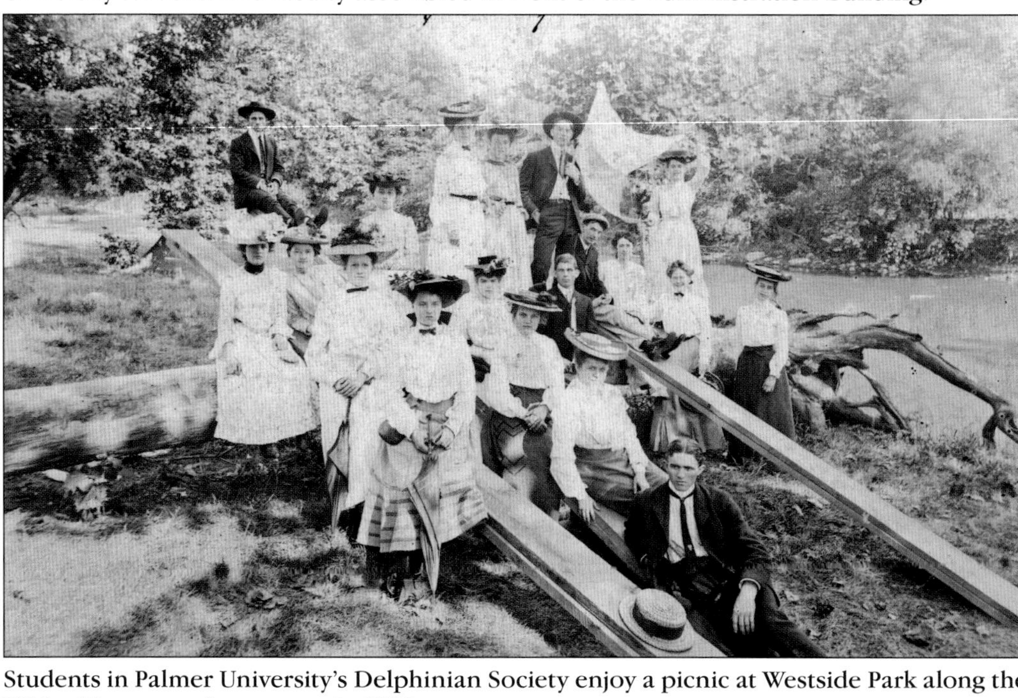

Students in Palmer University's Delphinian Society enjoy a picnic at Westside Park along the White River near the campus in 1903.

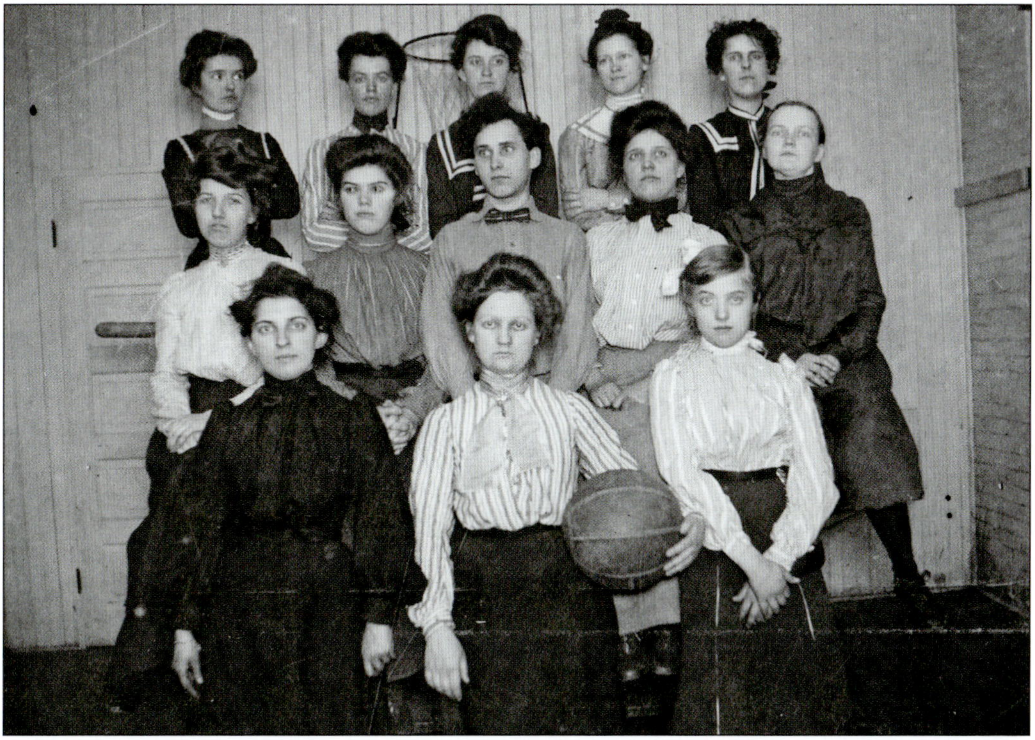

Members of the Palmer University women's basketball team are assembled in this April 7, 1903, group photograph. From left to right are (first row) Winogene Shirey, Nettie Jarrett, and Miss Frazee; (second row) Grace Daniels, Iva Rench, Walter Knothe, Ivy Shirey, and Mae Latchaw; (third row) Nina Blakely, Aura Baxla, Nettie Bartlett, unidentified, and Laura McGee.

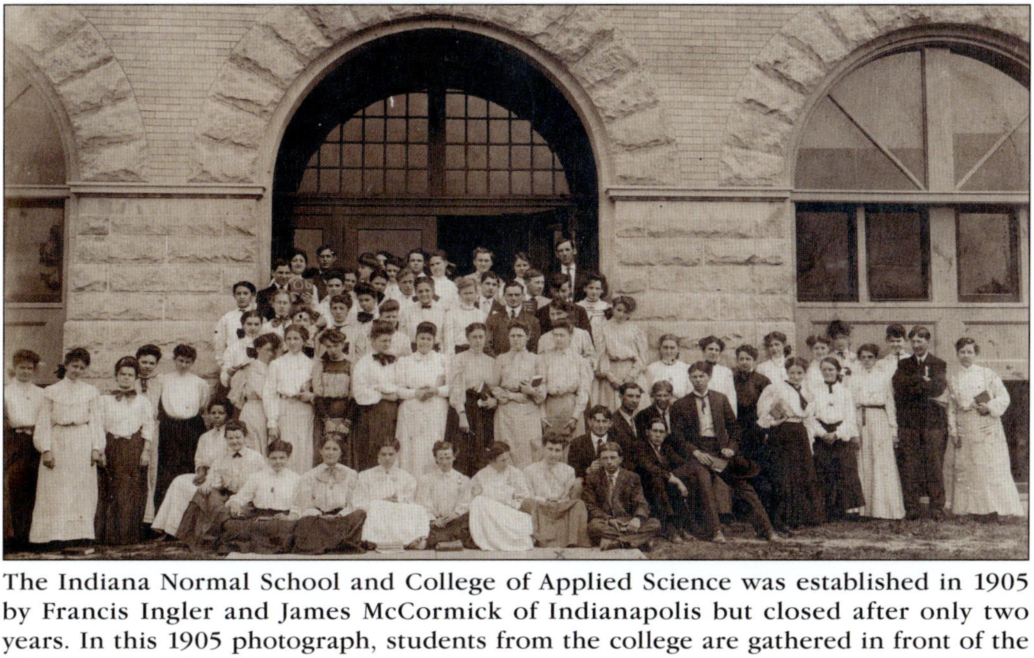

The Indiana Normal School and College of Applied Science was established in 1905 by Francis Ingler and James McCormick of Indianapolis but closed after only two years. In this 1905 photograph, students from the college are gathered in front of the Administration Building.

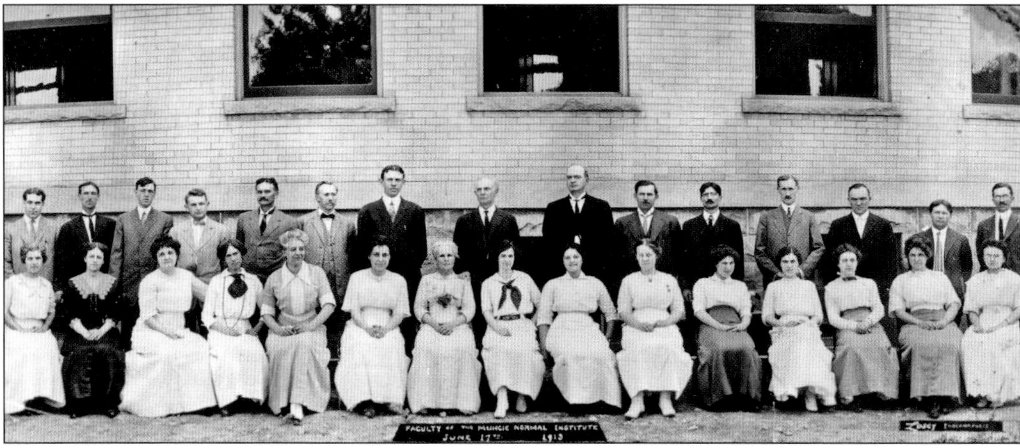

The Muncie Normal Institute was established in 1912 through the efforts of Wisconsin educator Michael D. Kelly in conjunction with the Eastern Indiana Normal University Association. In this photograph taken by Indianapolis photographer North H. Losey on June 17, 1913, faculty of the Muncie Normal Institute are gathered in front of the Administration Building. President Kelly is standing in the second row, ninth from the left.

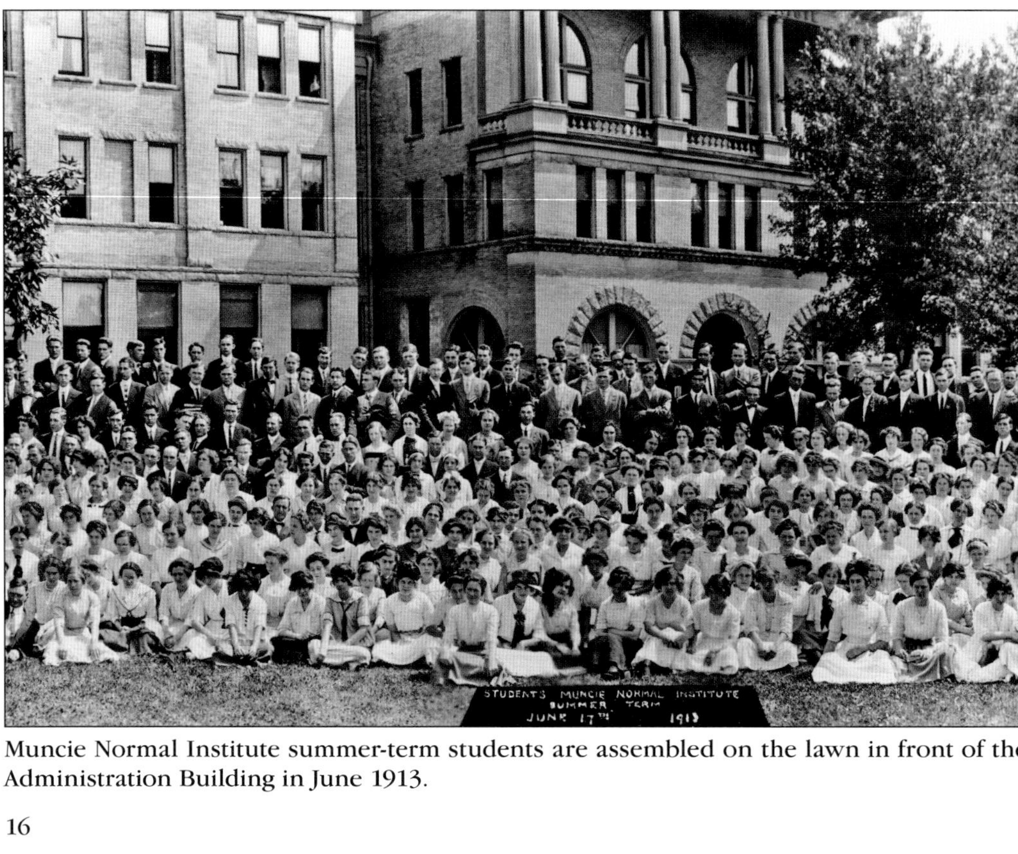

Muncie Normal Institute summer-term students are assembled on the lawn in front of the Administration Building in June 1913.

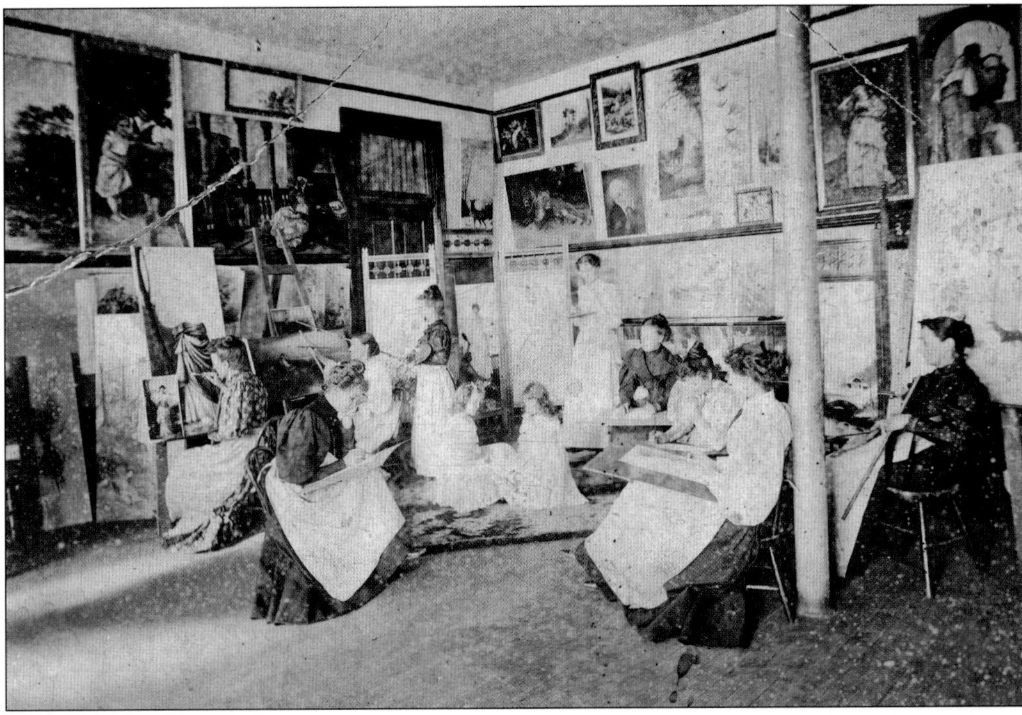

The Muncie Normal Institute was later rebranded as the Muncie National Institute in recognition of financial support the school received from the National Manual Training Corporation. The Muncie National Institute closed on January 27, 1917, due to bankruptcy. Here, students work on their painting during an art class at the Muncie National Institute around 1912–1917.

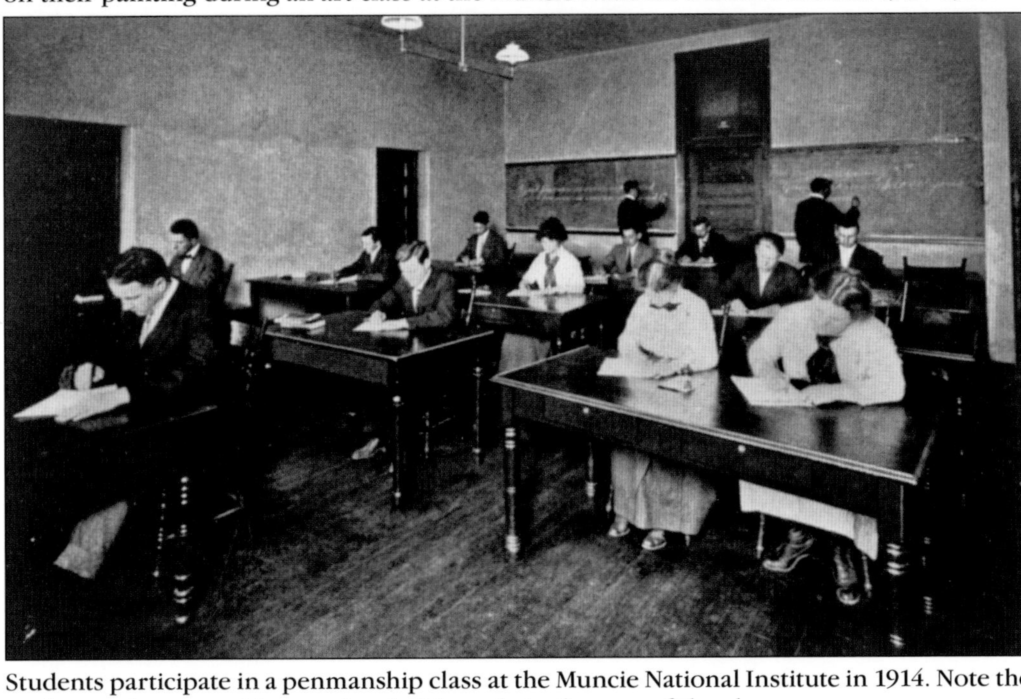

Students participate in a penmanship class at the Muncie National Institute in 1914. Note the students who are writing on the chalkboards in the rear of the classroom.

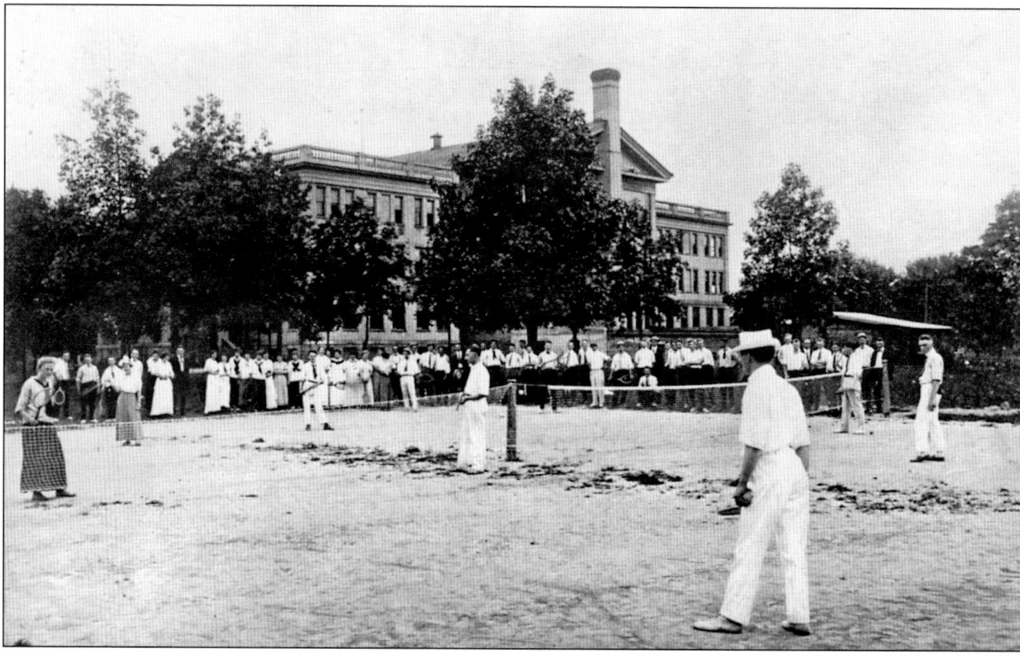

The lawn south of the Administration Building served as a recreation area for students at the Muncie National Institute. This group of students engages in a game of tennis around 1912–1917. Note the large group of spectators gathered to watch the contest.

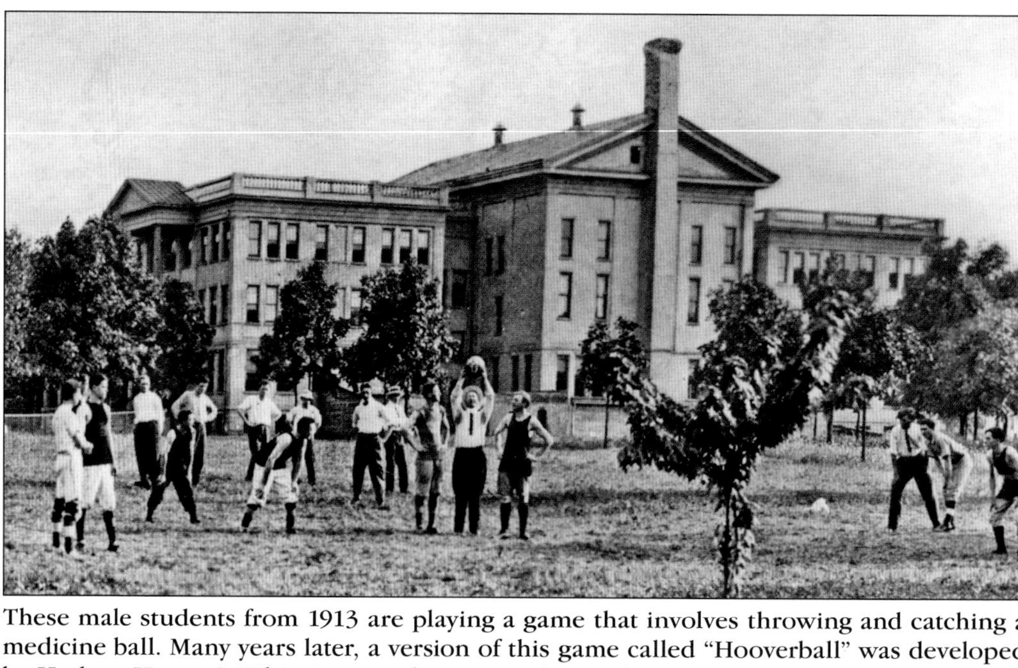

These male students from 1913 are playing a game that involves throwing and catching a medicine ball. Many years later, a version of this game called "Hooverball" was developed by Herbert Hoover's White House physician, Adm. Joel T. Boone, as a method of physical conditioning and fitness for the president.

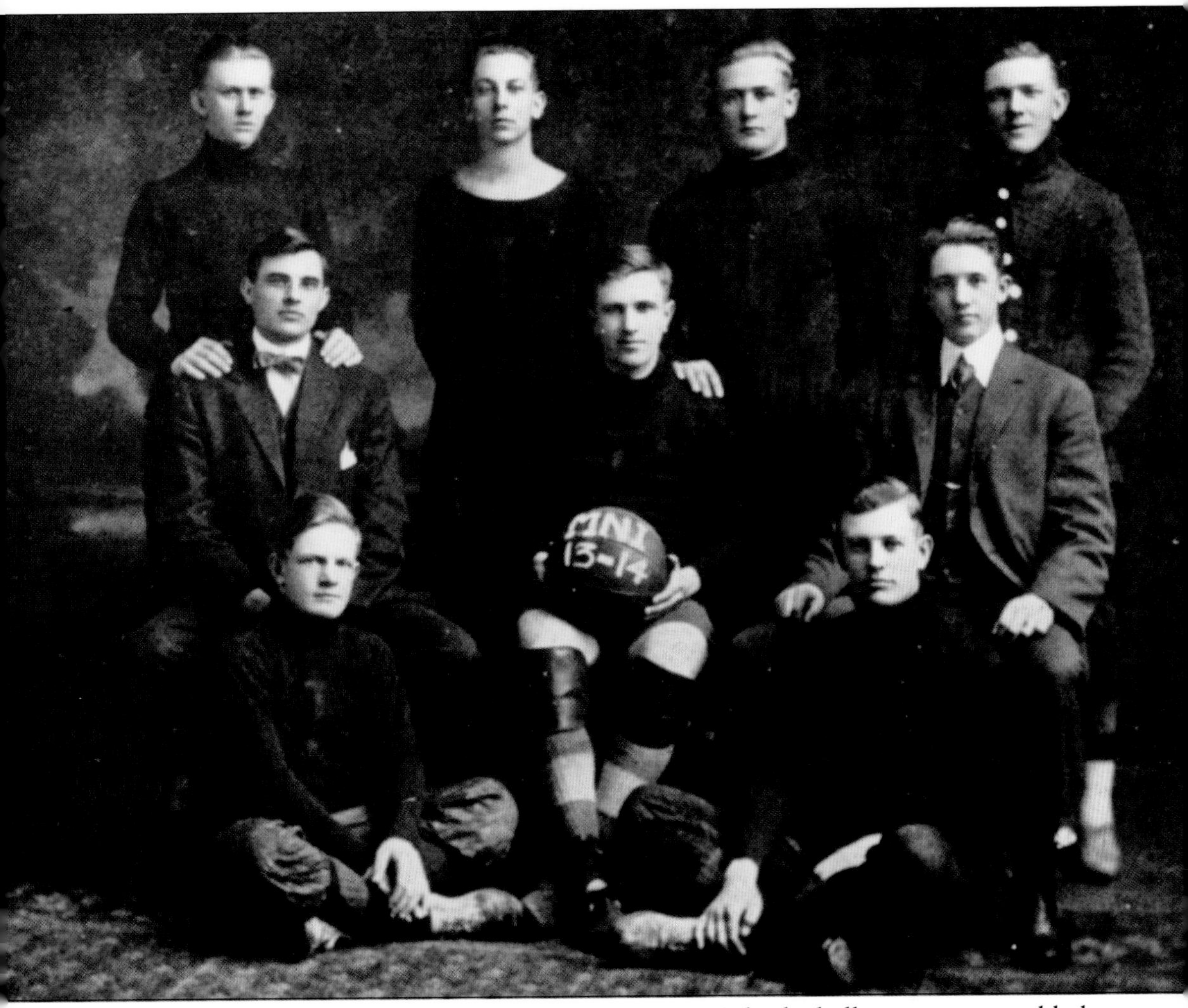

Members of the 1913–1914 Muncie National Institute men's basketball team are assembled for a group photograph for the 1914 *Arbor Vitae* yearbook.

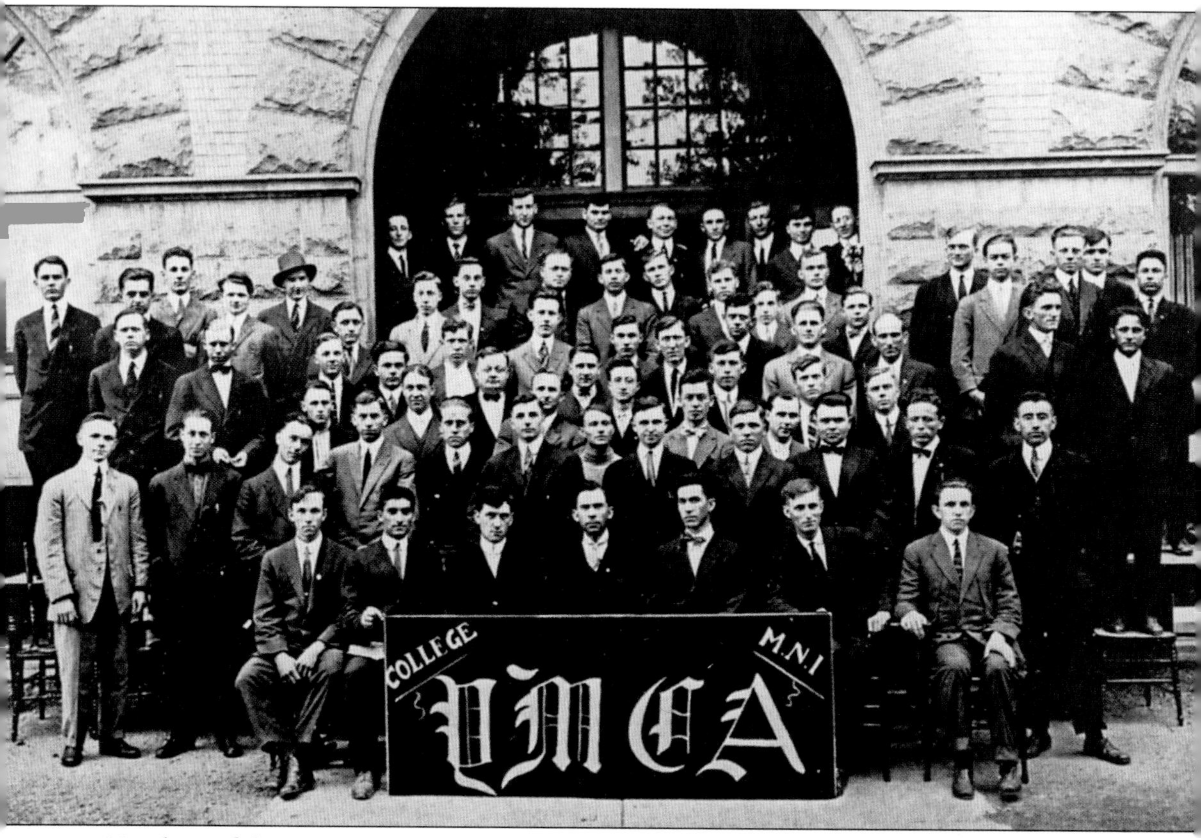

Members of the Muncie National Institute YMCA gather for a group photograph for the 1914 *Arbor Vitae* yearbook. According to the yearbook, "the aim of the association is service and it has cheerfully aided the new students in finding friends and congenial homes."

Two

The Emergence of Ball State Teachers College 1918–1945

Between the end of World War I and the end of World War II, Ball State experienced a momentous period. In 1921–1922, the college adopted a master plan for the main campus, known as the Quad (Quadrangle), and a wave of new construction began immediately. The State of Indiana provided the funds for the construction of Science Hall, opening in 1923, the Library and Assembly Hall, opening in 1927, and Burris Laboratory School, which opened in 1929. In 1929, Ball State acquired its independence from Indiana State and became Indiana's fourth public institution of higher education.

However, it was the lavish philanthropy of the Ball family that secured the permanence of the school during the interwar period. The Ball family provided the funding for Ball Gymnasium, opening in 1925; Lucina Hall, the first women's residence hall, which opened in 1927; and Elliott Hall, opening in 1938. Lucina Hall was named after Lucina Amelia Ball, the eldest sister of the five Ball brothers, who was also an accomplished educator. Elliott Hall was named for Frank Elliott Ball, the younger son of Frank and Elizabeth Ball, who was killed in a tragic plane crash in 1936. In 1935, Ball State's Arts Building was constructed with funds provided by the State of Indiana, the federal government, and the Ball family.

In 1937, Ball State unveiled the beautiful sculpture *Beneficence*, designed by Daniel Chester French and built with donations from the community in recognition of the Ball family's generosity to Muncie. Situated on campus between the Administration Building and Lucina Hall, *Beneficence*, referred to as "Benny" by the college's students, became Ball State's most visible symbol.

Ball State's student enrollment grew during the interwar period, except for declines during the austere years of the Great Depression and World War II. Leading the academic enterprise was a trio of administrators: Pres. Lemuel A. Pittenger, Dean Ralph W. Noyer, and Treasurer Winfred E. Wagoner. Pittenger stepped down as president in 1942, and W.E. Wagoner served as Ball State's wartime president until the appointment of John R. Emens as Pittenger's successor in 1945.

By the end of World War II, Ball State possessed all the elements necessary to survive in the postwar environment: an experienced faculty, a strong curriculum, active social organizations such as clubs, fraternities, and sororities, and an athletics program for both men and women. It had secured its rightful place in the Hoosier state's educational community.

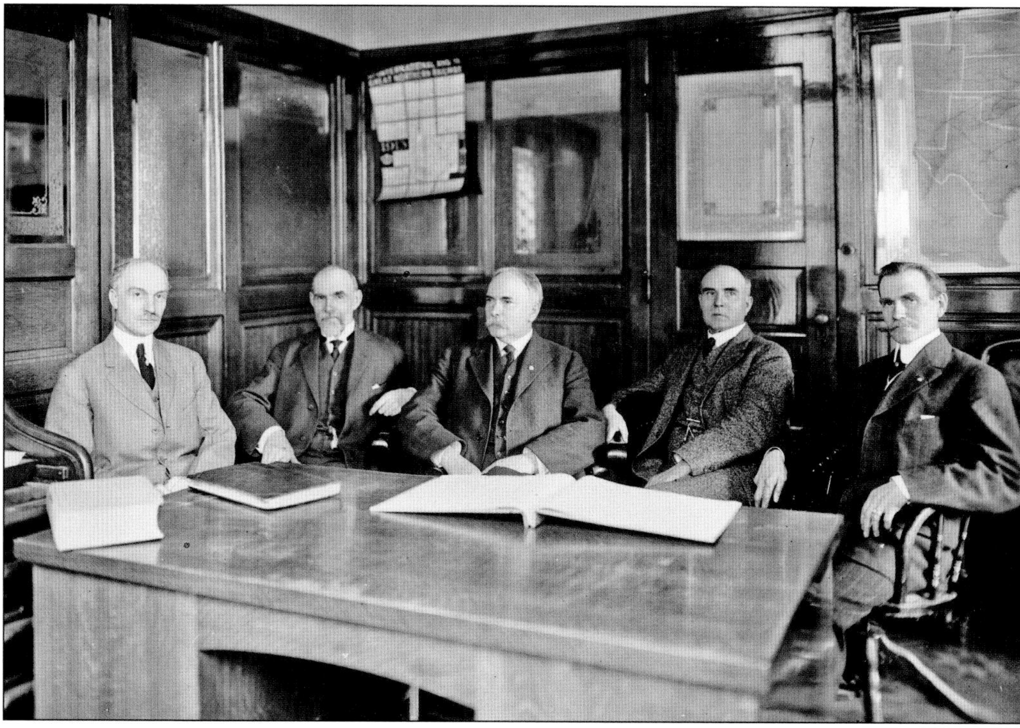

The five Ball brothers—(pictured from left to right) George A., Lucius L., Frank C., Edmund B., and William C.—were instrumental in establishing and providing critical early support for the Eastern Division of the Indiana State Normal School. Their donation of the campus property in 1918 and subsequent gifts of Ball Gymnasium (1925) and Lucina Hall (1927), the women's residence hall, gave the school the momentum it needed to survive well past the 1920s.

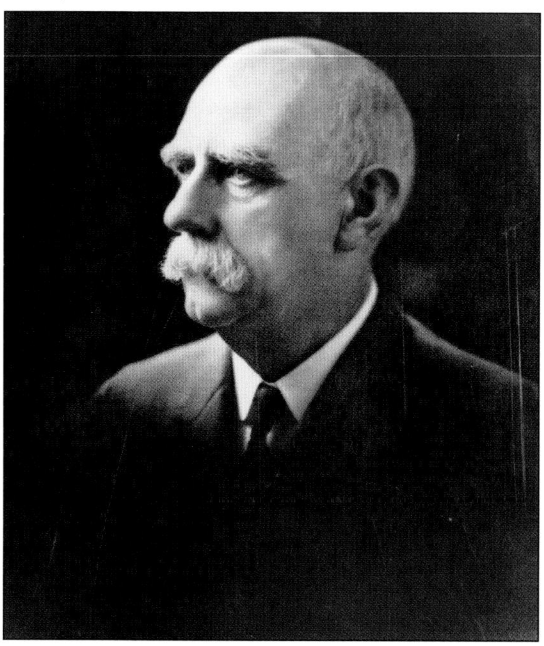

William Wood Parsons was president of the Indiana State Normal School from 1918 to 1927. Once the manpower requirements for America's participation in World War I took effect, Parsons found himself "with a complete faculty but only half a student body." By agreeing to accept the Eastern Division as a branch campus, Parsons received a much-needed infusion of students for Indiana State. Parsons had second thoughts about his decision, however, when World War I ended in November 1918 and the men started returning home from France early in 1919. Parsons was later said to have commented, "If I had known World War I was going to end so quickly, I never would have agreed [to accept the property in Muncie]."

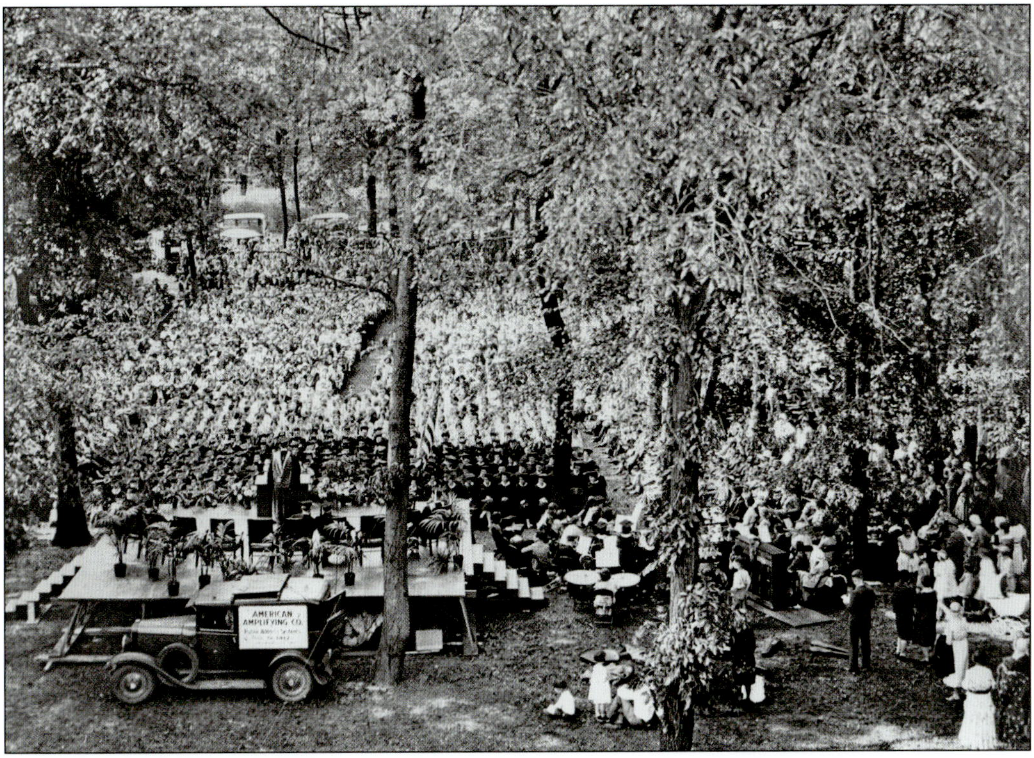

Graduates of the Indiana State Normal School Eastern Division are assembled outside for the 1918 commencement ceremony. The presence of the truck in the foreground indicates that the public address system for the event was provided by the American Amplifying Company.

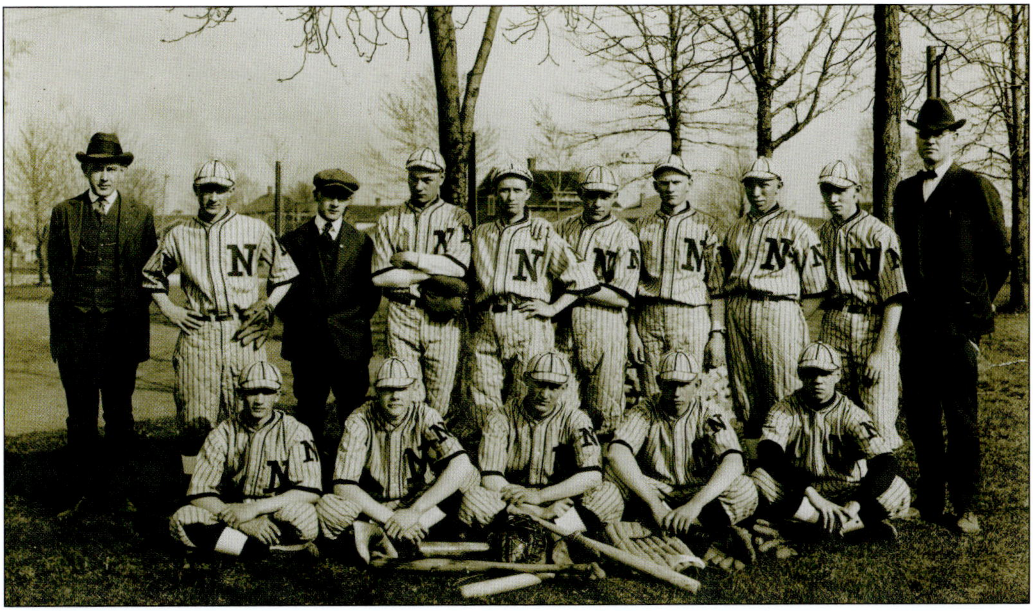

This is the team portrait for the Eastern Division of the Indiana State Normal School men's baseball team for the 1919–1920 season.

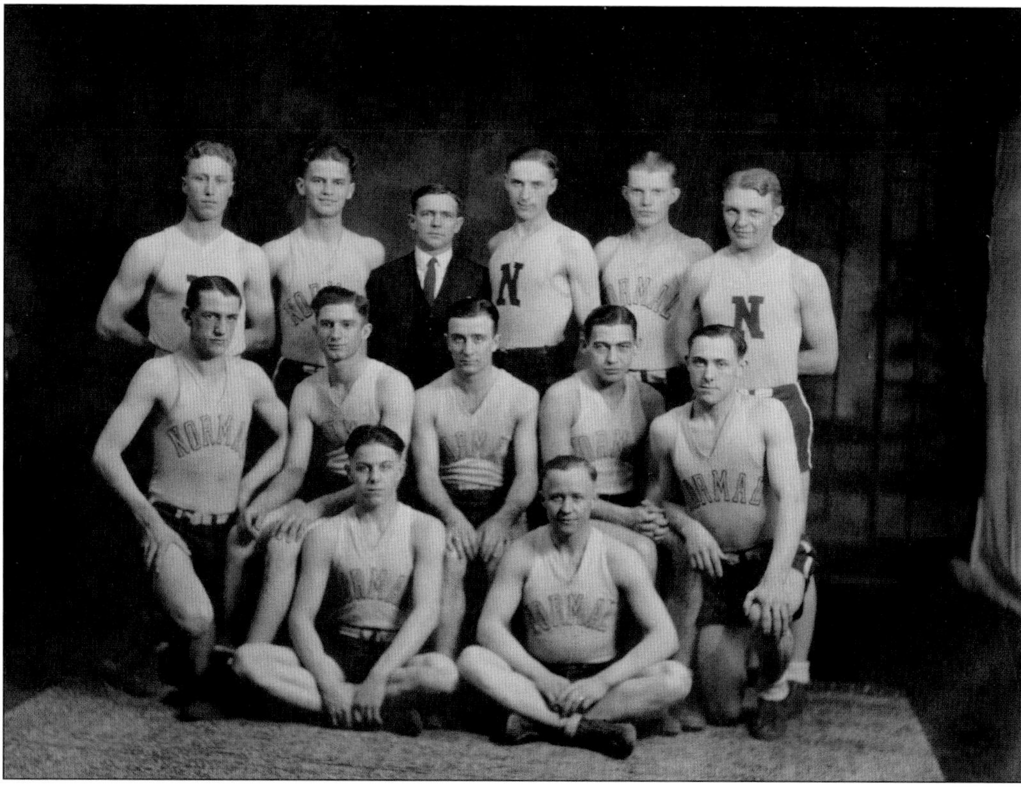

This is the team portrait for the Eastern Division of the Indiana State Normal School men's basketball team around 1921–1925. The coach of the team was Paul "Billy" Williams (top row, third from left), who served as athletic director at Ball State from 1921 to 1958.

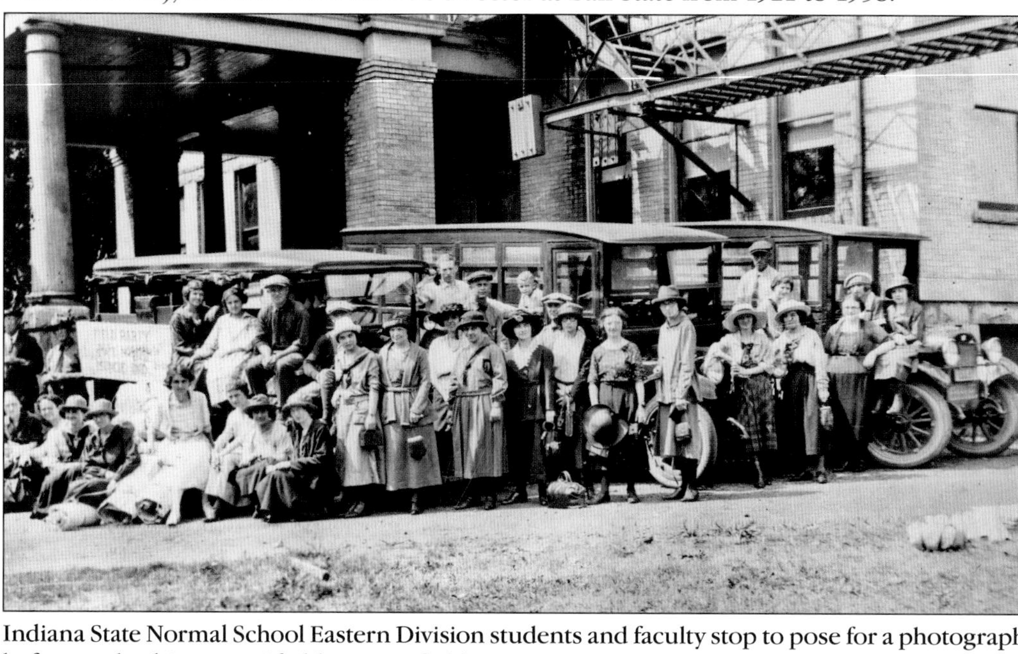

Indiana State Normal School Eastern Division students and faculty stop to pose for a photograph before embarking on a "field party" (field trip) in 1921.

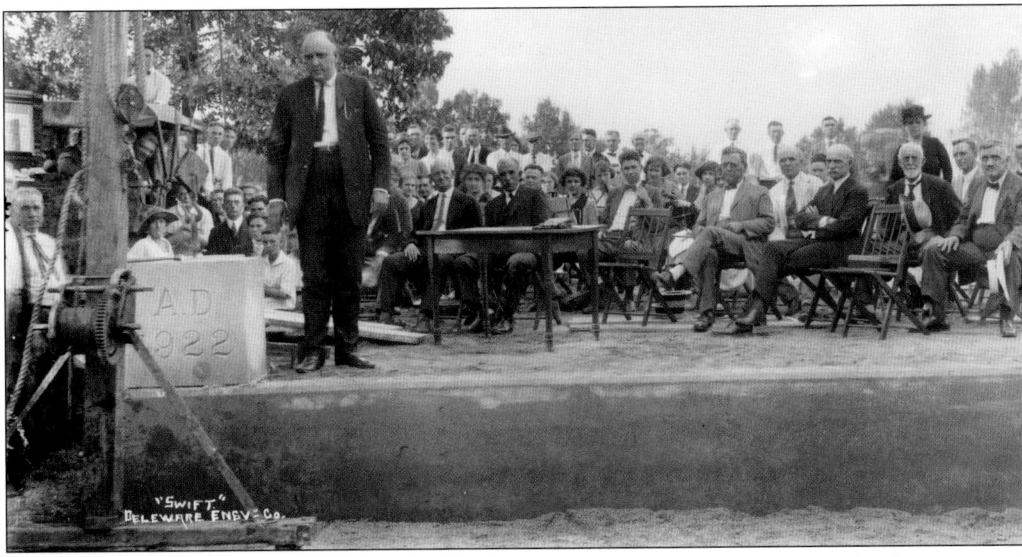

The cornerstone laying ceremony for the construction of Science Hall took place in 1922. Pictured in this photograph by W.A. Swift are Linnaeus N. Hines, president of the Indiana State Normal School (standing near cornerstone), George A. Ball (front row, seated far right), and Edmund Burke Ball (second row, third from the right). Still in use, the former Science Hall has undergone several renovations and name changes over the course of its existence. It has also been known as Old Science Hall and East Quad and is presently the Richard W. Burkhardt Building.

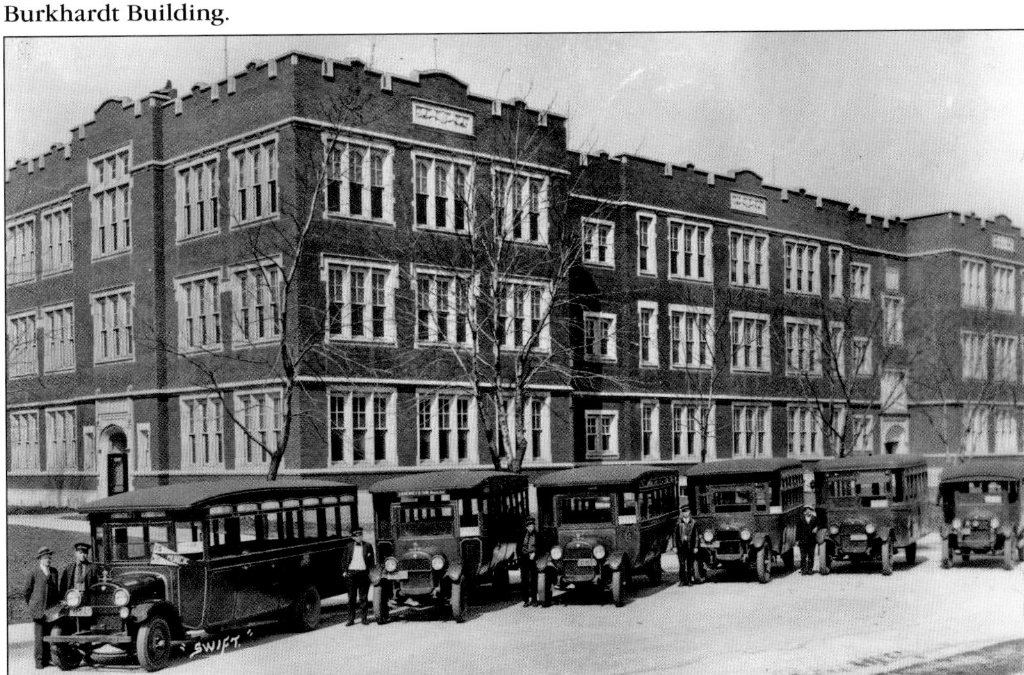

This c. 1926–1928 photograph shows the southern end of Science Hall, with S.D. Denney and Sons buses parked outside. Note the large windows all around Science Hall at every level of the building. These were a characteristic feature of Science Hall, letting in ample sunlight throughout the building and into the separate classrooms.

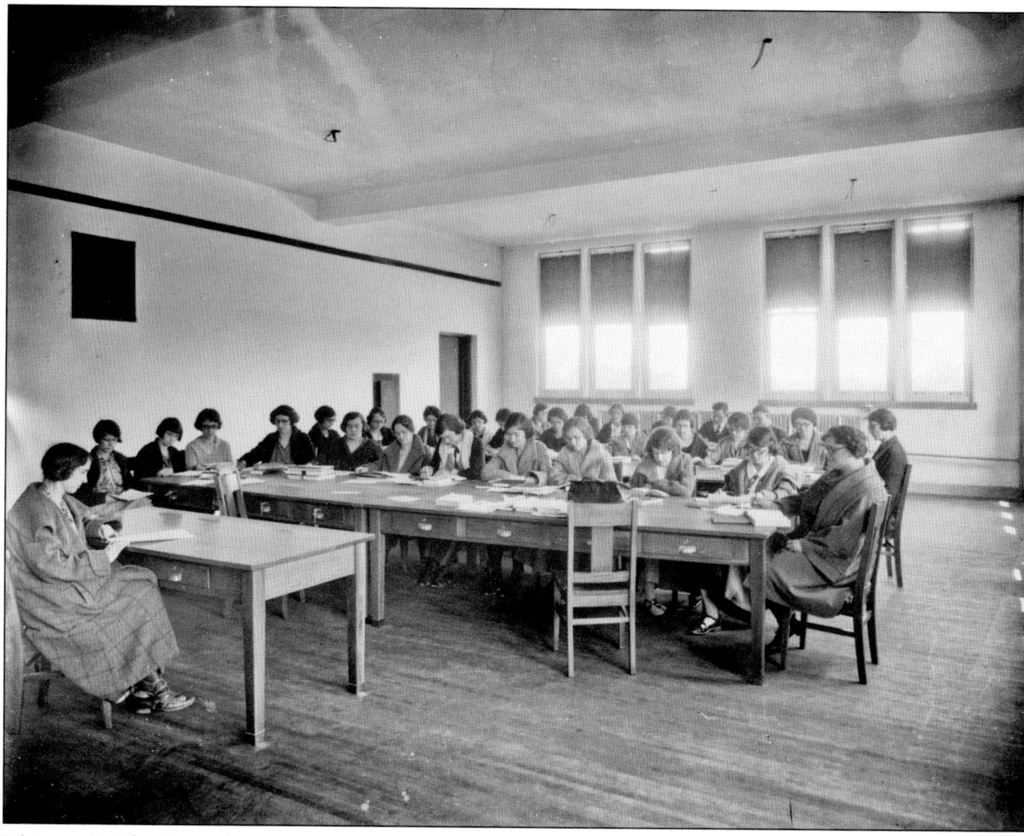

This c. 1926–1928 photograph shows a typical classroom with students in Science Hall.

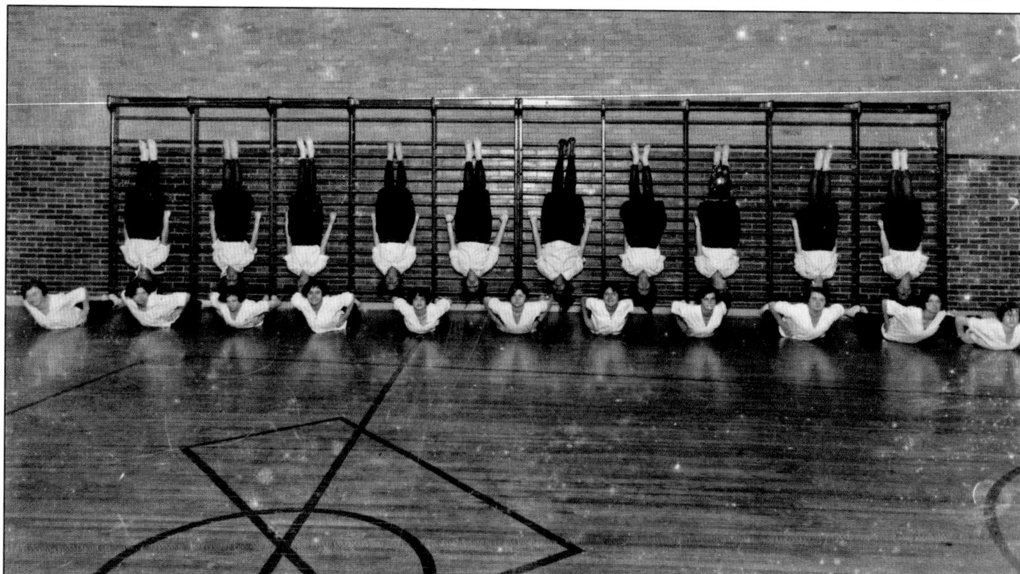

Female students are pictured in a physical education class in Ball Gymnasium around 1925. It is not clear as to the exact nature of the exercises that the ladies are doing.

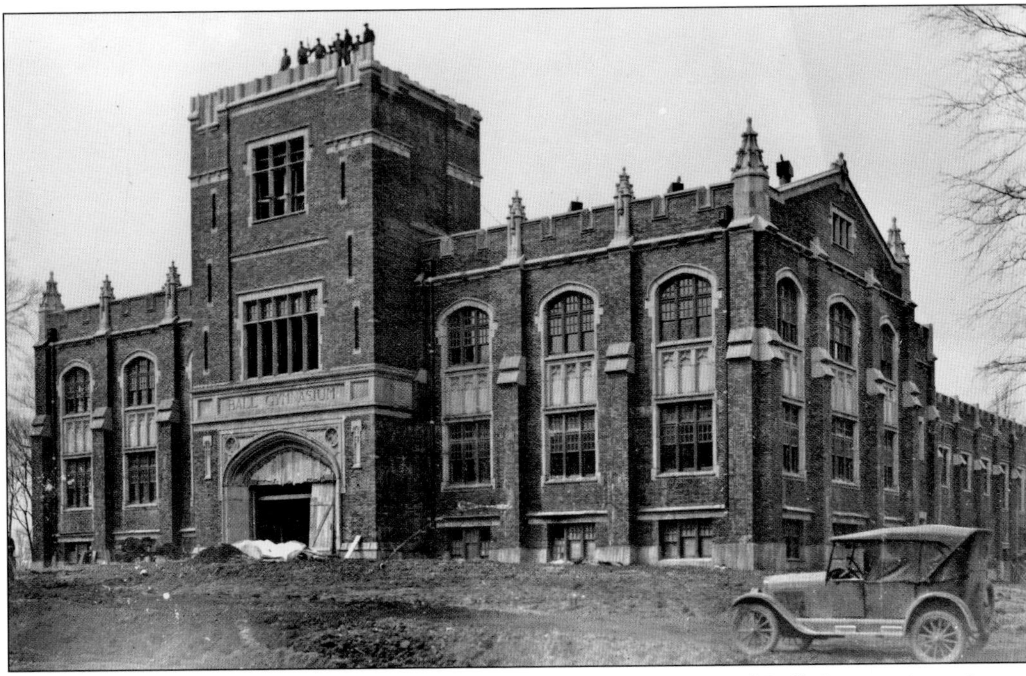

This photograph, taken by W.A. Swift during the construction of Ball Gymnasium, is one of the earliest of the building. Note what appear to be construction workers standing on the roof.

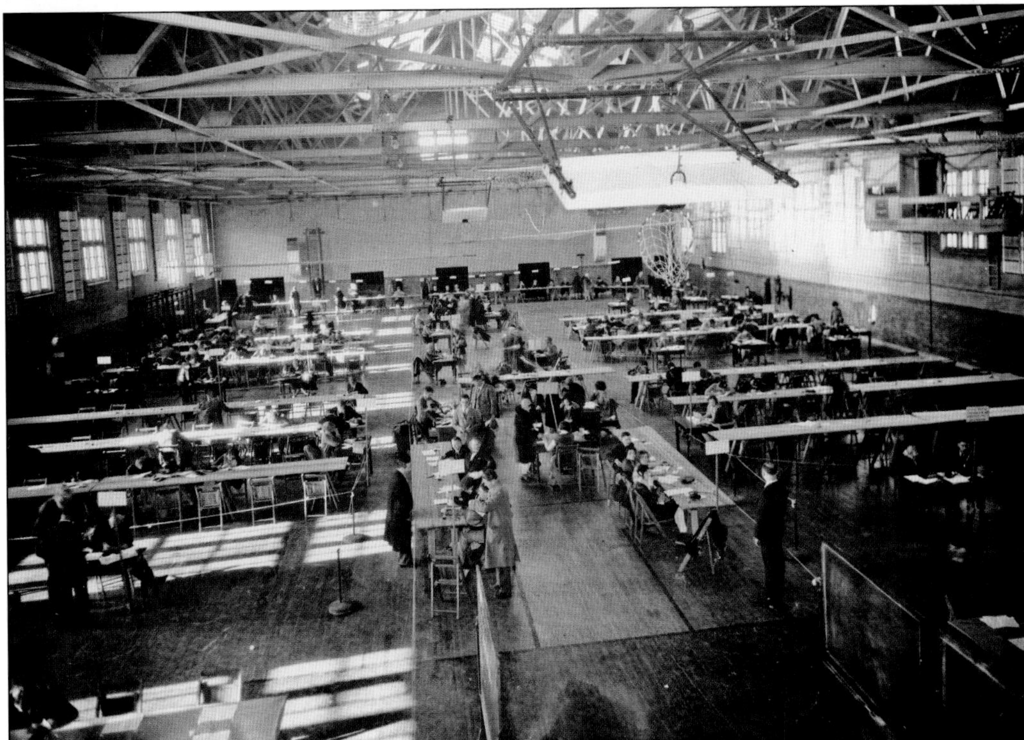

Ball State students line up for course registration in Ball Gymnasium around 1932–1933.

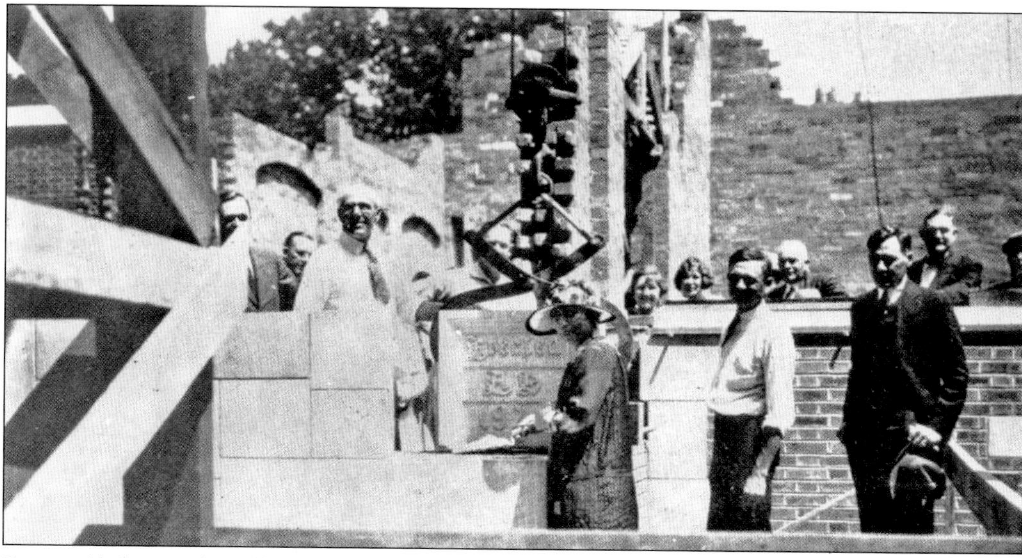

Barcus Tichenor, head librarian at Ball Teachers College, lays the cornerstone for the new Library and Assembly Hall in 1926. Barcus Tichenor served as head librarian at Ball State from 1921 to 1947. During her tenure, the library's collection expanded to more than 75,000 books. In 1960, Ball State recognized Tichenor's contribution to the school by naming a residence hall in her honor in the Grace DeHority complex of residence halls.

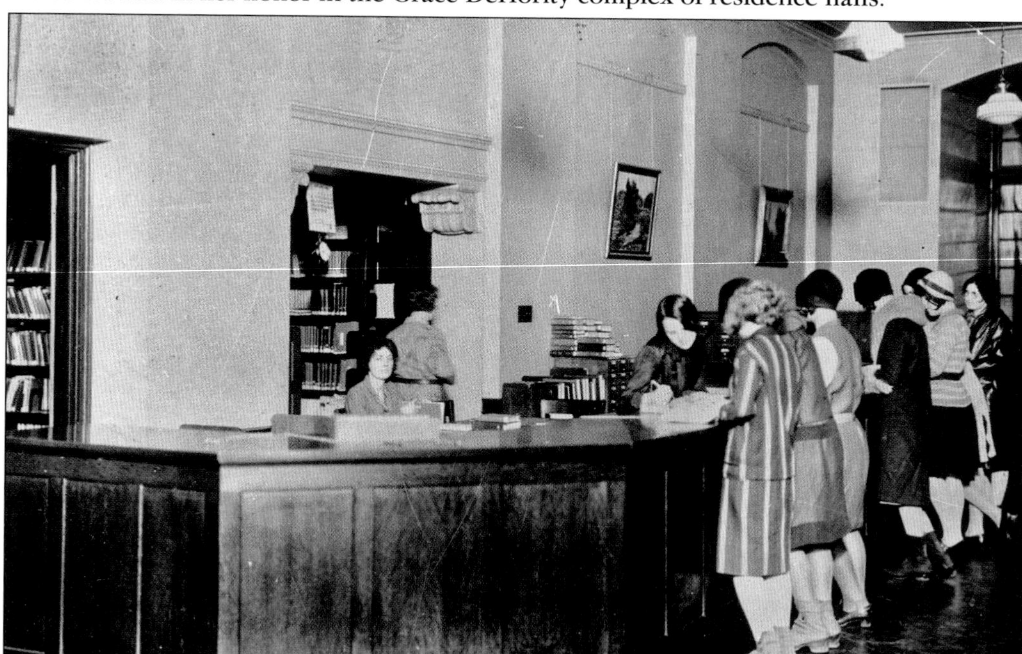

Students and faculty alike were regular patrons of the college library. In this photograph, students are shown at the library's circulation desk.

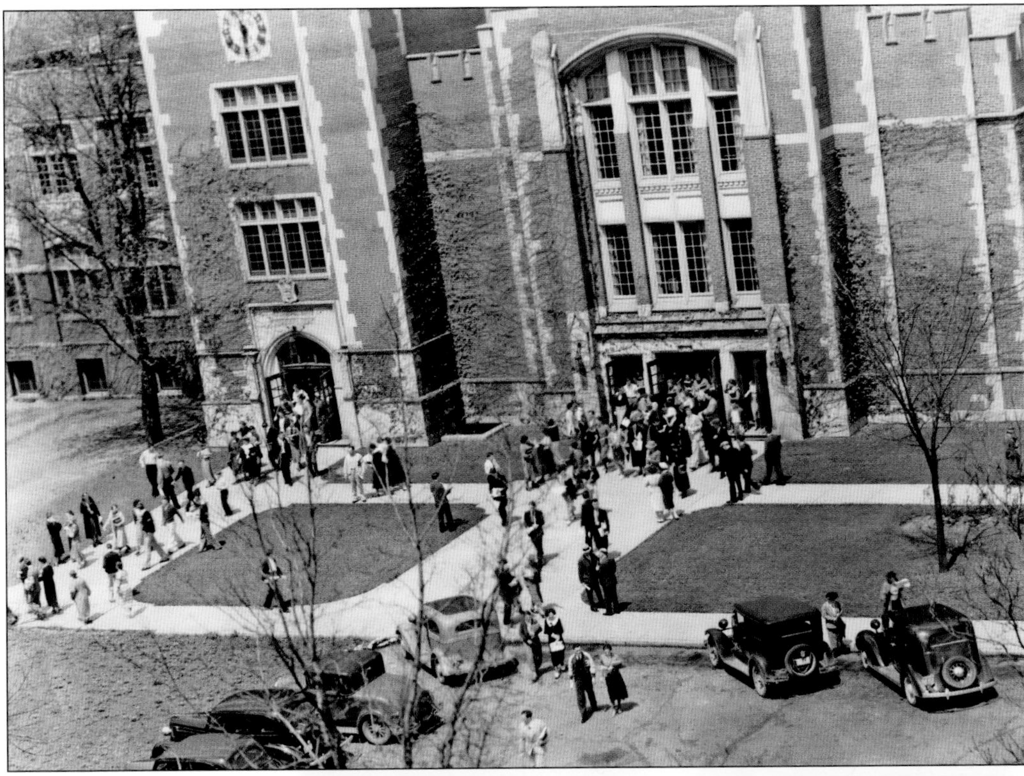

Numerous vehicles are parked outside the Library and Assembly Hall during the 1920s. Ease of transportation, including spaces to park cars on campus, was one of the factors in the growth of the school in the 1920s.

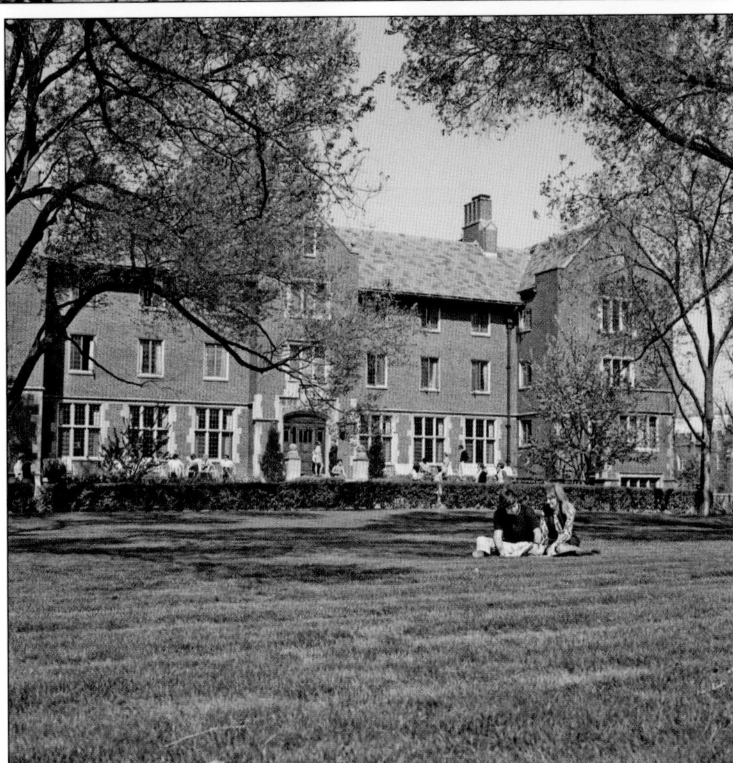

Lucina Hall was completed in 1927 with funds supplied by the Ball brothers. The namesake of the hall is Lucina Amelia Ball, the oldest sister of the five brothers, who was a renowned educator in her own right.

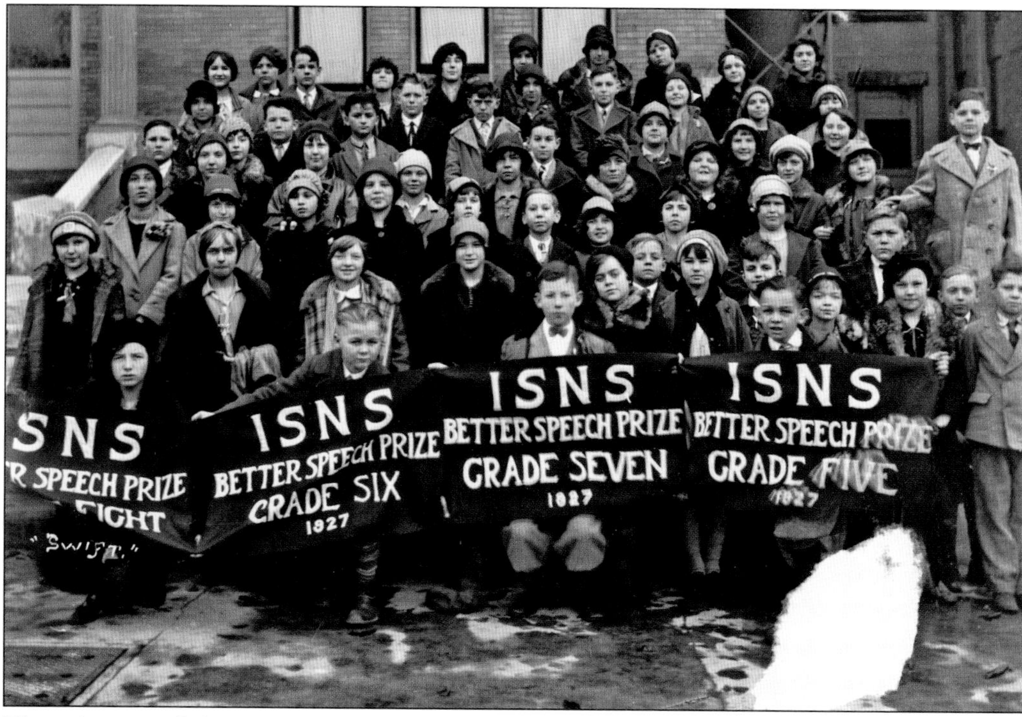

The winners of the Better Speech Prize, grades five through eight, gather for a group photograph outside the Administration Building. Note the acronym "ISNS" on the banners of the contestants for Indiana State Normal School.

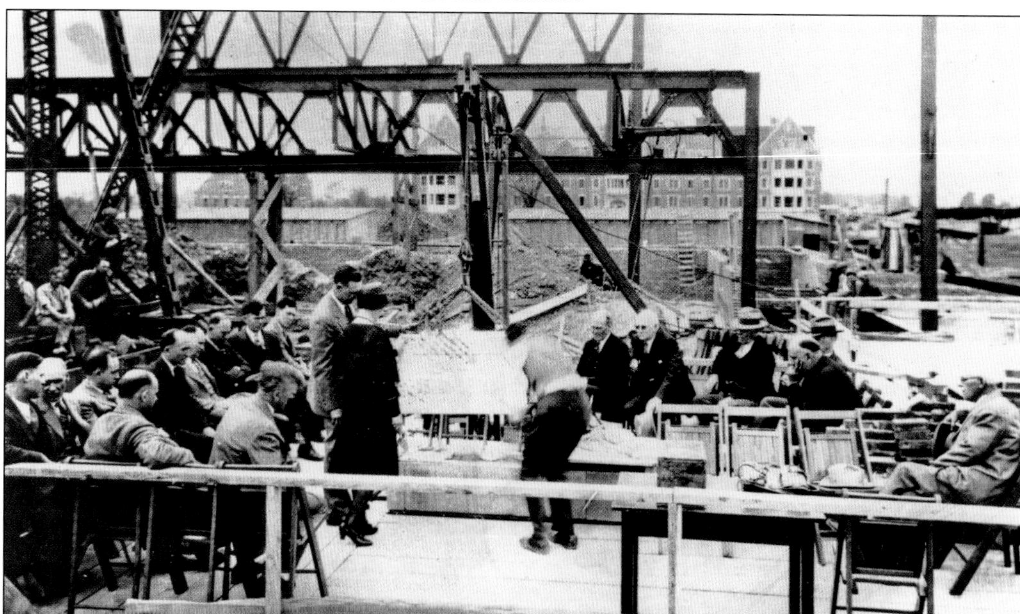
In 1928, students, faculty, and trustees gathered for the laying of the cornerstone for the Burris School, one block south of the main campus. Named after former president Benjamin Burris, the school includes kindergarten through the 12th grade and is the laboratory school for Ball State.

Benjamin Burris was the president of Ball Teachers College from 1924 to 1927. Young, energetic, and politically astute, Burris was a popular leader who enjoyed the support of students and faculty. He died after he collapsed following a high school commencement speech.

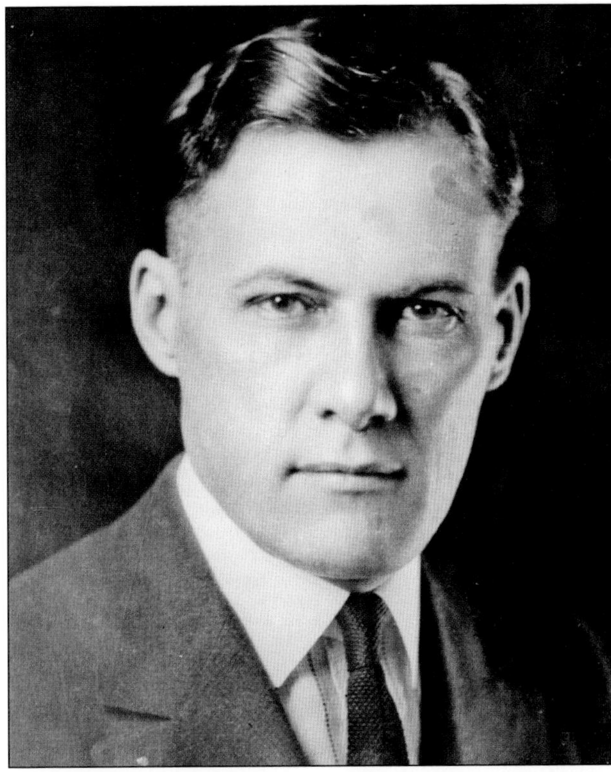

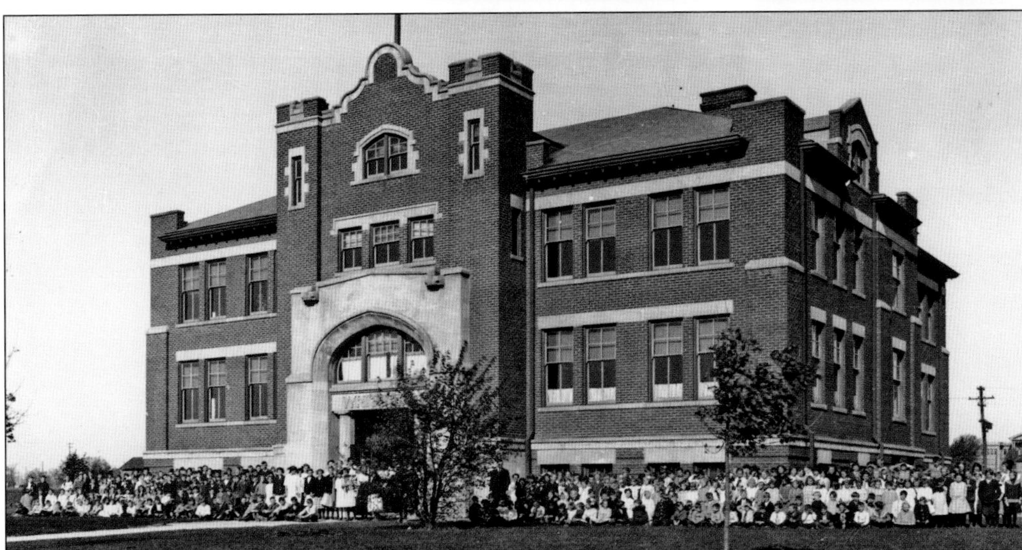

Before Burris Laboratory School was completed in 1929, Ball State education students completed some of their classroom observations and instruction at the Whittier Public School, located at the corner of North McKinley Avenue and West Main Street. The Whittier School housed grades one through eight but was closed with the establishment of Burris. The building was purchased by the congregation of College Avenue United Methodist Church (formerly the Normal City Methodist Episcopal Church, located at the corner of Calvert and Gilbert Streets) and ultimately razed in the early 1970s.

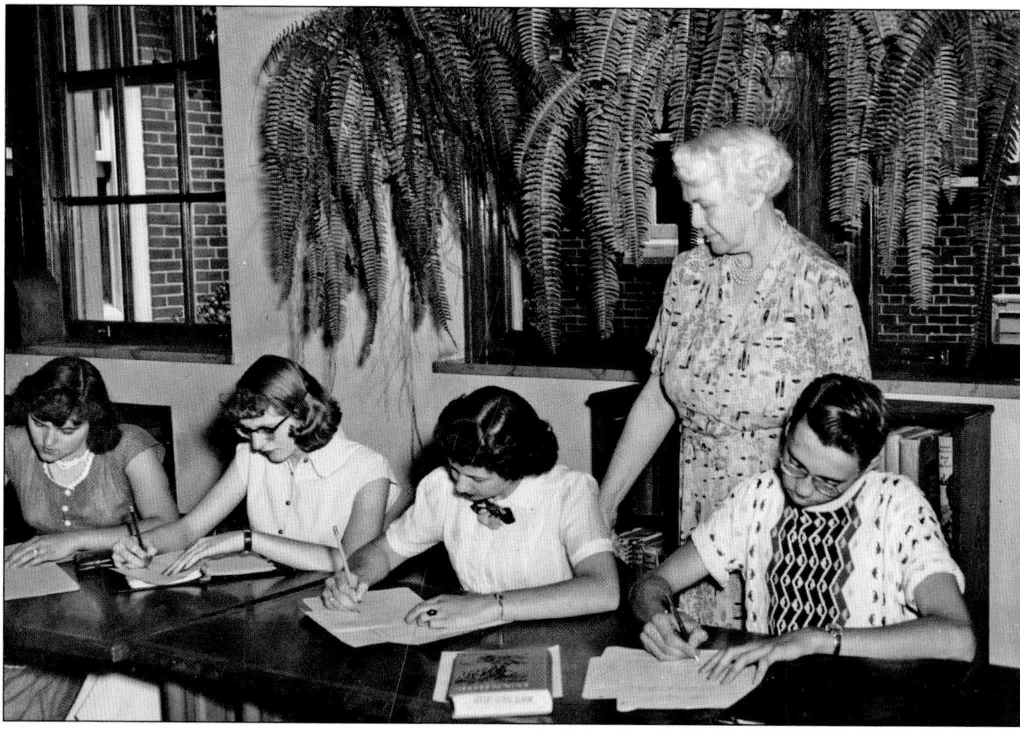

At Burris, many seniors learned English and composition from Lucille Knotts, shown in this 1930s photograph. In 1967, Ball State recognized Knotts's contribution to the college by naming a residence hall in her honor in the Robert R. LaFollette complex of residence halls.

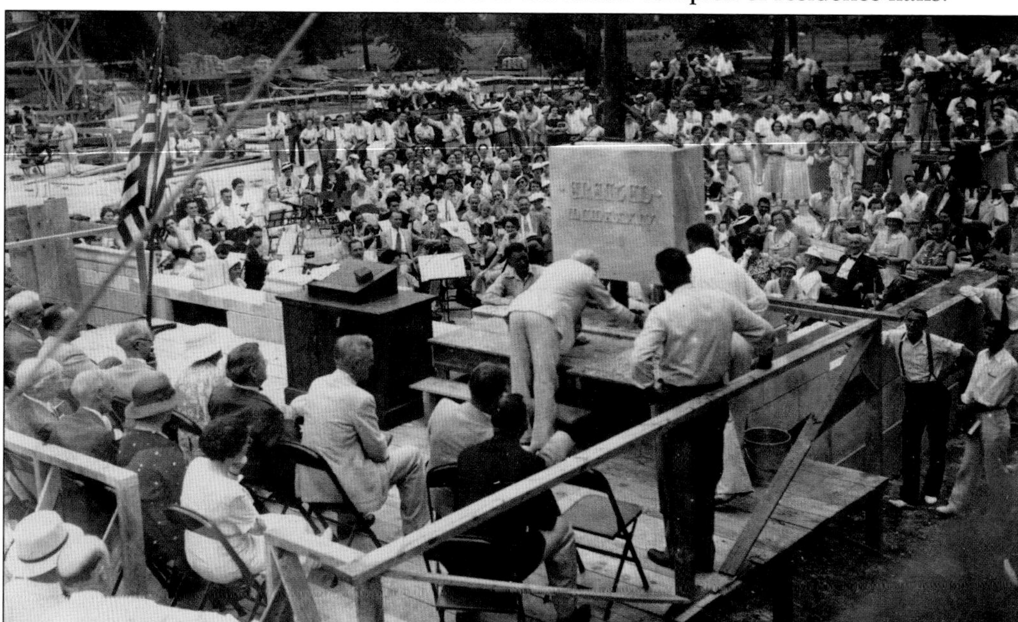

In 1934, George A. Ball (bending down in front of cornerstone) helped to lay the cornerstone for Ball State's Fine Arts Building. The Fine Arts Building was funded through a combination of funds from the State of Indiana, the federal government, and the Ball family.

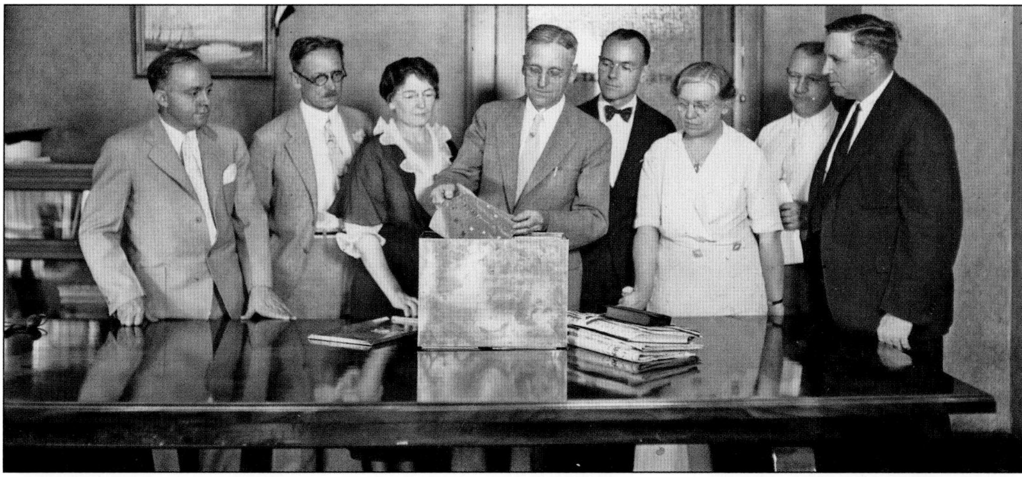

In 1935, several of Ball State's faculty and administrators participated in a cornerstone box filling ceremony. According to the 1935 yearbook, the box included a Bible, US and Indiana flags, a photograph of the Ball brothers, an aerial photograph of campus, newspaper articles, an architectural drawing of the building, a list of students and faculty from the first summer term of 1934, wood-block prints and watercolors, musical compositions, and a history of the Muncie Art Association. From left to right are Robert R. LaFollette, chair of the Social Science Department; project architect Walter Schreiber; Grace DeHority, dean of women; Pres. Lemuel A. Pittenger; Claude Palmer, chair of the Music Department; Susan M. Trane, chair of the Art Department; Ralph W. Noyer, dean of the college; and Winfred A. Wagoner, registrar and treasurer. In the 1950s, the Ball State Student Center was named in honor of L.A. Pittenger. In the 1950s and 1960s, as new residence halls opened, individual halls were named in honor of each of these faculty members and administrators.

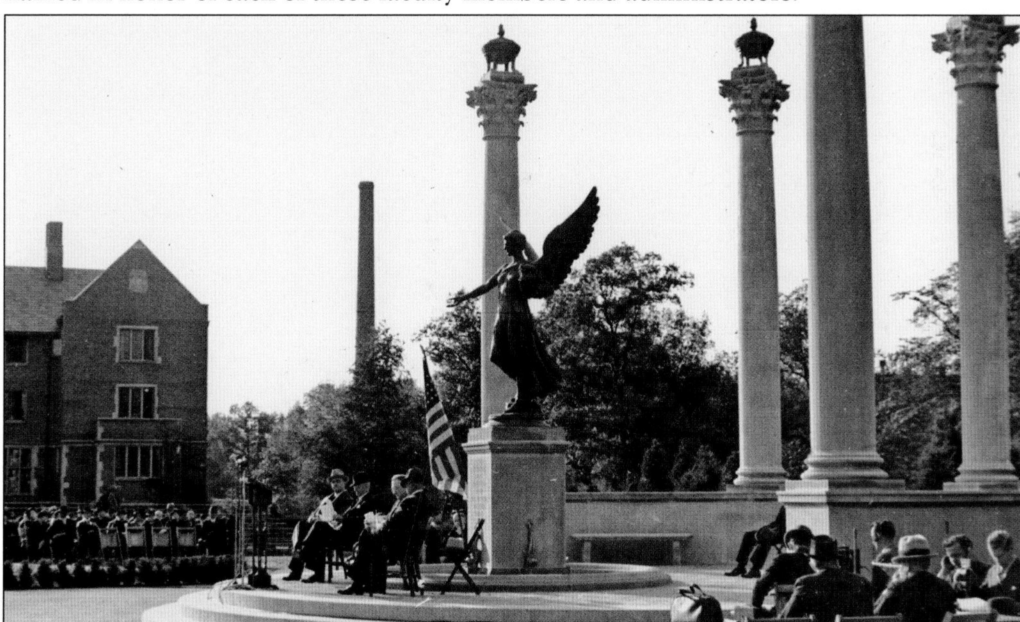

In 1937, Ball State dedicated *Beneficence*, by the noted sculptor Daniel Chester French. Known on campus as "Benny," the statue is an enduring symbol of Ball State.

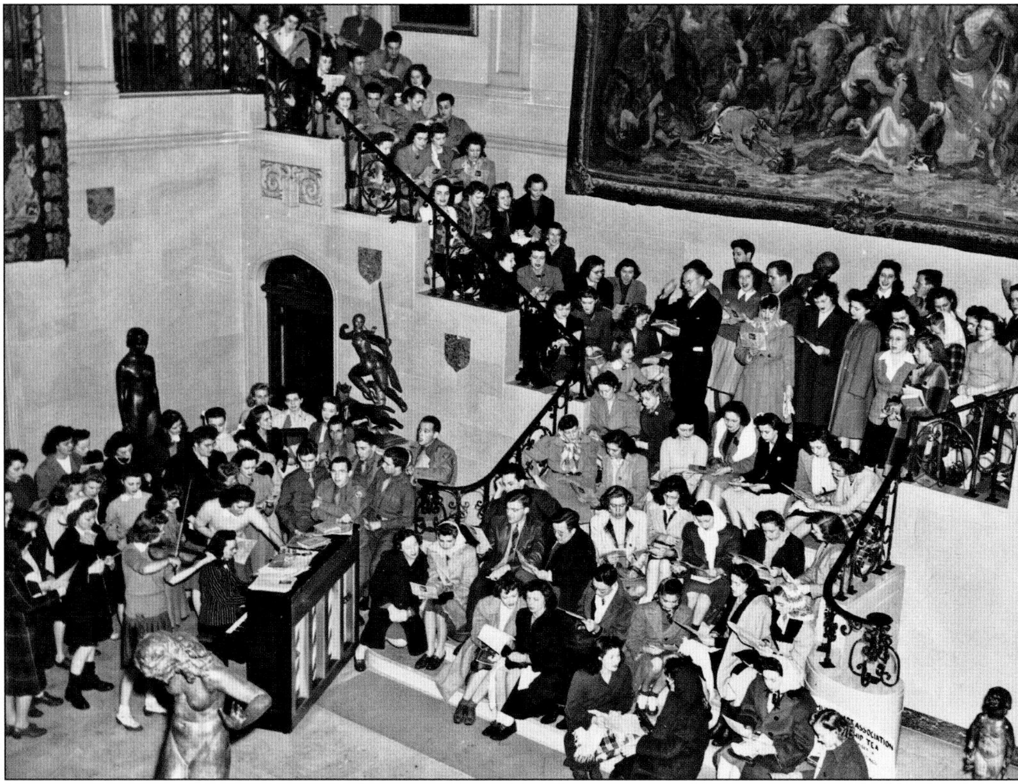

Another active student organization in the interwar period at Ball State was the college Choral Society, shown here singing at the Fine Arts Building in 1944.

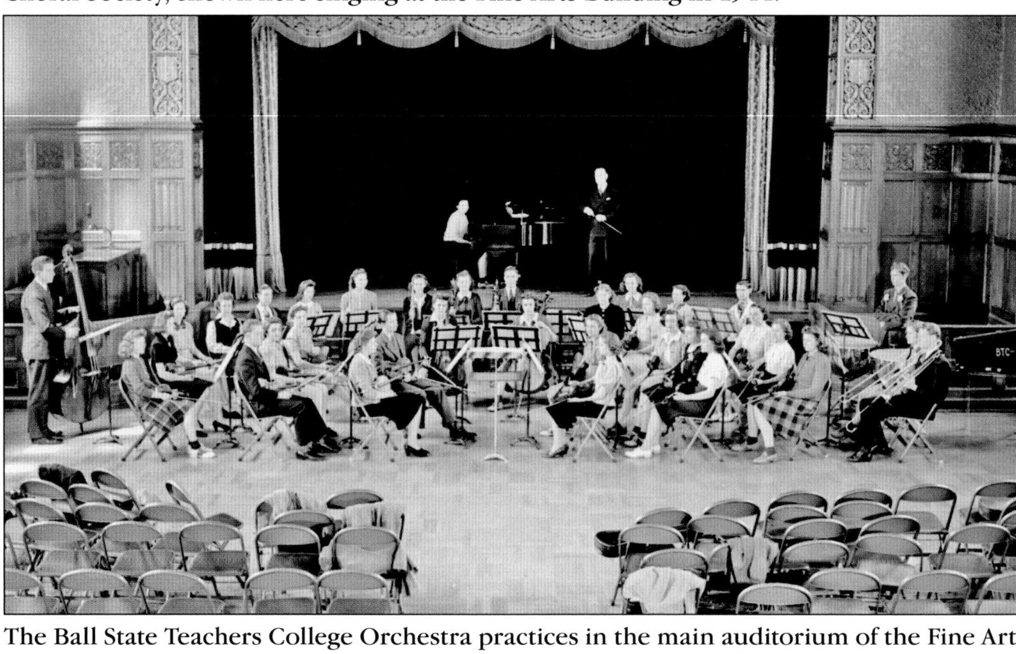

The Ball State Teachers College Orchestra practices in the main auditorium of the Fine Arts Building prior to a performance in 1941. Performances by student musicians were an ever-growing feature of the college in the 1930s and 1940s.

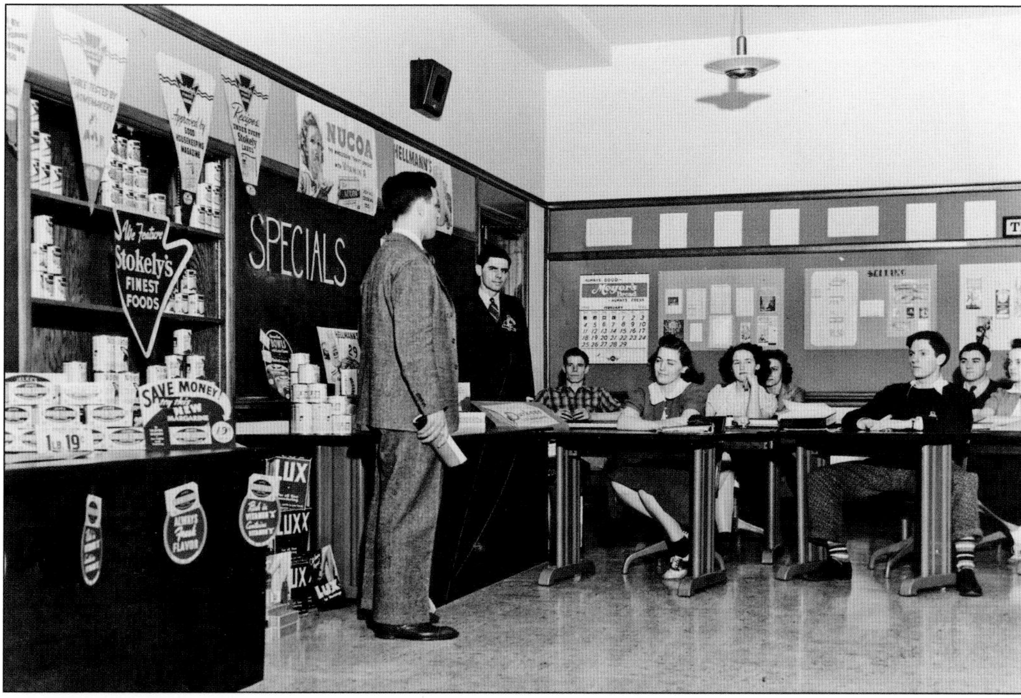

A student makes a presentation in a salesmanship class at Ball State Teachers College in 1940. Perhaps this is evidence of an early focus on entrepreneurial education at Ball State.

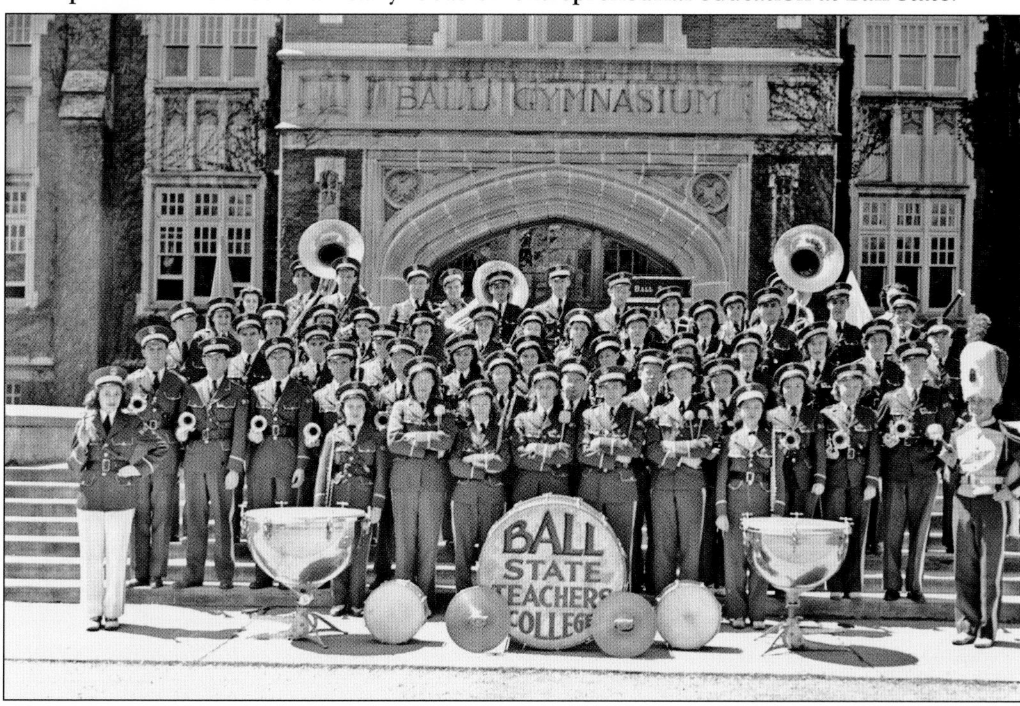

Members of the Ball State Teachers College Marching Band are gathered for a group photograph outside of Ball Gymnasium around 1940–1941. Judging by the number of male students, the United States had not yet begun to call up college-age men for military service.

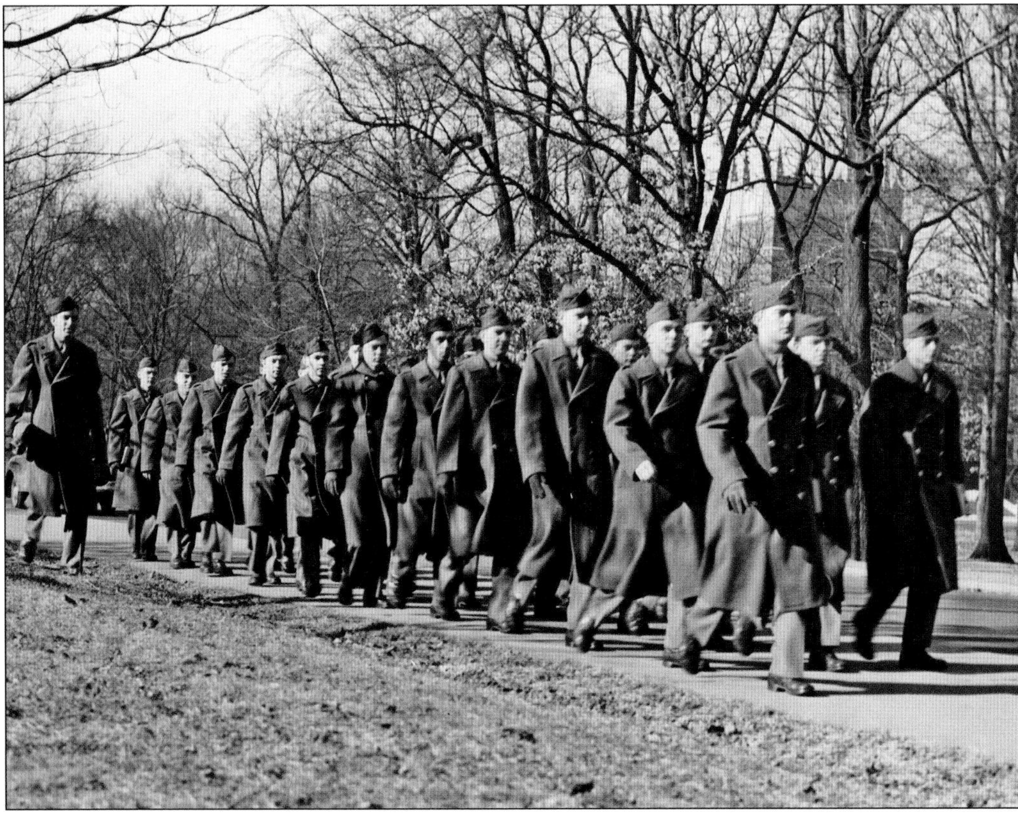

During World War II, War Training Service cadets were a familiar sight on campus. In this 1944 photograph, the cadets are shown on the Main Quad marching to their next class.

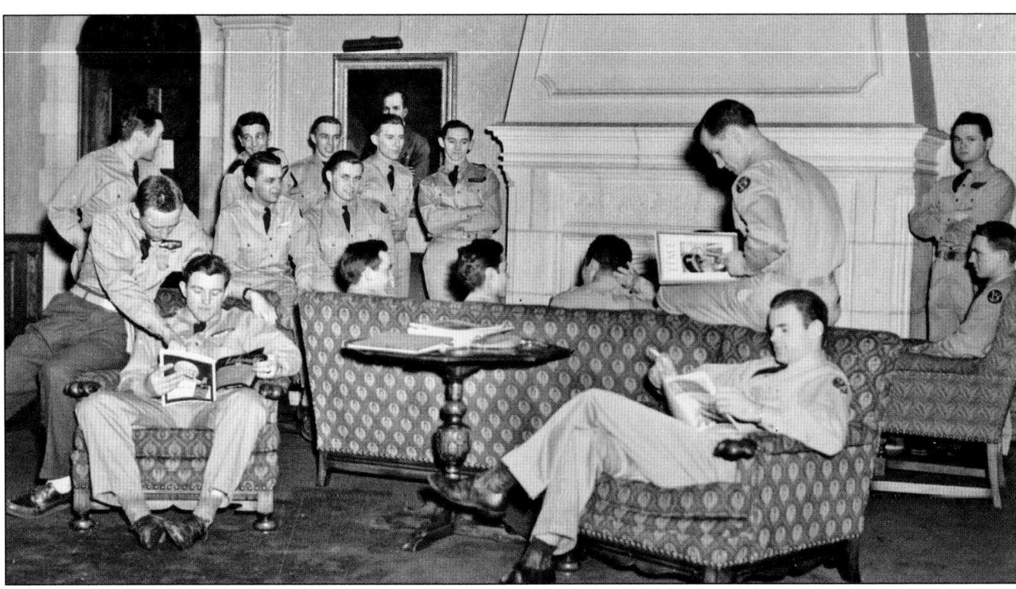

During World War II, War Training Service cadets were housed in Elliott Hall on campus. In this c. 1942 photograph, cadets relax in the main lounge of Elliott Hall.

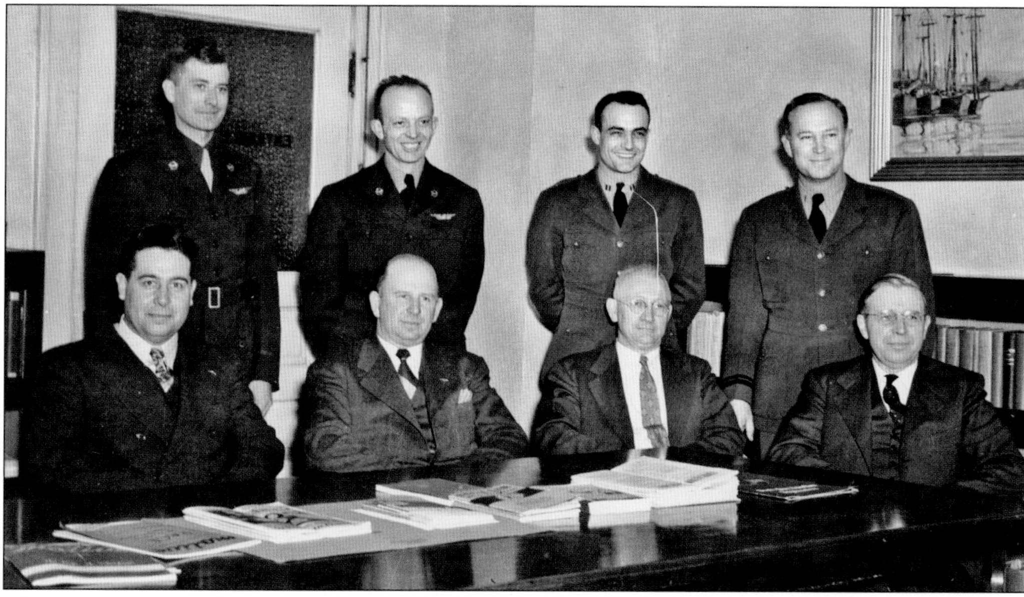

The Ball State Teachers College's War Training Service coordinating staff gather for a group photograph during World War II. From left to right are (first row) James Bolby, Clyde Shockley, Ralph Noyer, and Winfred Wagoner; (second row) Lawrence Herschinger, Lawrence Spearman, Donald Oren, and Robert H. McIntyre.

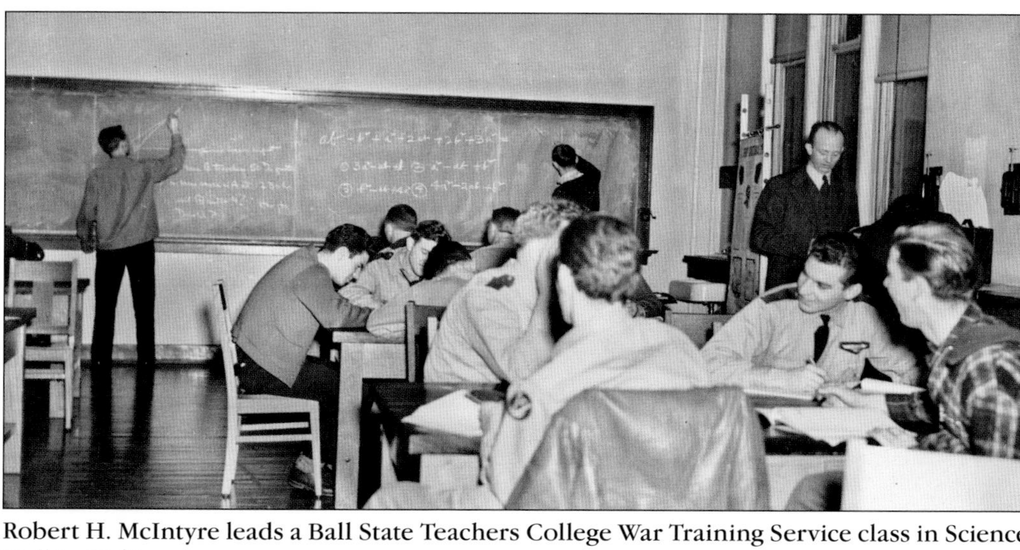

Robert H. McIntyre leads a Ball State Teachers College War Training Service class in Science Hall in 1943.

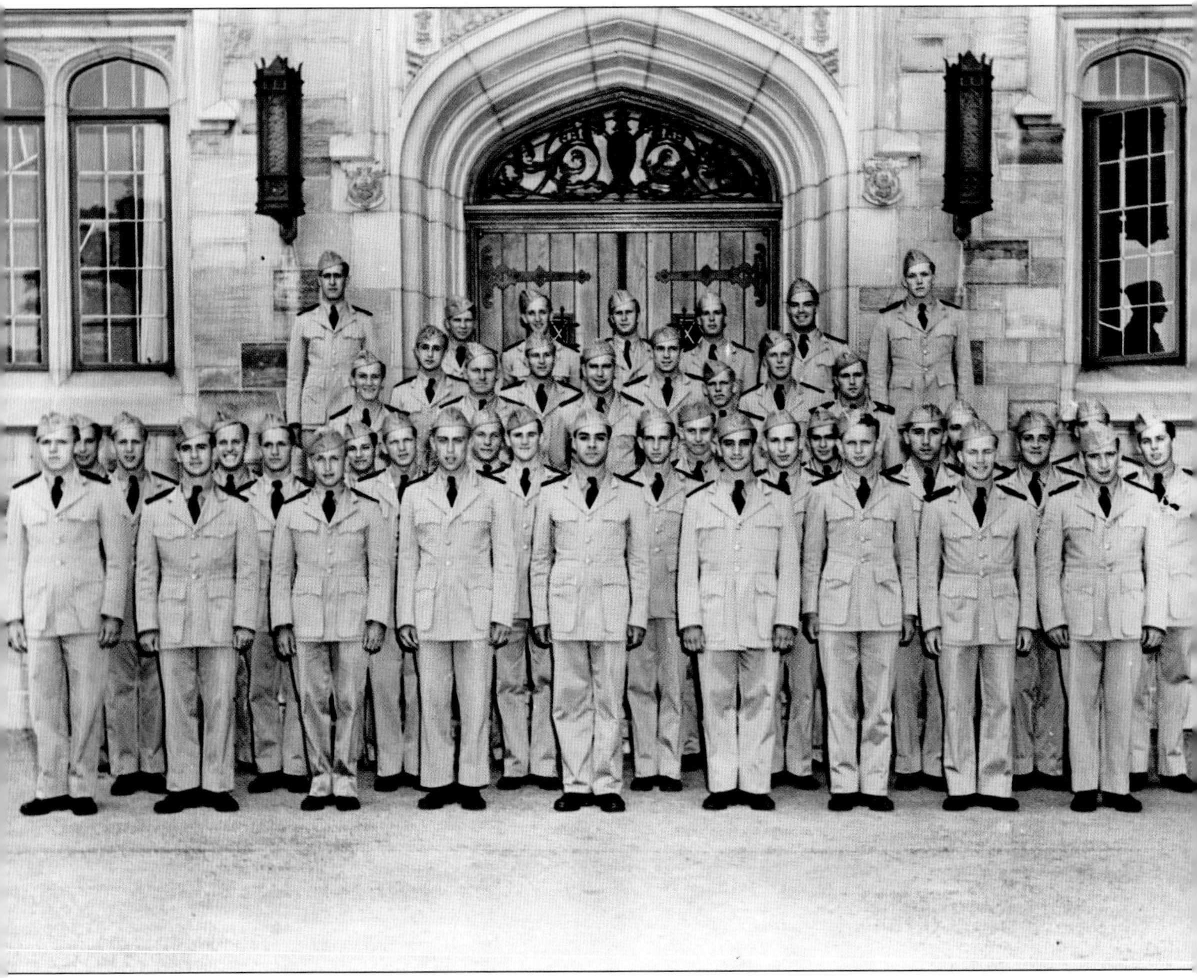

Members of the first graduating class of the Ball State Teachers College's War Training Service gather for a group photograph outside Elliott Hall in 1942.

Three

From Teachers College to University 1945–1965

In the two decades after World War II, Ball State Teachers College moved steadily in the direction of becoming a university. By 1965, more than 10,000 students were enrolled at Ball State, a milestone that led the Indiana General Assembly to grant university status to the school on February 8, 1965. On March 11, 1965, the General Assembly also passed legislation granting Ball State its College of Architecture, the first public college of architecture in Indiana.

The postwar decades at Ball State were the era of John R. Emens. Emens came to Ball State as its president in September 1945 and served until his retirement in 1968. It was Emens who presided over Ball State's unprecedented growth and became, in a sense, the keeper of Ball State's traditional emphasis on student-faculty interaction as its hallmark. A firm believer in the value of teacher education, Emens was also a realist who understood that institutional growth required a diversified curriculum and new connections with the wider world of higher education.

Ball State responded quickly to the surge of growth that it experienced after World War II, growth that was fueled first by the GI Bill in the late 1940s and then in the 1960s by the Baby Boomer children of the World War II generation. In 1945, Ball State's student enrollment was slightly more than 1,000. By 1968, enrollment had climbed to more than 13,500 students. The physical growth of the campus, especially south of University Avenue and north of Riverside Avenue, also accelerated. New residence halls (DeHority, Noyer, Woodworth, Studebaker, and LaFollette), new classroom buildings (Practical Arts, Music, English, Physical Science and Mathematics, and Nursing Education) and athletic facilities (Men's Gym and University Pool) took their places on campus, extending it geographically well beyond the bounds of the original Quad.

Ball State changed permanently after World War II, and yet, it also symbolized the times in which it grew: forward thinking, largely positive in outlook, and optimistic for the future. The years from 1945 to 1968 were fast-paced and memorable, as Ball State quickly transcended its earlier history as a single-purpose institution.

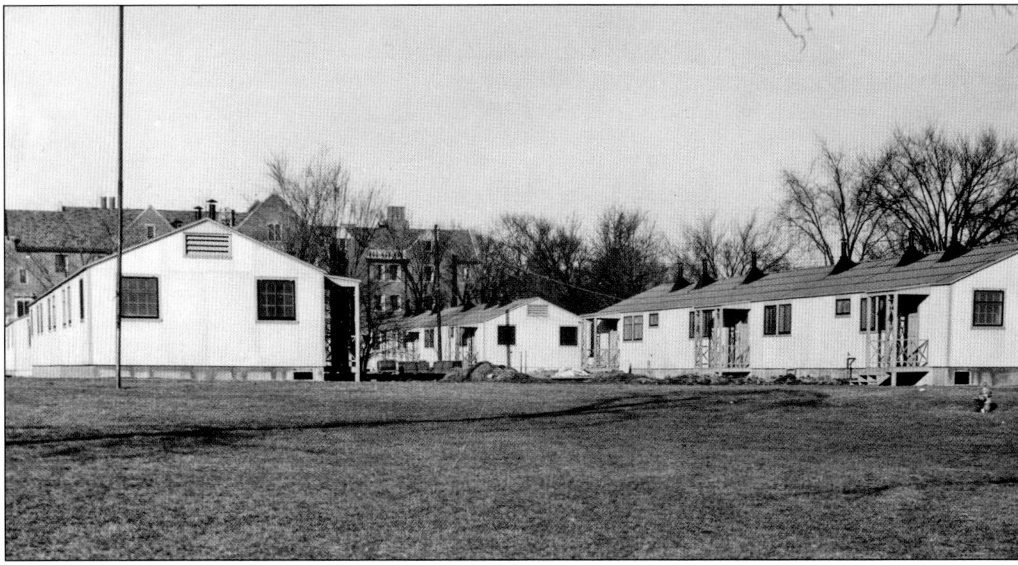

Spurred by available tuition funding through the GI Bill, student enrollment soared at Ball State in the immediate postwar period, tripling from over 1,000 to over 3,100 from 1945 to 1950. Temporary housing units brought to campus during the postwar period allowed the campus to accommodate the rapid growth. The Elliott Hall annex, erected in 1947 and razed in 1960, provided housing for 64 students on the green space west of Elliott Hall.

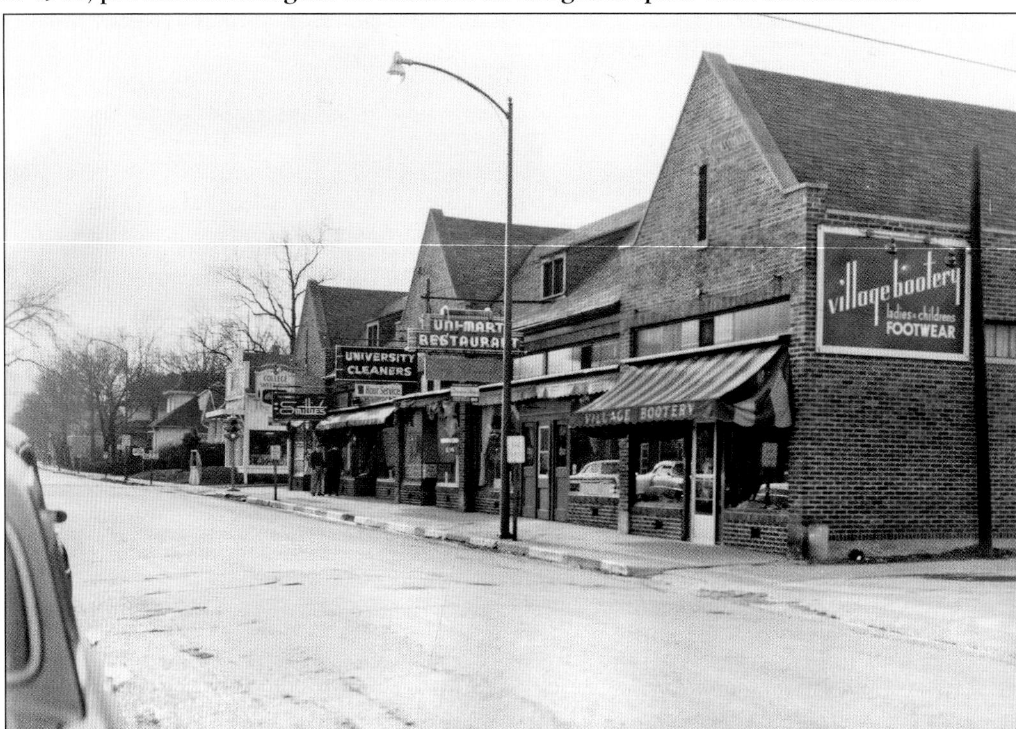

The Village neighborhood, just off the Ball State Teachers College campus, featured many popular hangouts for the students of the era. Favorite destinations included the Tally-Ho, the Pine Shelf, and the Uni-Mart Restaurant, pictured here along University Avenue.

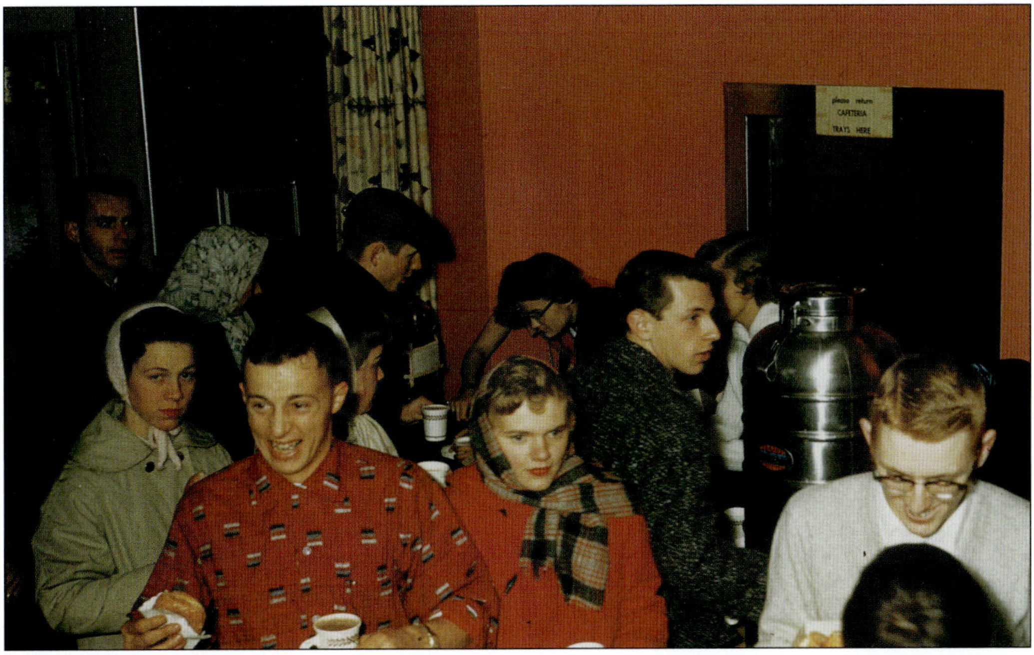

The opening of the L.A. Pittenger Student Center in 1952 (later expanded in 1959 and 1961) greatly enriched life on campus, providing students with much-needed space for social events and student organization activities. Here, students grab some coffee and doughnuts after an evening of caroling in December 1956.

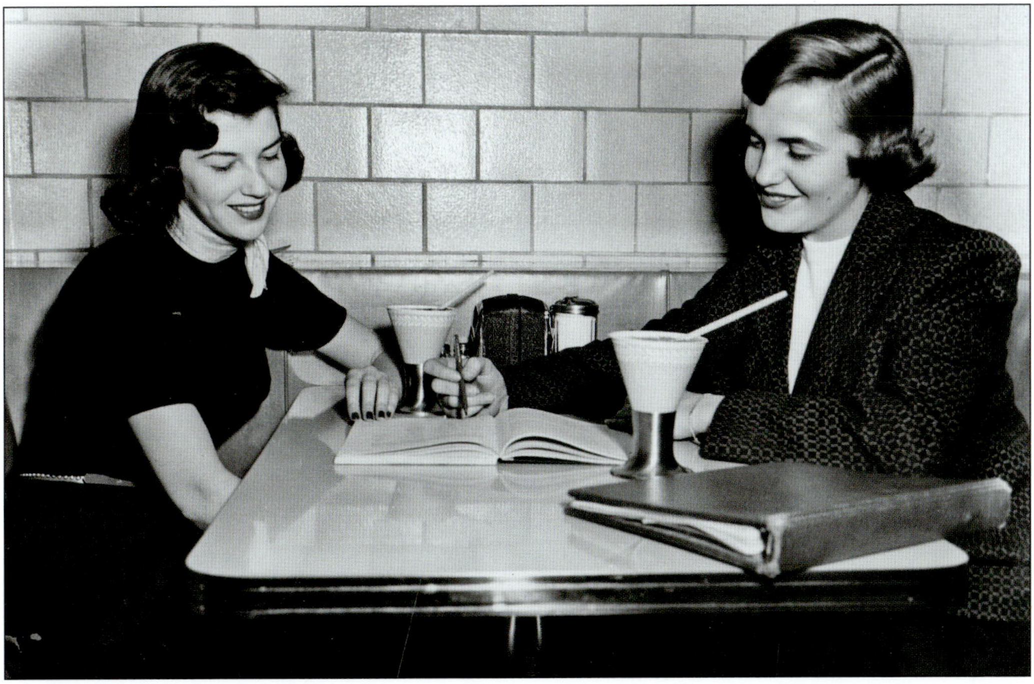

The student center quickly became a popular place to meet, gather, socialize, study, and grab a milkshake like these students enjoyed in 1954. When completed, the student center included a bookstore, a hotel, a bowling alley, a barbershop, and meeting rooms for conferences.

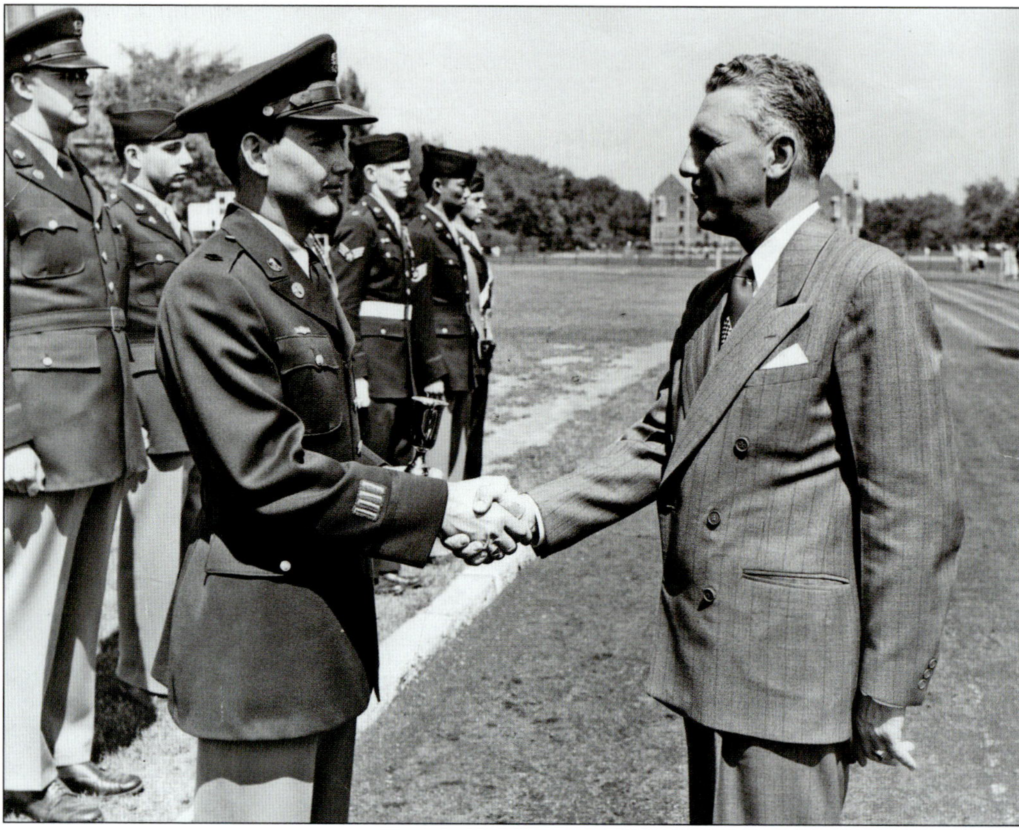

From 1948 to 1971, Ball State's Air Force ROTC program provided training for would-be officers in courses of study including air navigation, meteorology, marksmanship, and military law. Pictured above, Ball State Teachers College president John R. Emens greets cadet Joe Walker during a ceremony in 1950.

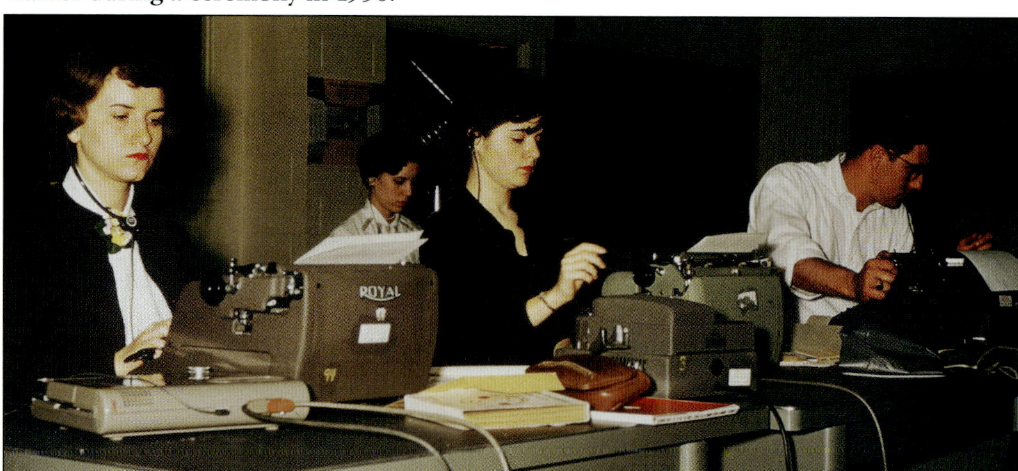

Completed in stages from 1950 to 1953, the Practical Arts Building (now Applied Technology Building) housed departments including Industrial Arts, Home Economics, and Business Education. Dictation, a valuable office administration skill, was studied and practiced by business education students at Ball State Teachers College.

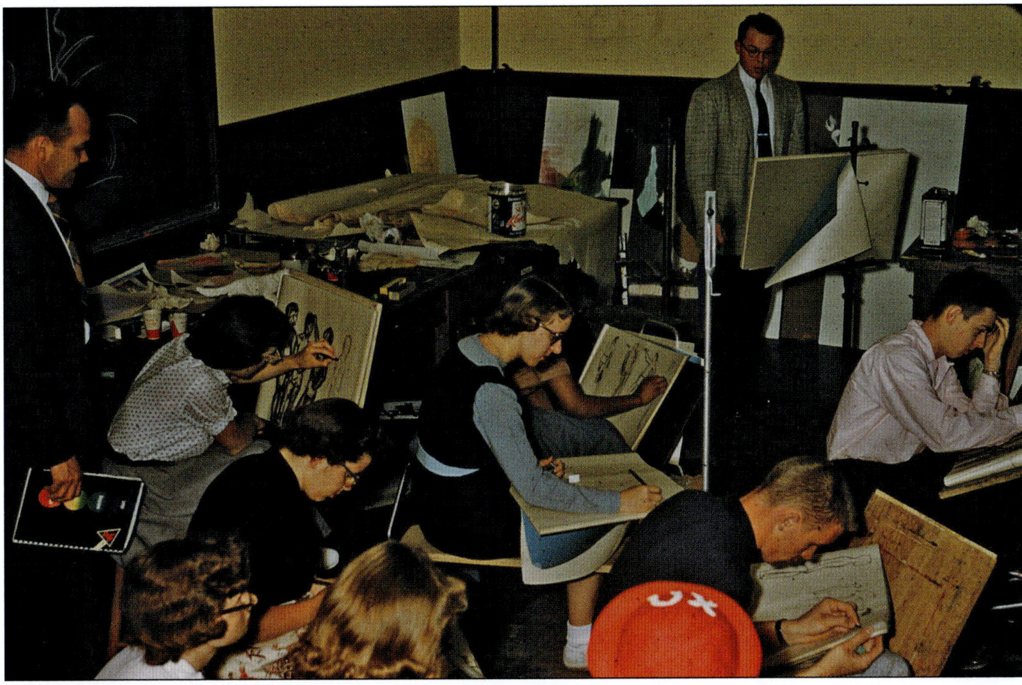

South of Riverside Avenue in the Arts Building, Ball State students took courses in painting, sculpting, drawing, and weaving. Here, art professor Warren Casey oversees a figure drawing class during the 1950s.

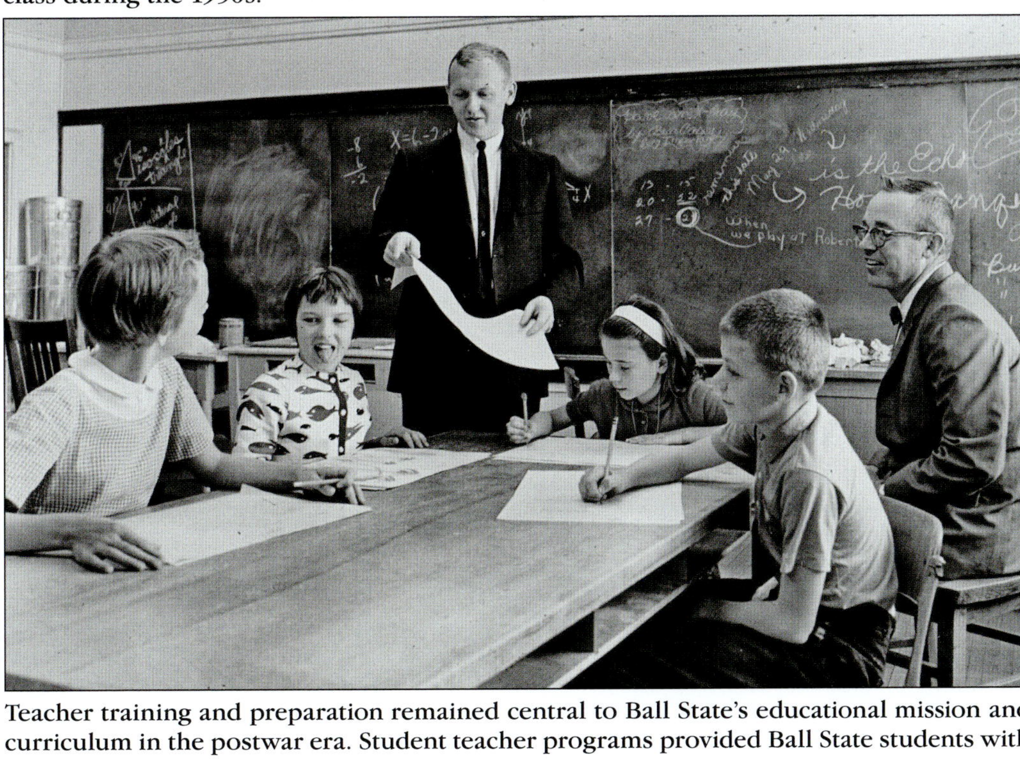

Teacher training and preparation remained central to Ball State's educational mission and curriculum in the postwar era. Student teacher programs provided Ball State students with valuable practice and experience at the head of the classroom.

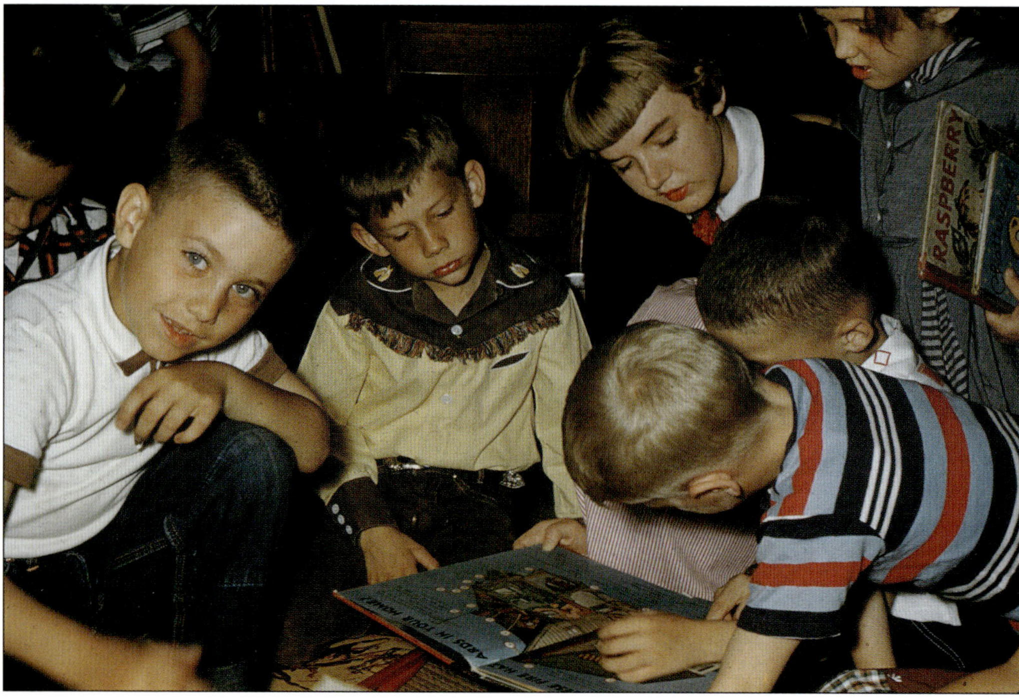

Student teacher Virginia O'Connell works with a second-grade reading class at the Burris Laboratory School around 1953–1957.

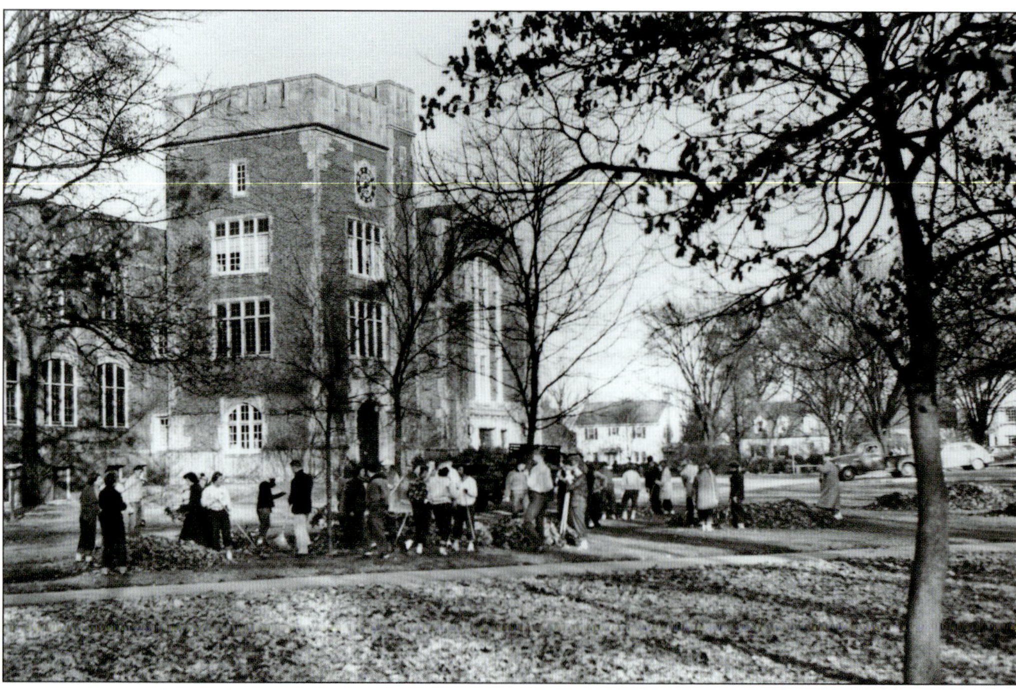

Beginning in the 1940s, the Leaf Rake was quickly established as one of the most prominent Ball State campus traditions. Every fall, students, faculty, and administrators alike pitched in to keep the Quad clear and tidy.

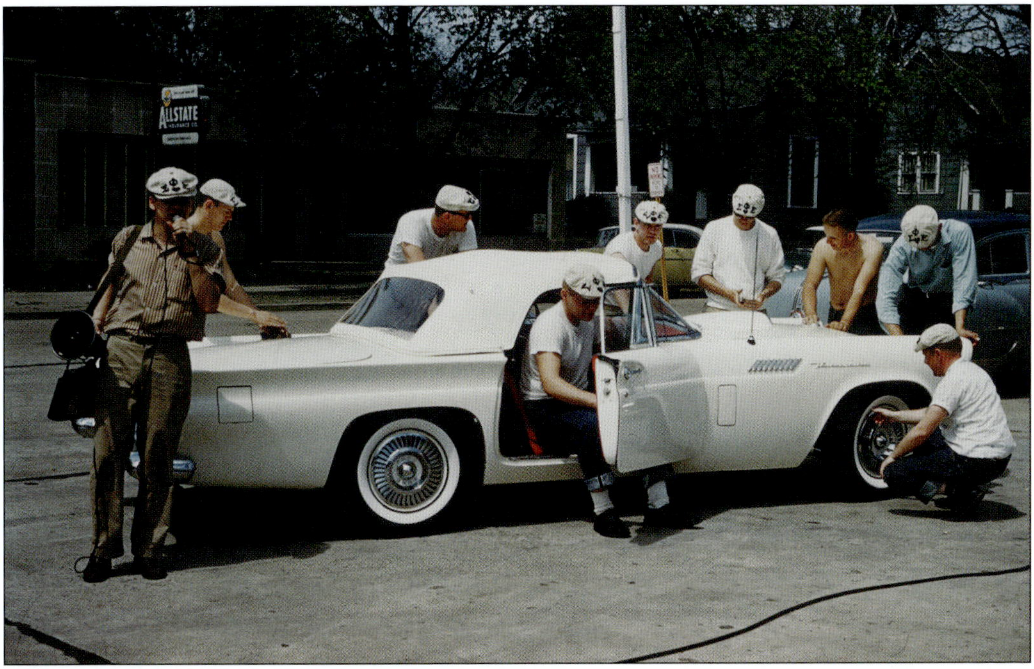

The period from 1945 to 1965 saw a burgeoning Greek scene at Ball State, with 11 new fraternities and sororities organizing on campus. The recruitment process put pledges to work, including these soon-to-be Sigma Phi Epsilon pledges holding a car wash at a service station in the Village.

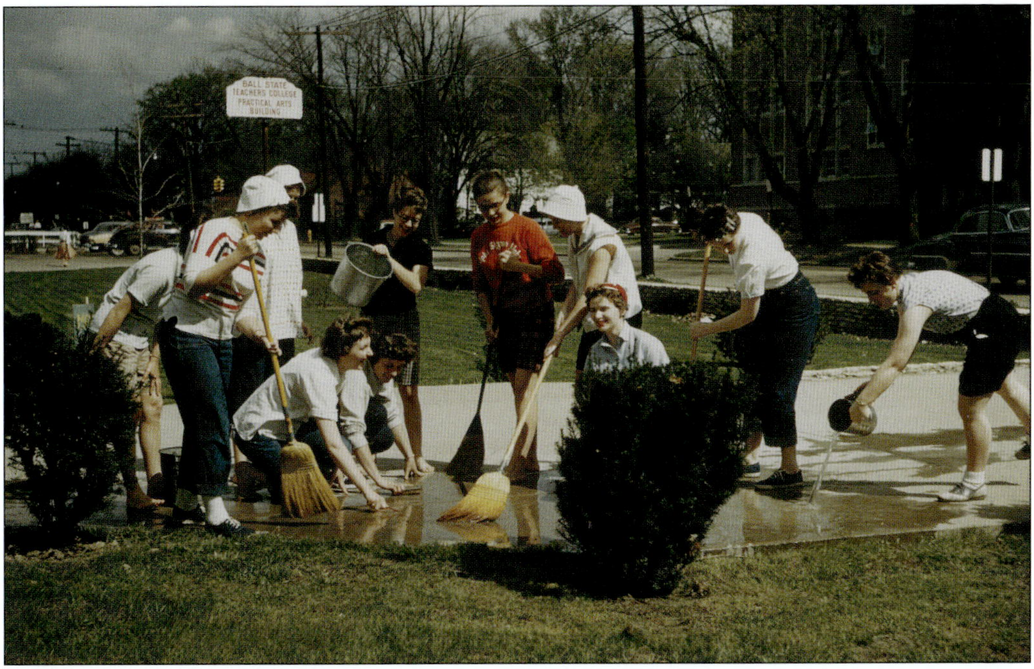

Across campus, sorority pledges scrub the sidewalk along Riverside Avenue in the spring of 1957.

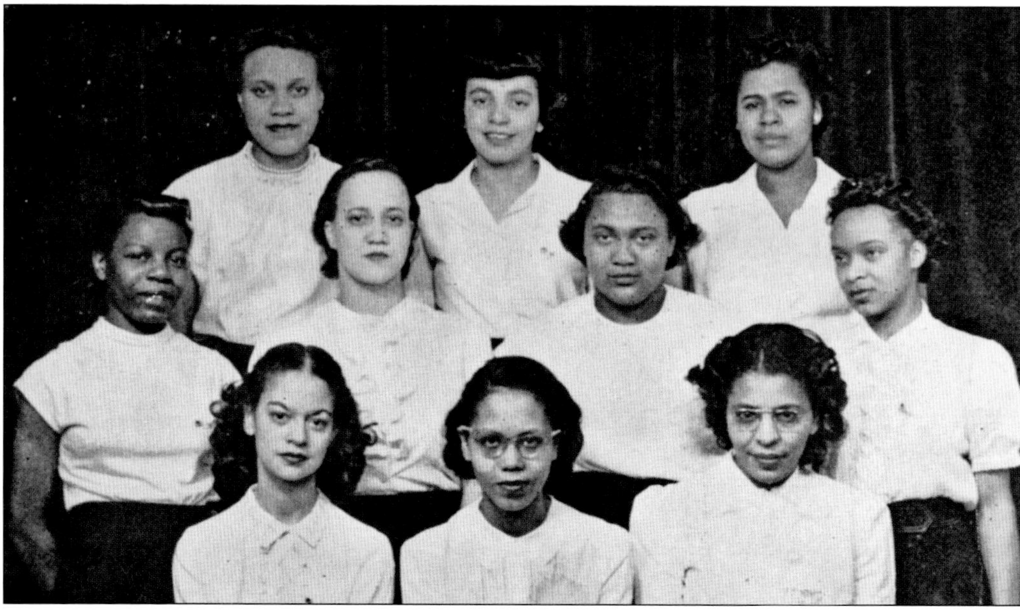

Organized in 1940, Sigma Gamma Rho became the first African American sorority on the Ball State Teachers College campus. The 1947–1948 class pictured here, led by Pres. Juanita Smith (front row, left), was sponsored by professors Ruth Dutro and Mary Beeman.

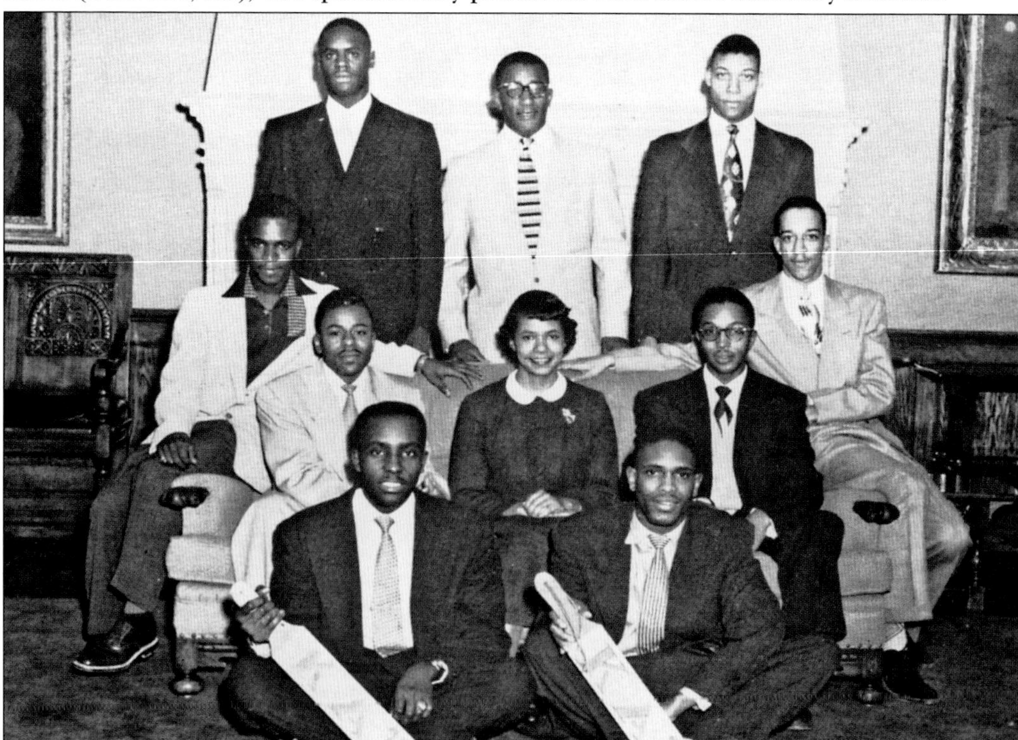

Kappa Alpha Psi became the first African American fraternity on campus, initiated on February 22, 1953. The chapter's first president was Leonard Edwards, seated here on the far right of the second row.

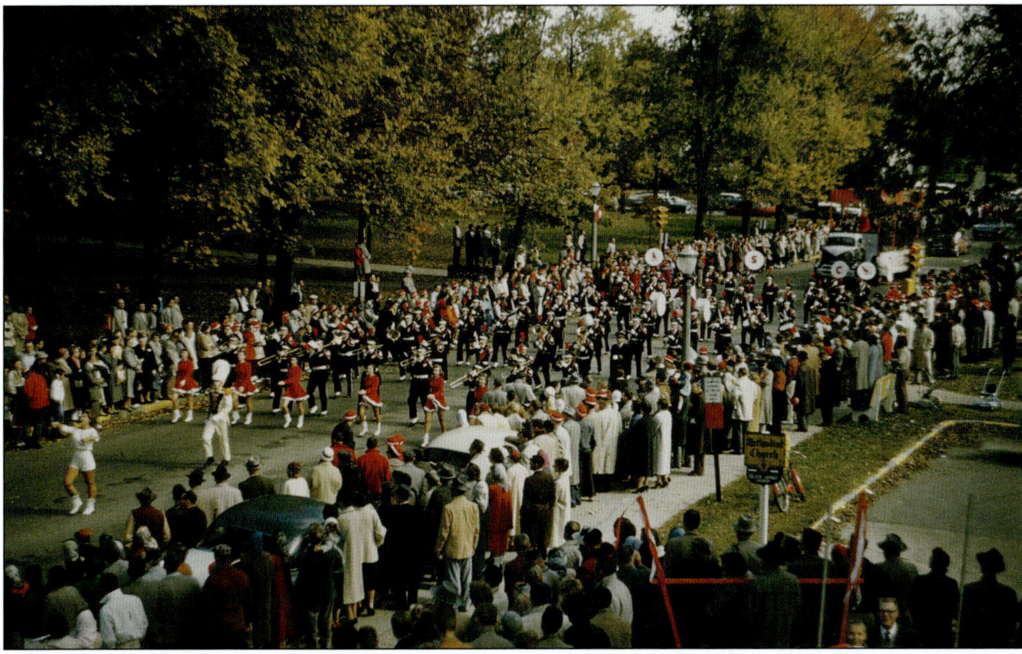

Homecoming brought alumni young and old back to campus to revisit old friendships and take in the changing, growing college. Here, parade goers line University Avenue to ring in Homecoming 1957 as the Ball State Teachers College Marching Band leads the way to the football field.

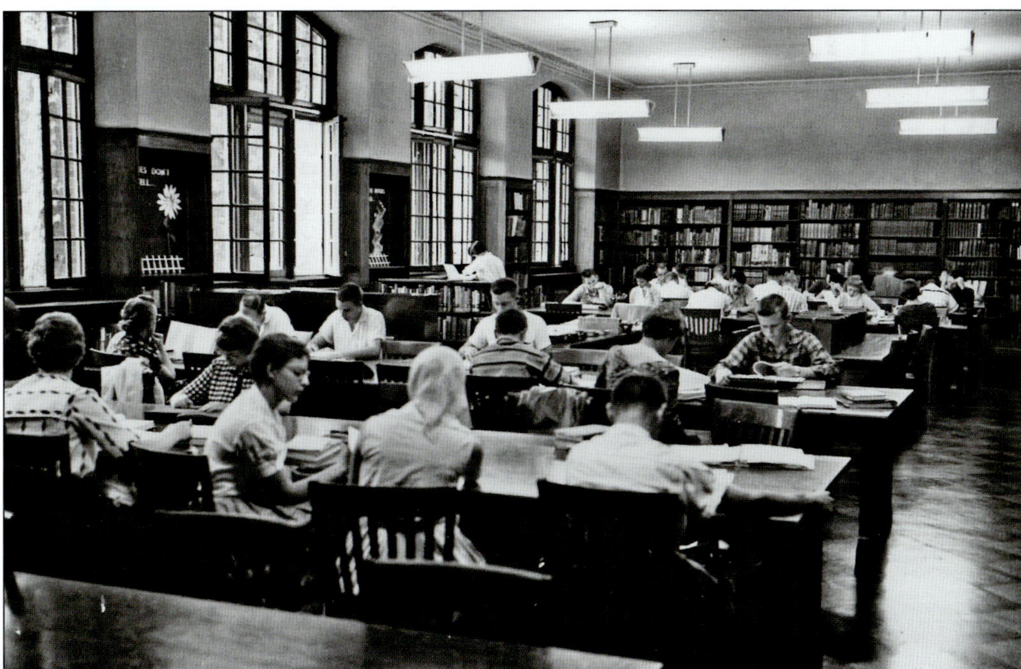

The college library, then housed in today's North Quadrangle Building, was frequently packed with students seeking access to books, periodicals, films, audio recordings, and teaching tools—and quiet study space.

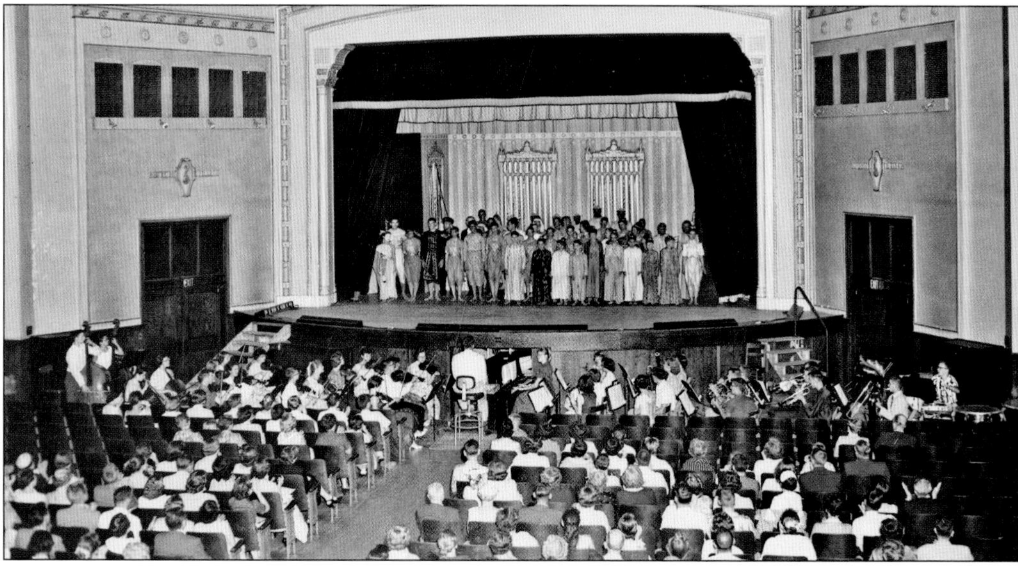

Sharing a building with the library was the Assembly Hall, which housed major performances, lectures, and programs until the opening of Emens Auditorium in 1964.

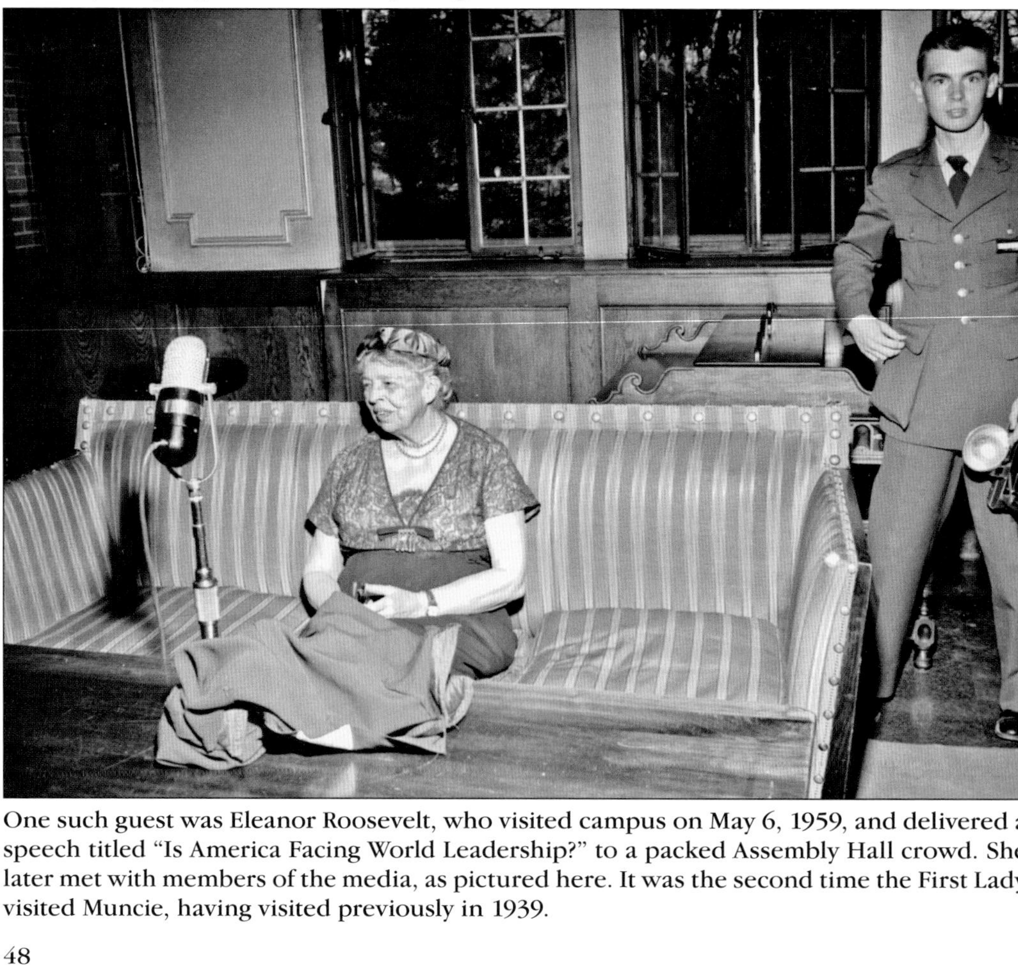

One such guest was Eleanor Roosevelt, who visited campus on May 6, 1959, and delivered a speech titled "Is America Facing World Leadership?" to a packed Assembly Hall crowd. She later met with members of the media, as pictured here. It was the second time the First Lady visited Muncie, having visited previously in 1939.

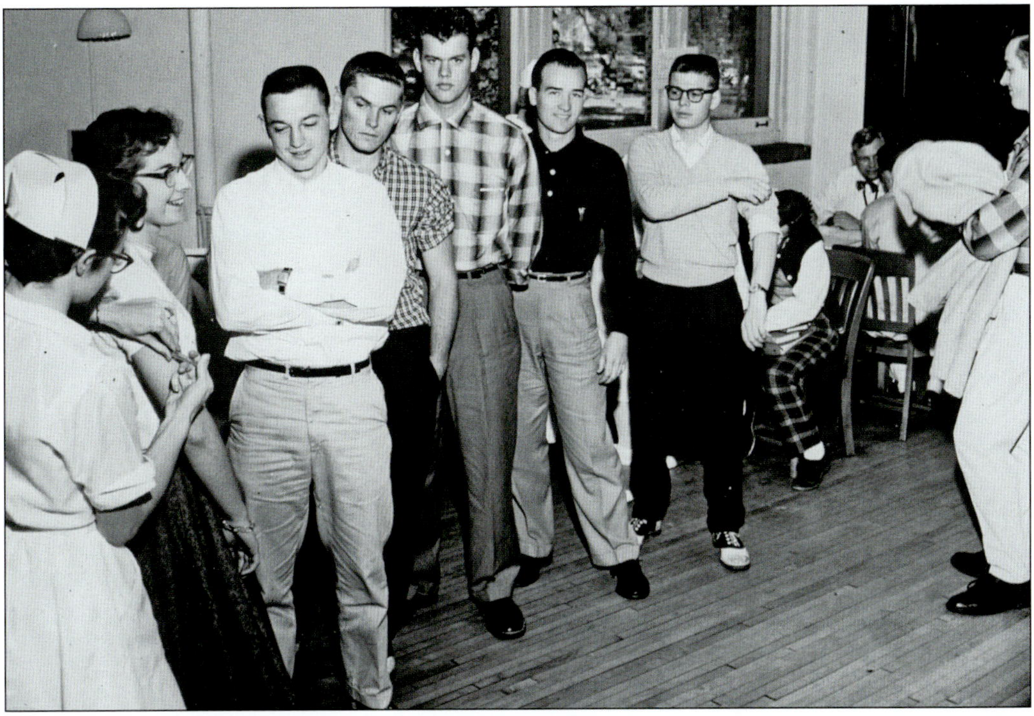

Ball State provided robust healthcare for its students in the 1950s via the College Health Service, including a vaccination program.

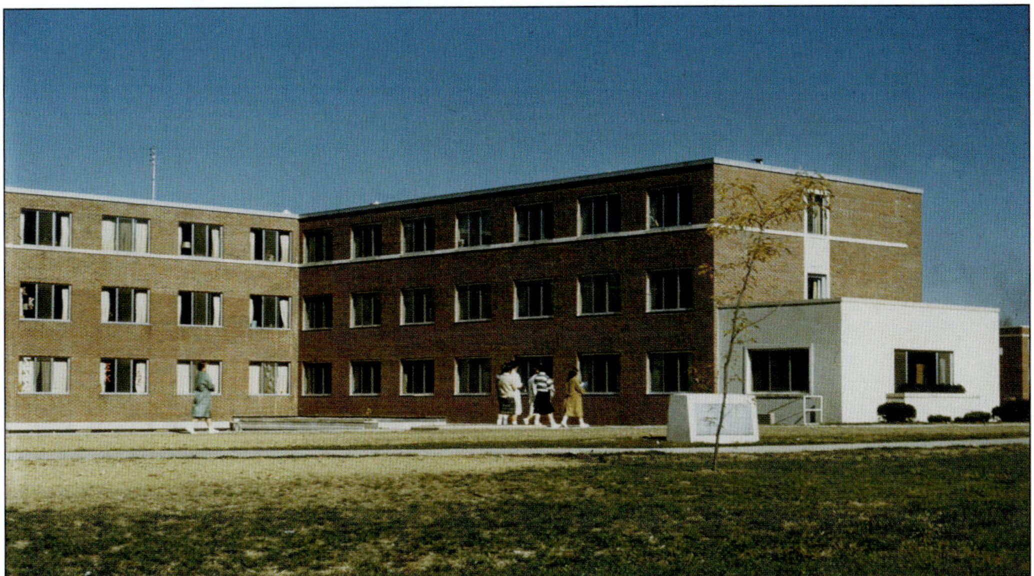

By the start of the 1960–1961 school year, over 7,000 students were enrolled at Ball State Teachers College. Temporary housing gave way to permanent, modern structures. Frances Woodworth Ball Halls (named after Frances Woodworth, wife of George A. Ball), pictured here, opened in 1956, accommodating 624 women. Wagoner Hall (now home to Indiana Academy for Science, Mathematics, and Humanities students) opened a year later, housing 413 men.

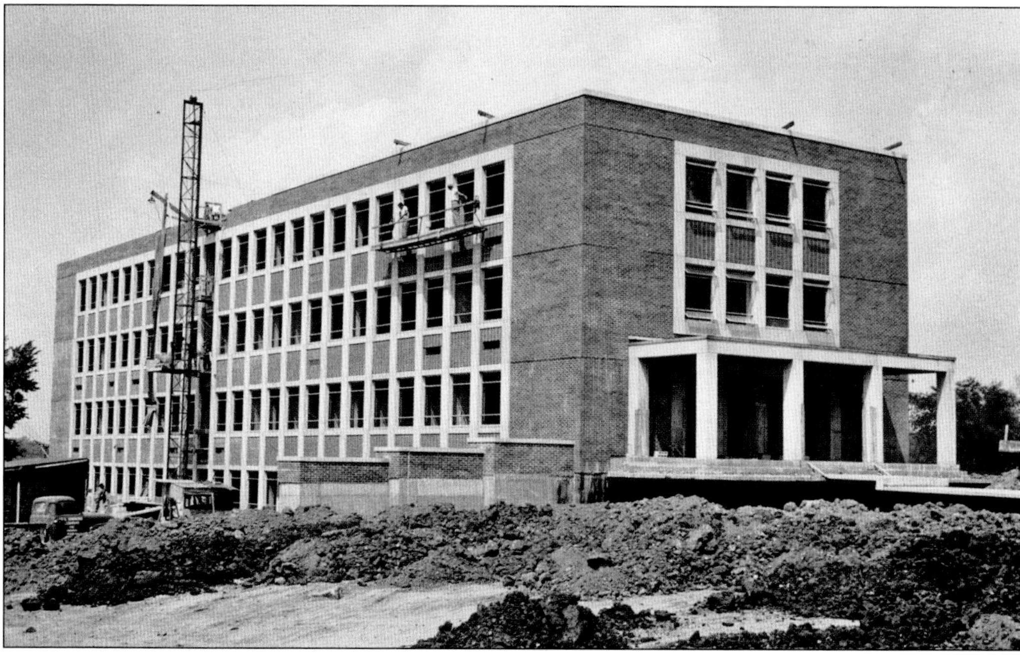

Classroom buildings were a focus of campus development as well in order to accommodate a growing faculty and larger, more specialized, modern classroom spaces to support advancing academic programs. Such buildings included the Music Building (opened in 1957, seen here under construction) and the English Building (opened in 1959).

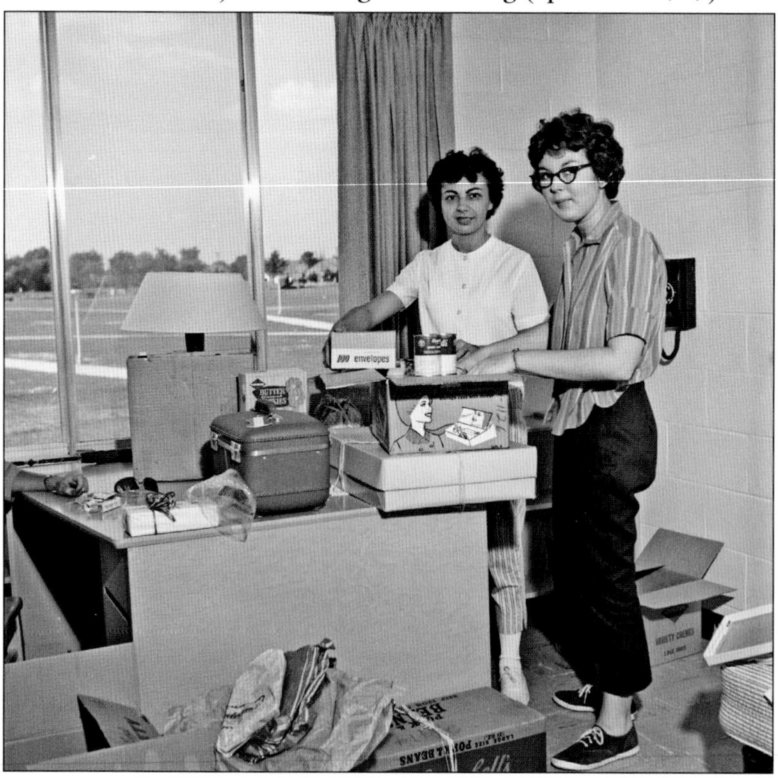

Additional residence halls built in the era include DeHority Halls (1960), named for Grace DeHority, dean of women at Ball State from 1922 to 1946, and Noyer Halls (1962), named for Ralph Noyer, housing 612 and 928 students respectively. Shown here is one of Noyer's first inhabitants with family in September 1962.

Overseeing Ball State's monumental and visionary growth in both size and reputation was Pres. John R. Emens, pictured in 1963 with Ball State first lady Aline Emens hosting a reception for graduating seniors.

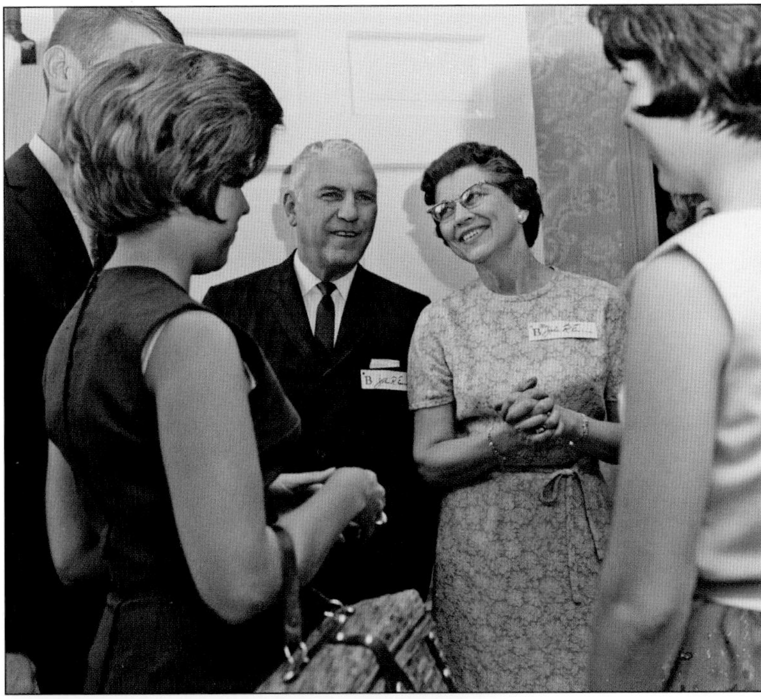

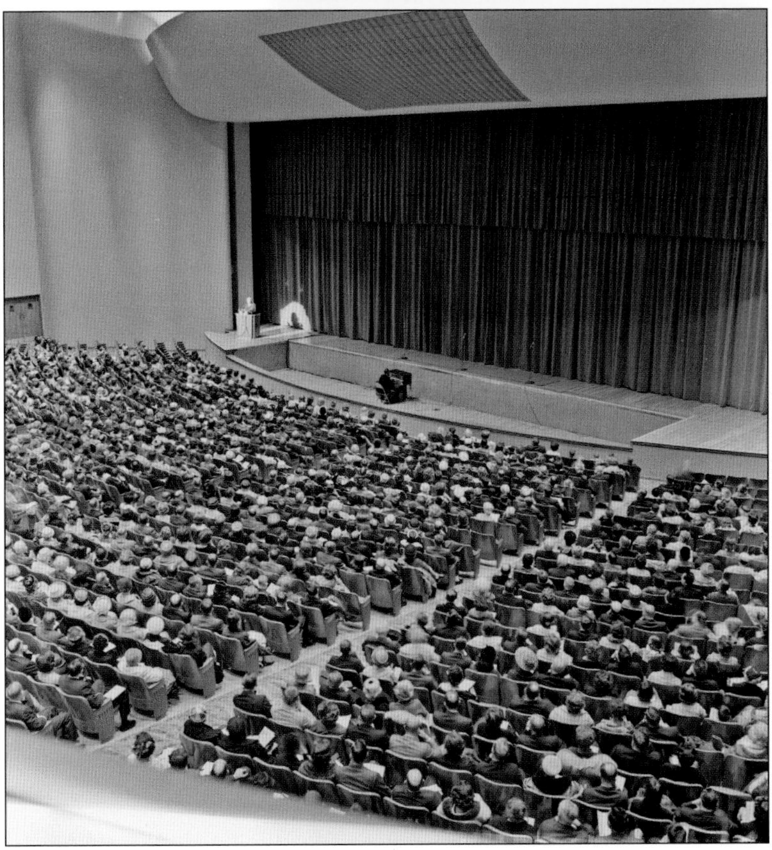

Emens Auditorium, opened in March 1964 with a sneak-peek performance by Fred Waring and his Pennsylvanians, became a Muncie landmark, providing invaluable cultural programming and event space for the Ball State and Muncie communities alike.

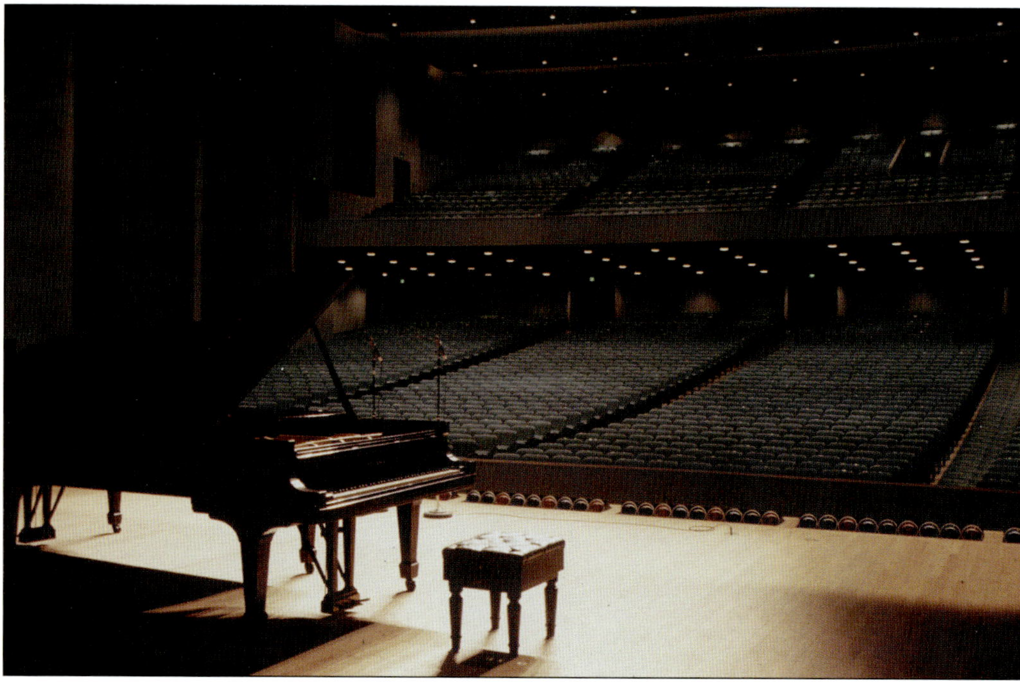

The auditorium, designed with a capacity of over 3,600, featured state-of-the-art acoustical engineering and hosted both Ball State University performances and national and international artists and acts.

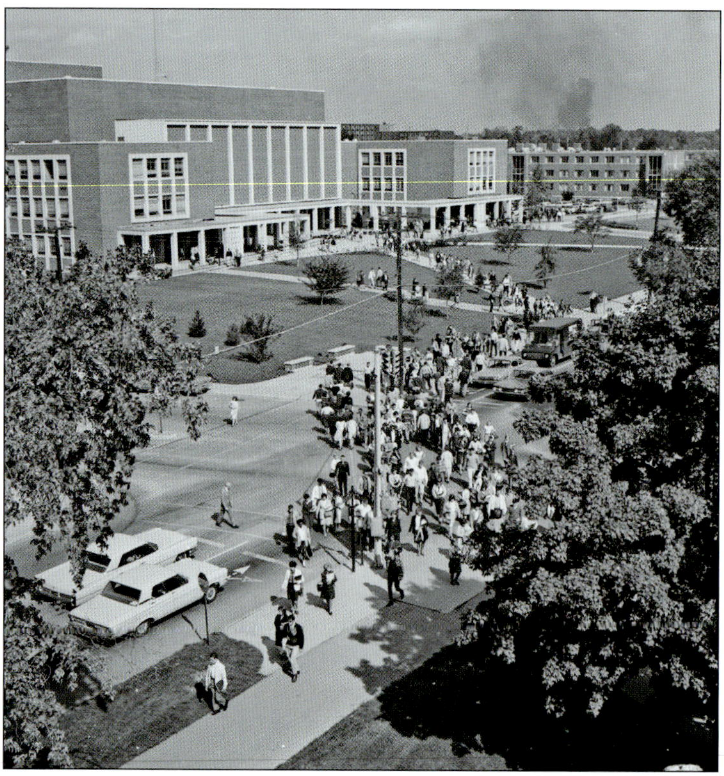

Ball State's iconic "scramble light," installed in 1959 and pictured in 1965, allowed students to traverse their growing campus by crossing the McKinley Avenue and Riverside Avenue intersection diagonally.

In 1962, student actors and actresses perform *Where's Charley?* in a series of performances in the University Theatre. Along with performances and exhibits in art and music, the theatrical scene became increasingly popular at Ball State in the 1960s.

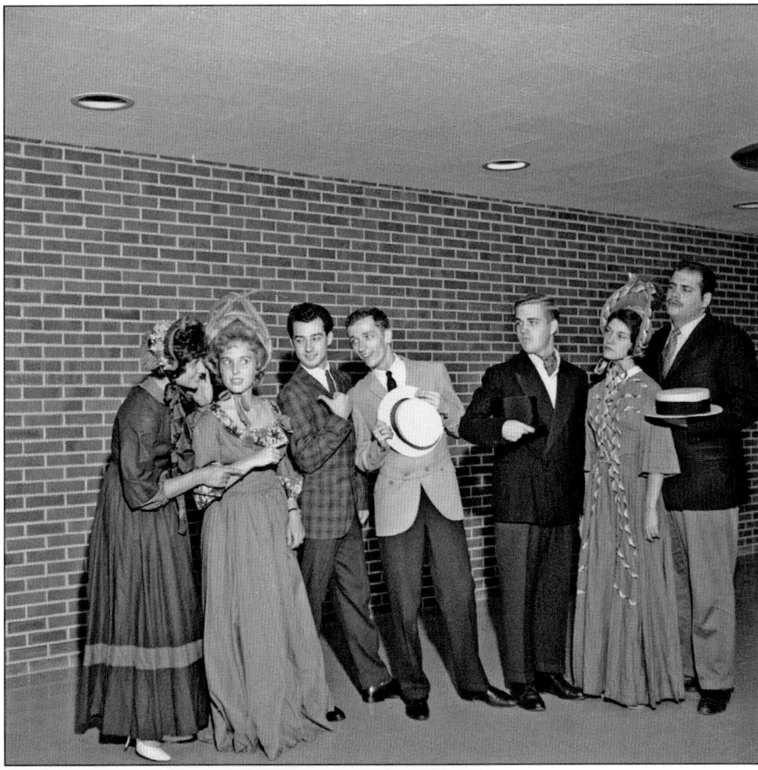

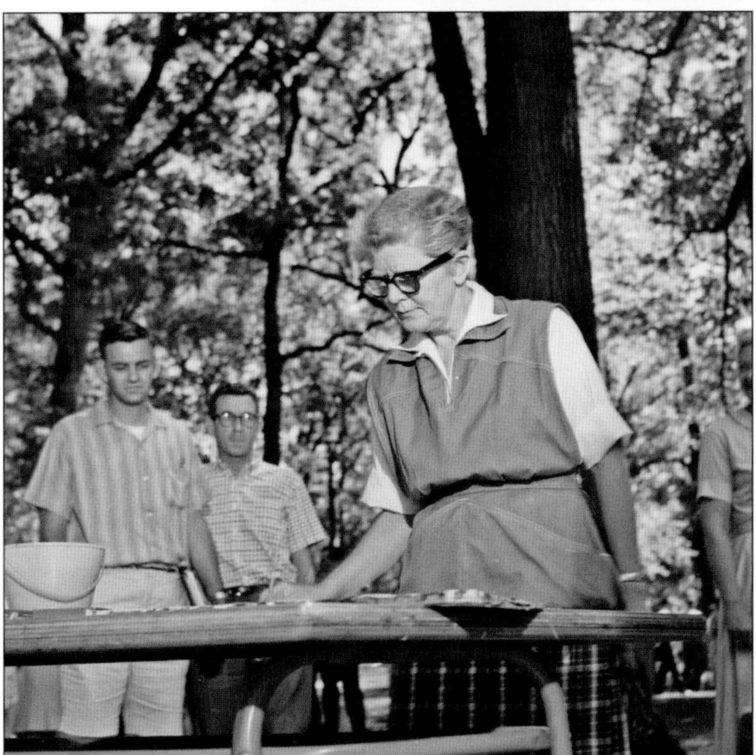

Alice Nichols, head of the Ball State Art Department from 1947 to 1968, is shown giving a painting demonstration at the annual Ball State Arts Festival in 1962. The Ball State Museum of Art (now the David Owsley Museum of Art) greatly enriched the depth and diversity of its collection under Nichols's leadership.

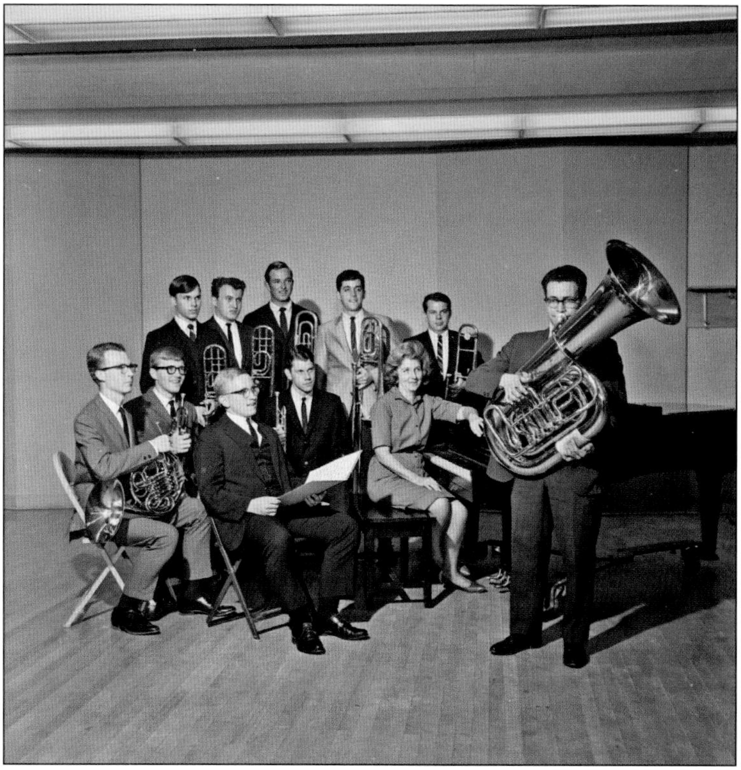

Members of the Ball State University Brass Ensemble gather for a practice and a performance in 1965. Ball State's newly constructed Music Building attracted an increasingly specialized and renowned faculty and a growing population of both undergraduate and graduate music students.

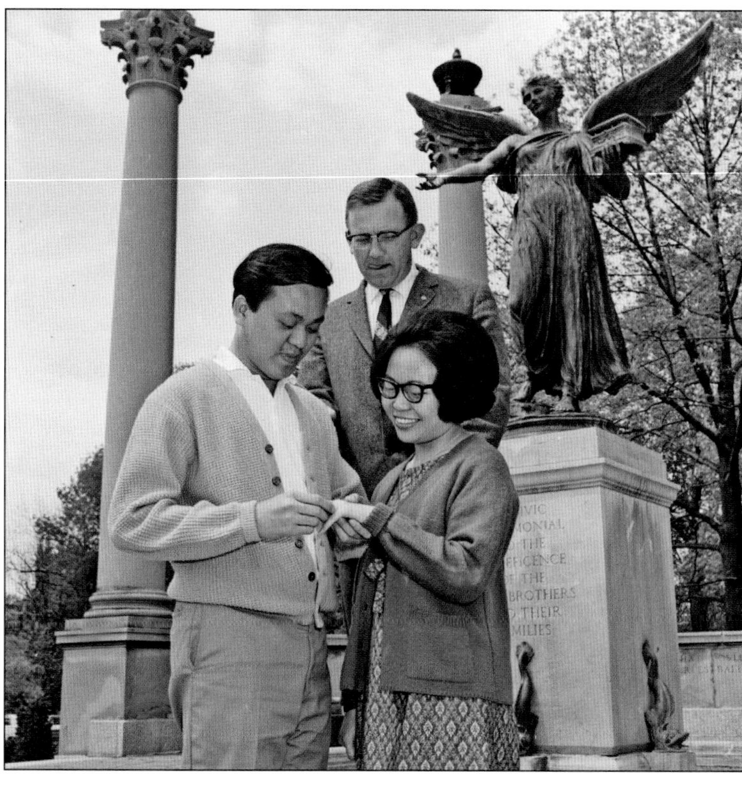

Ball State first began actively recruiting international students in the postwar era and by 1965 boasted an international enrollment of over 60 students from over 25 different countries. In May 1964, international students Phanich Hansa and Julia Shuai Hansa celebrate their engagement alongside Richard Alexander, director of international student programs at Ball State from 1959 to 1965.

Robert Russell LaFollette, namesake of the LaFollette Complex, was a member of the Ball State faculty from 1921 to 1961, serving as chair of the Social Science Department for much of his tenure. He was known for his legendary ability to know, and call, all of his students by their first names when he met them outside the classroom. LaFollette tragically died in a plane crash in 1967 during a higher education consulting visit to South Vietnam.

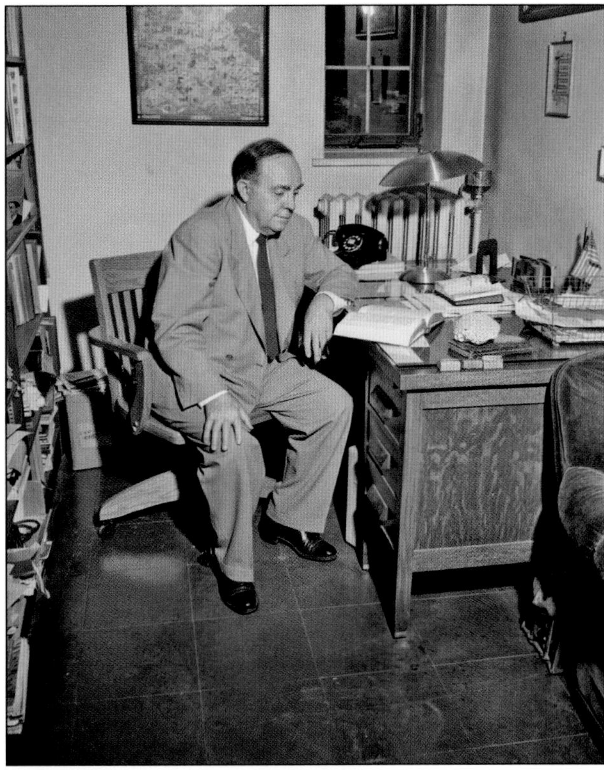

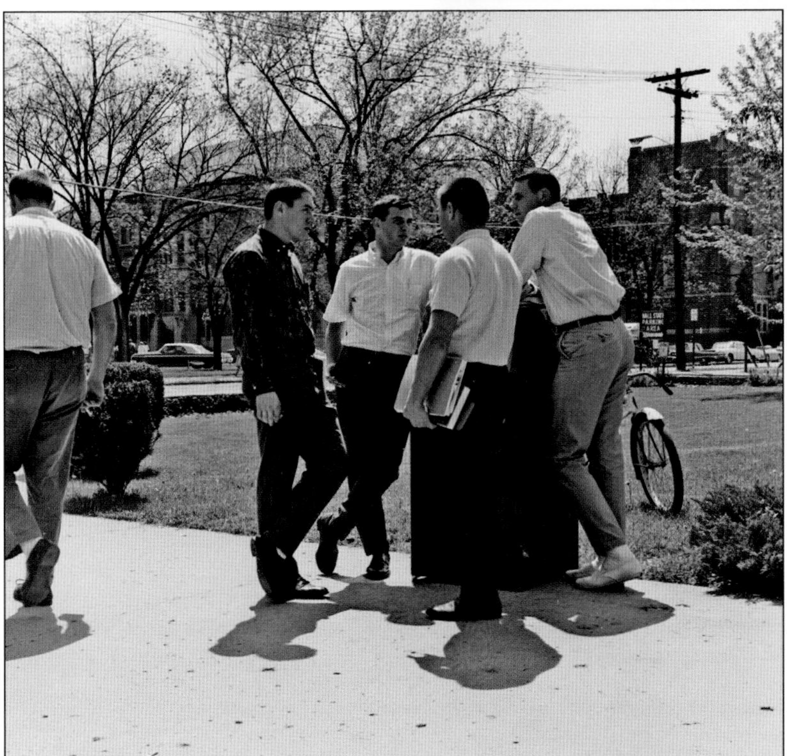

Several men enjoy a lovely afternoon on campus in May 1963, their thoughts undoubtedly turning toward the end of the academic year, coming up later that month.

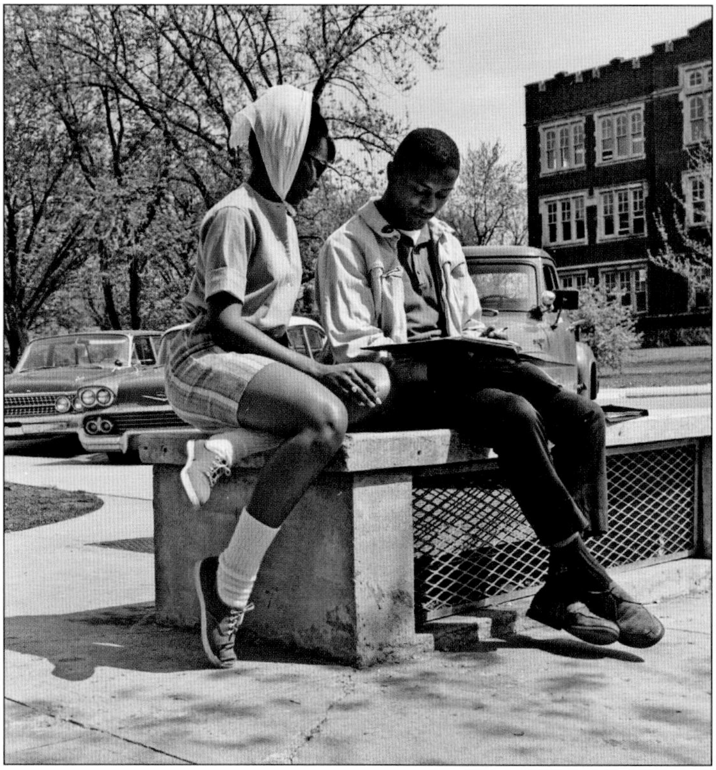

Two students take a break to read on a bench along Ball State's circular drive just north of the Administration Building.

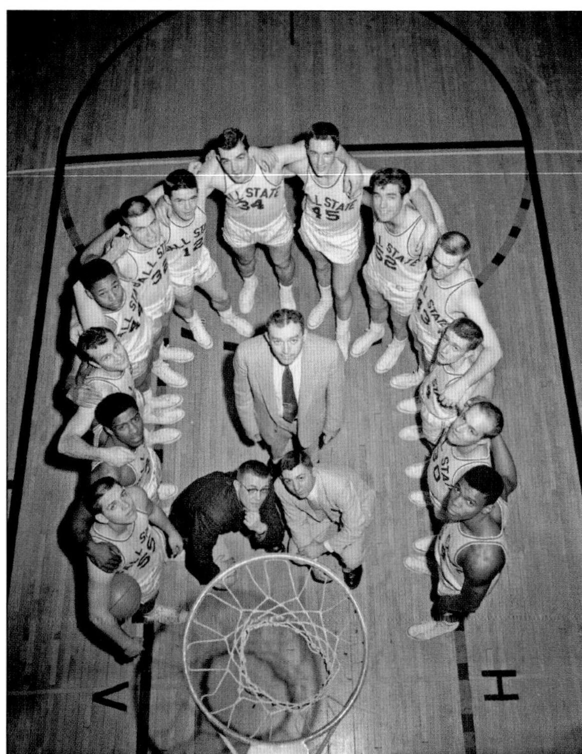

On the heels of a strong season, compiling a regular season record of 16 wins and 7 losses, the Ball State men's basketball team earned an invitation to the 1957 NAIA Division I Men's Basketball Tournament. The team was coached by Jim Hinga (center) and led by all-conference forwards Tom Dobbs (45) and Wayne Van Sickle (43).

Ball State's football team thrived in the Indiana Collegiate Conference under the leadership of head coach Ray Louthen, who led the team to a 37-13-3 record during his tenure from 1962 to 1967. Here, Louthen leads Ball State to victory over Butler in 1964 alongside student athletes Merv Rettenmund (15), who went on to greater fame as a 13-year Major League Baseball player.

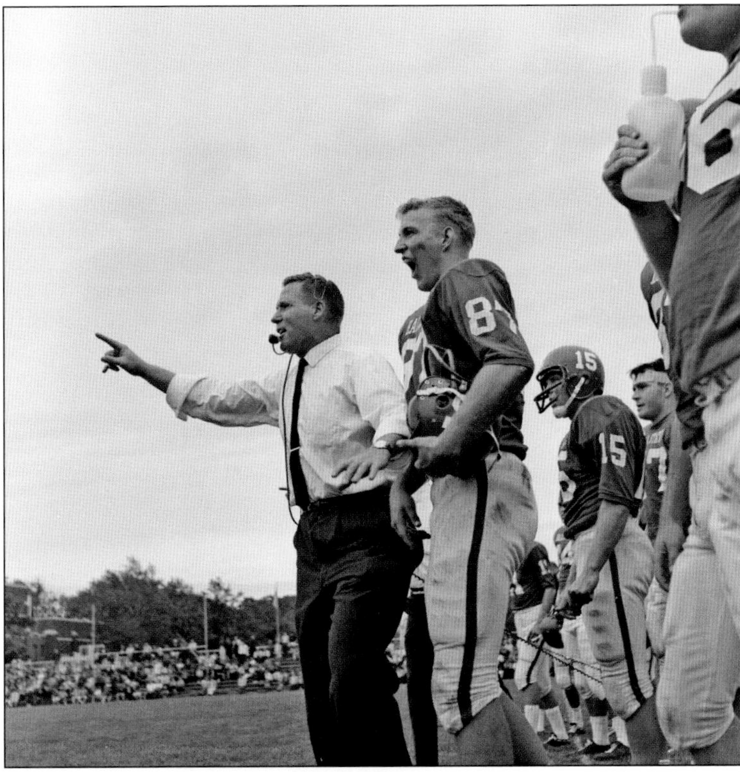

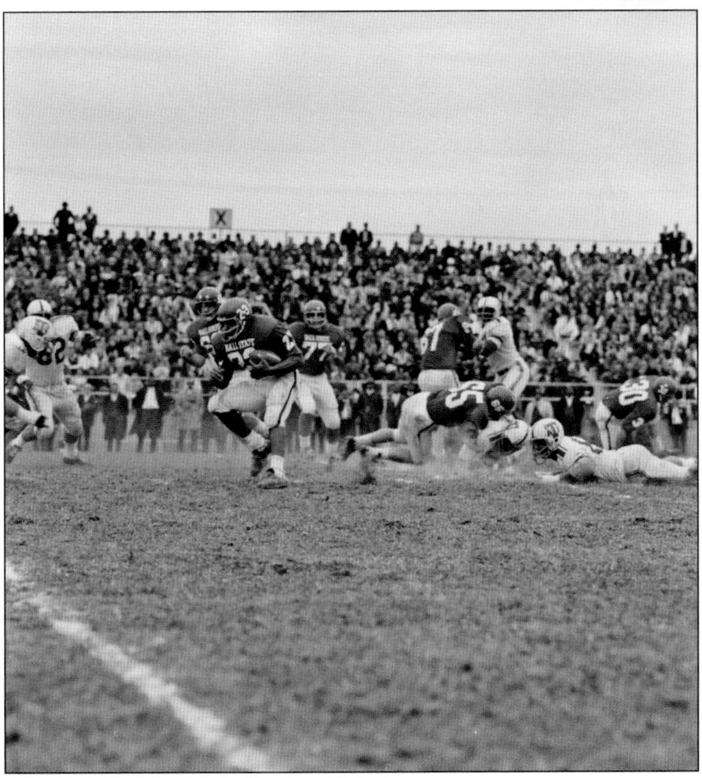

Ball State's star halfback Jim Todd carries the ball against Tennessee State University when the two schools met at the Grantland Rice Bowl in Murfreesboro, Tennessee, in December 1965. The contest ended in a hard fought 14-14 deadlock, preserving Ball State's undefeated season. The Cardinals finished the year with a 9-0-1 record and a conference championship.

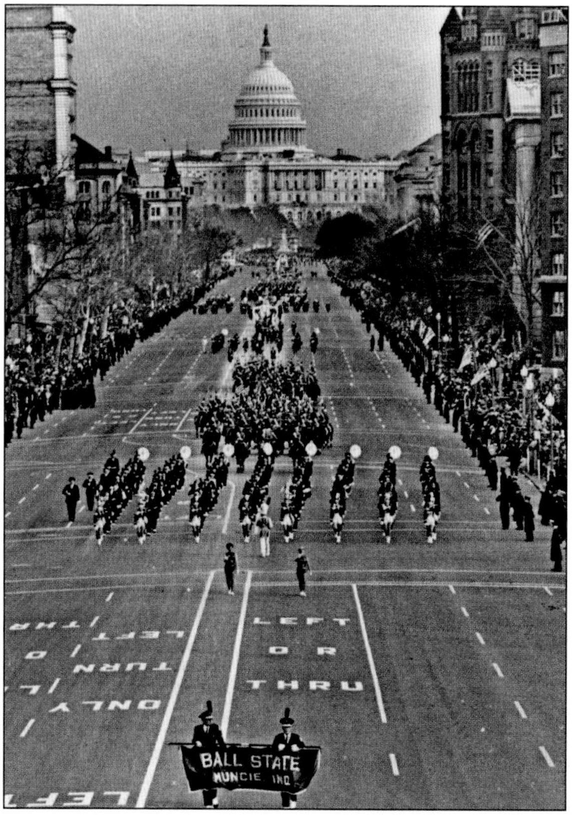

Earl Dunn directed the Ball State Marching Band from 1957 to 1969 and greatly increased the regional and national profile of the band, which earned invitations to perform at numerous prominent sporting events, parades, and celebrations. In January 1965, the Ball State Marching Band performed in the inaugural parade of Pres. Lyndon Johnson in Washington, DC.

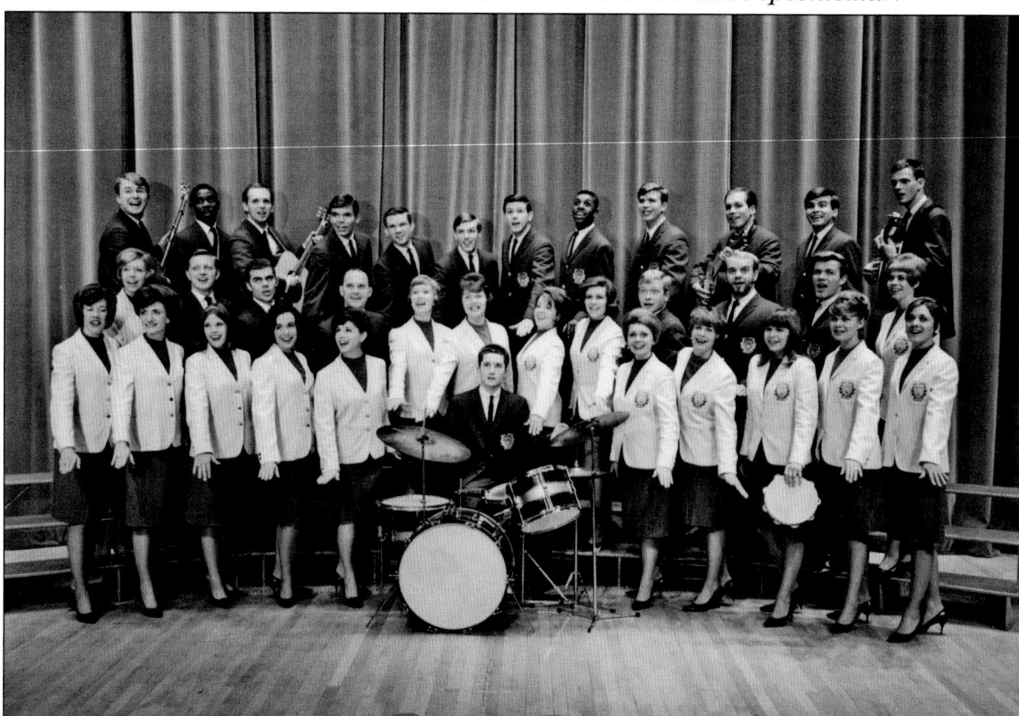

Ball State's University Singers were officially formed in 1965. Soon to become known as Indiana's Official Goodwill Ambassador, the University Singers were comprised of 40 students, including singers, dancers, instrumentalists, and sound technicians. Their annual feature performance was the production of the *Ball State Spectacular*.

Four

A Regional Public University 1965–1984

When Ball State Teachers College became Ball State University in 1965, it ventured into a new realm of expectations. Ball State's new challenge was to become a comprehensive regional public university that emphasized undergraduate education while also offering selective graduate programs.

With university status came a new administrative structure that focused on five colleges: the College of Architecture and Planning, the College of Business, the College of Fine and Applied Arts, the College of Sciences and Humanities, and the Teachers College. Not surprisingly, as enrollment in Ball State's teacher education program declined in response to a national teacher surplus, newer programs in the other colleges expanded.

In the midst of this historic transition, Ball State developed some impressive strengths. Under the direction of Dr. David Costill, Ball State opened its Human Performance Laboratory (HPL) in the early 1970s with an emphasis on exercise physiology and improved athletic performance. Costill also succeeded in obtaining external funding from public and private sources for the HPL's research agenda.

Also, an emerging issue in higher education at the time was improving access to colleges and universities for students with physical handicaps. At the initiative of Dr. Merrill C. Beyerl, vice president for student affairs, Ball State established the Office of Handicapped Services (OHS) to provide academic support and ease of access across campus for students with disabilities. Under the direction of Richard W. Harris, the OHS was a pioneer in serving the needs of disabled students while also raising awareness of this issue throughout American higher education.

Finally, Ball State made its mark in intercollegiate athletics during this transitional period. Once Ball State became a member of the Mid-American Conference, its athletes and coaches rose to the occasion, winning conference championships in men's golf and men's cross country in 1975, in football in 1976 and 1978, in men's basketball in 1981, and in women's field hockey in 1983. The success of Ball State's athletes helped to raise the university's profile as a comprehensive regional public university. By 1984, Ball State was comfortably at home in the presence of other Midwestern regional universities.

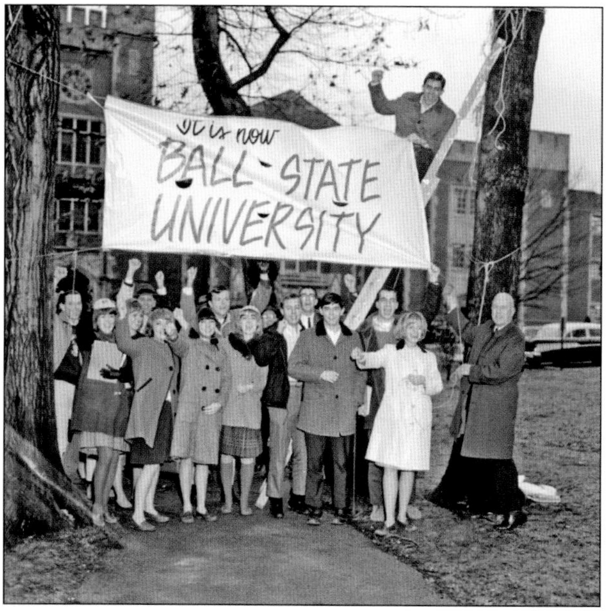

On February 8, 1965, Indiana governor Roger D. Branigin signed House Bill 1014, granting university status to the institution—Ball State Teachers College, with an enrollment exceeding 10,000 students, became Ball State University. Above, University president John R. Emens and students celebrate the momentous occasion under a banner in the Quad.

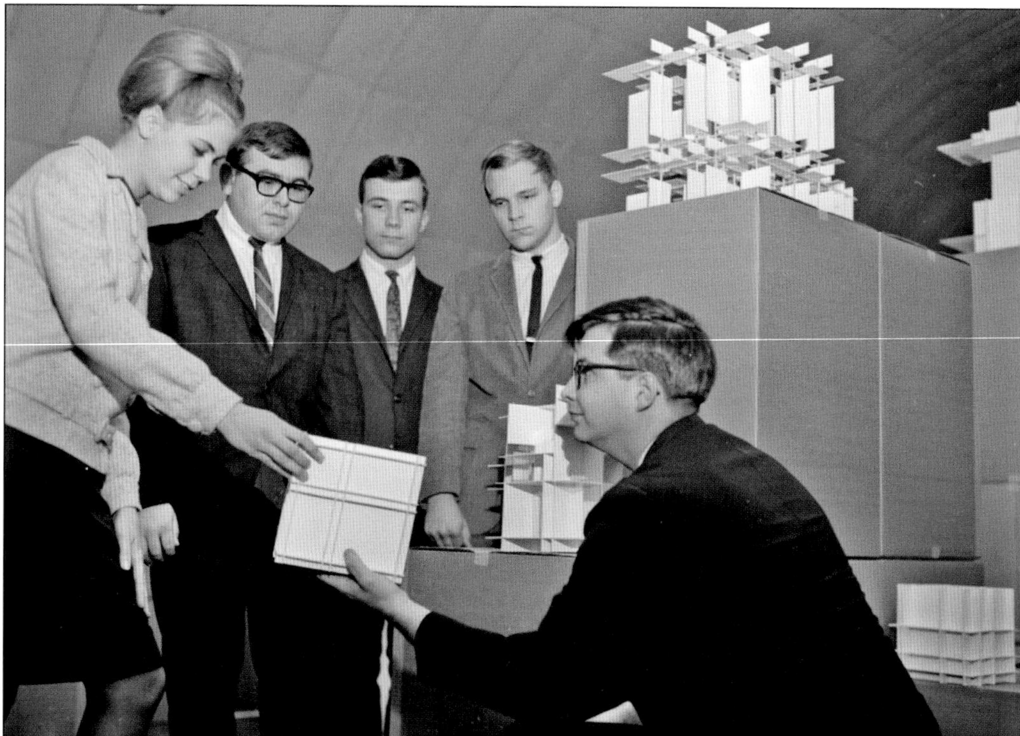

With Ball State's new university status came new colleges, including the College of Architecture and Planning, the first state-supported architecture program in Indiana higher education. The college first offered classes in 1966 and produced its first graduating class from the five-year bachelor of architecture program in 1971. Pictured here in 1967 is architecture professor Richard Pollak (kneeling) with students (from left to right) Barbara Downs, Eugene Deutsch, John Kemlo, and Charles Pfau.

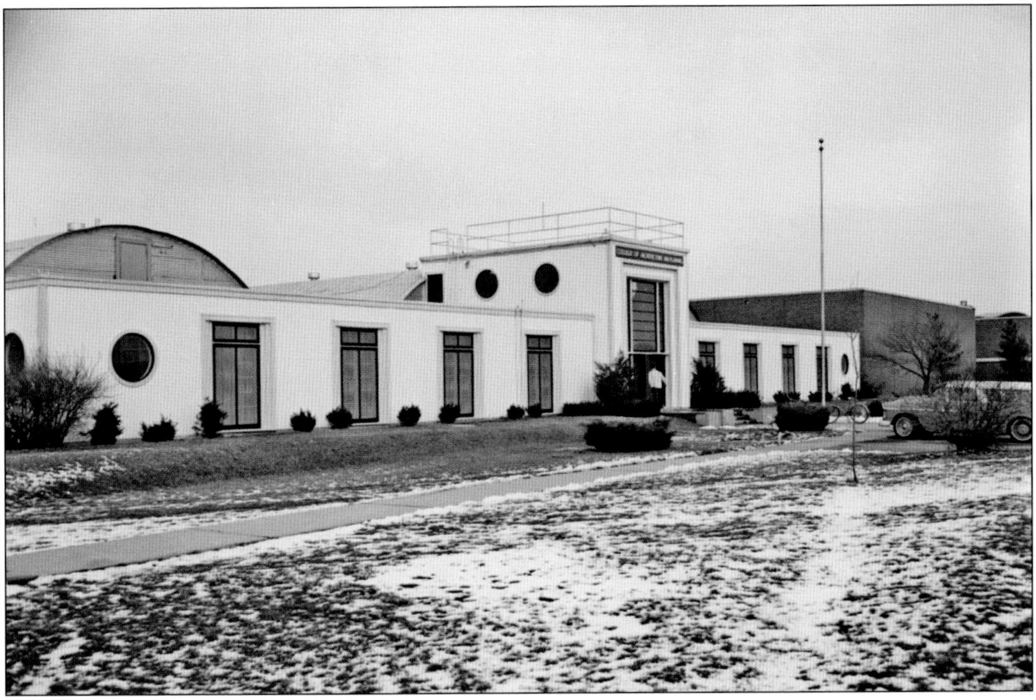

The College of Architecture and Planning's first dean was Charles M. Sappenfield, and its first building was a converted Naval Reserve Armory Quonset hut structure located just northeast of the McKinley Avenue and Neely Avenue intersection, pictured here in the winter of 1967. The College of Architecture and Planning received its permanent home with the completion of the Architecture Building, erected southeast of the intersection of McKinley Avenue and Neely Avenue. Constructed for $2.2 million, the building was designed by South Bend architect Melvin D. Birkey, winner of a design competition to develop a new permanent home for the college.

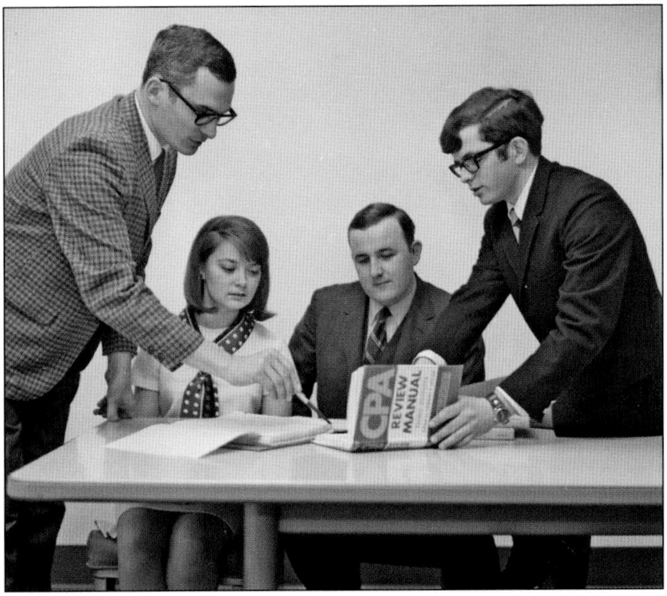

Also founded in 1965 was Ball State University's College of Business, bringing together programs in accounting, business education, office administration, business administration, and marketing. From left to right in April 1969 are accounting professor Paul Parkison, who served on Ball State's faculty from 1966 to 2001, and students Debbie Michael, Steve McGann, and Les Coop. Parkison, an alumnus of Ball State, held the title of Alumni Distinguished Professor of Accounting from 1994 until his retirement.

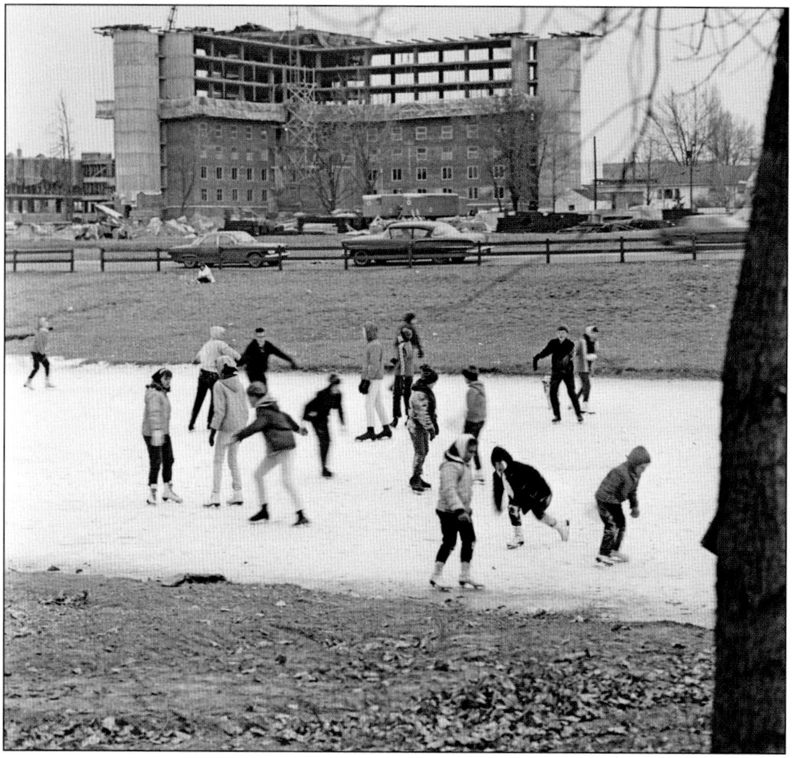

Beginning in the mid-1960s, Ball State expanded its residence halls upward as well as outward. The LaFollette Complex, which opened in stages from 1966 to 1967, featured nine individual residence halls housing nearly 2,000 students in total with vast space for dining halls and student meeting spaces.

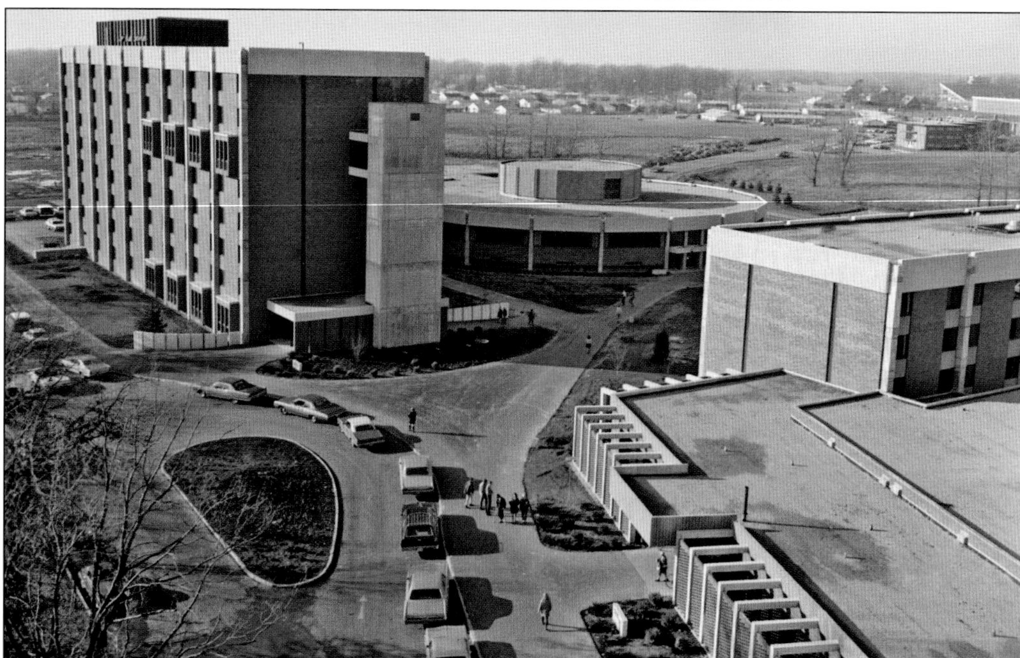

The Johnson Complex, consisting of the residence halls Botsford Hall, Swinford Hall, Wilson Hall, and Schmidt Hall and the classroom building Carmichael Hall, opened in 1969. The Johnson Complex was readily identifiable on the northern part of campus across from the Duck Pond.

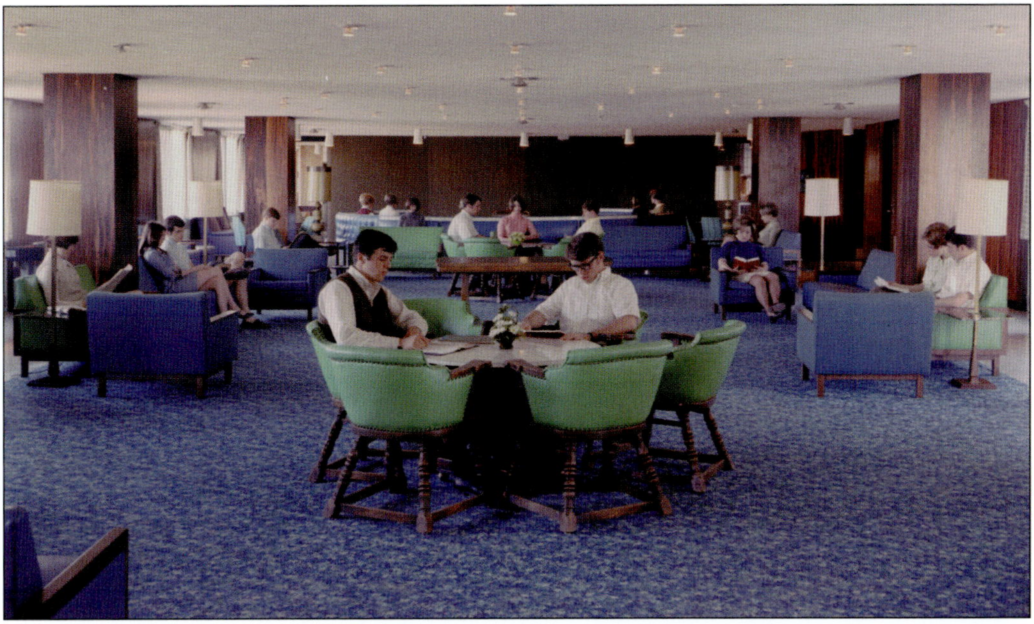

The Studebaker West Complex (completed in 1964) and Studebaker East Complex (completed in 1965) expanded the campus footprint eastward, providing accommodations for over 1,300 student residents in total. The halls' lounges, like the one shown here in the summer of 1969, proved to be popular destinations for study and relaxation.

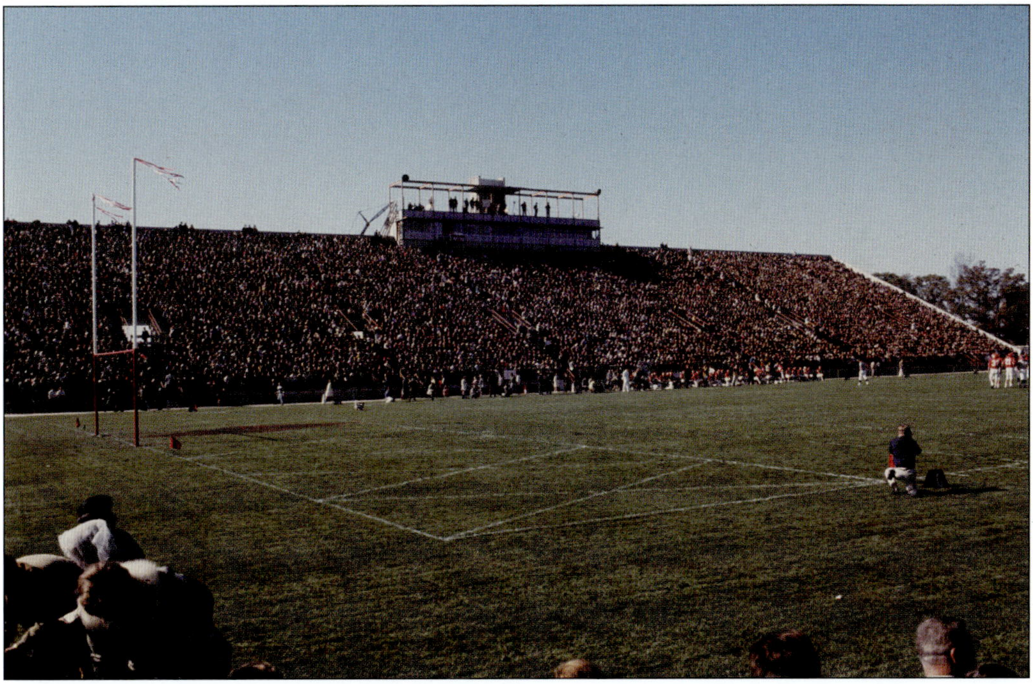

With success on the football field and a growing population of both students and alumni, Ball State outgrew its former football field just north of Ball Memorial Hospital. On October 21, 1967, Ball State Stadium (now Scheumann Stadium) was debuted as the Cardinals soundly defeated the Butler Bulldogs 65-7 in front of a homecoming crowd of over 17,000.

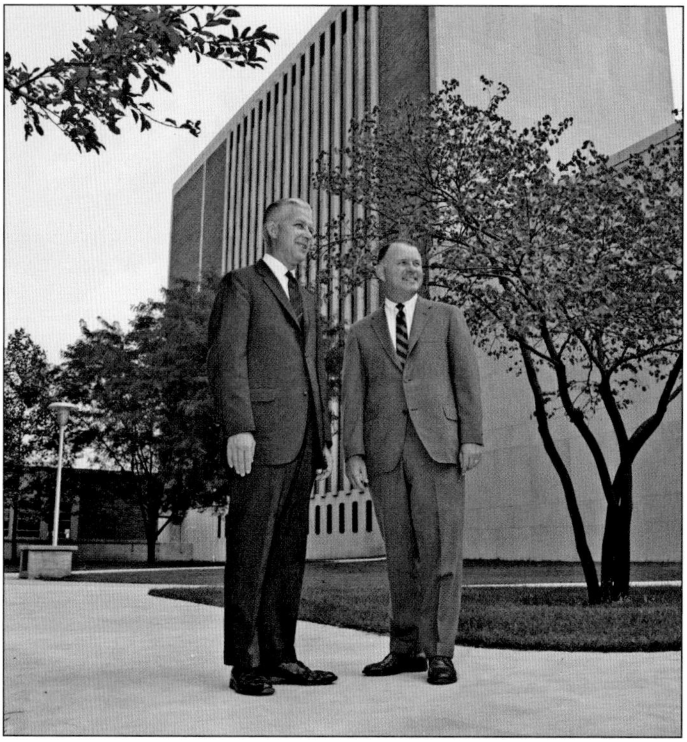

The completion of the Teachers College Building in the fall of 1968 vastly expanded academic space in the center of Ball State's growing campus. The 11-story building, featuring expanded office space, classrooms and lecture halls, and innovative laboratories, cost under $5 million to complete. Pictured here are John J Pruis (left), whose 10-year Ball State presidency began in 1968 and saw significant expansion of the university's academic programs and buildings, and John Dunworth (right), Teachers College dean.

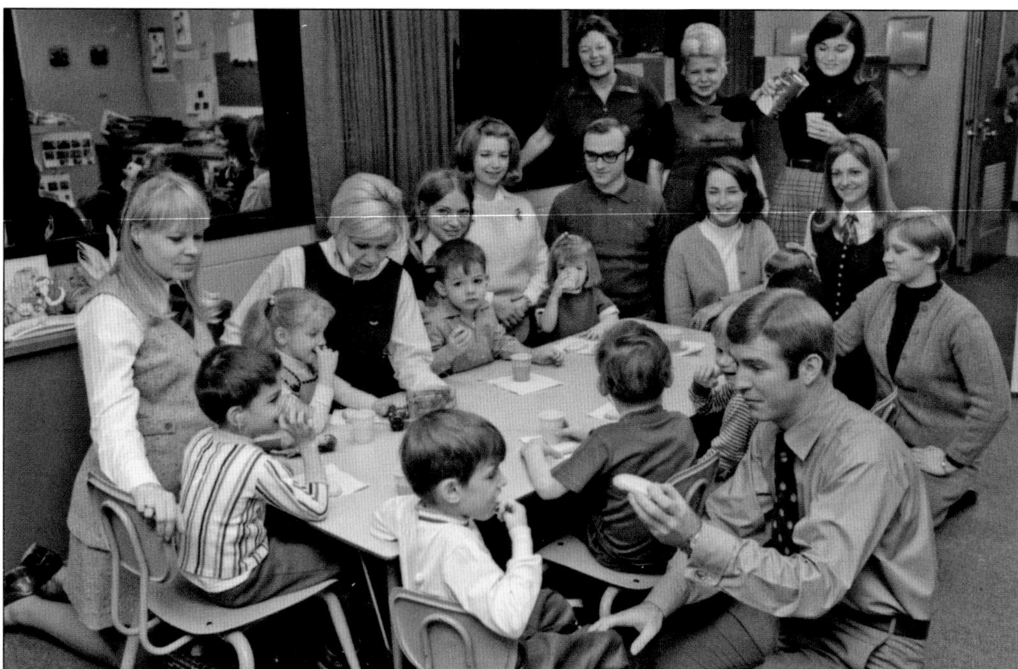

This new structure provided the necessary space and resources to continue the growth of Ball State's education and psychology programs in the Teachers College in the university era. Shown here are elementary education graduate students and faculty in one of the building's interactive laboratory and observational spaces.

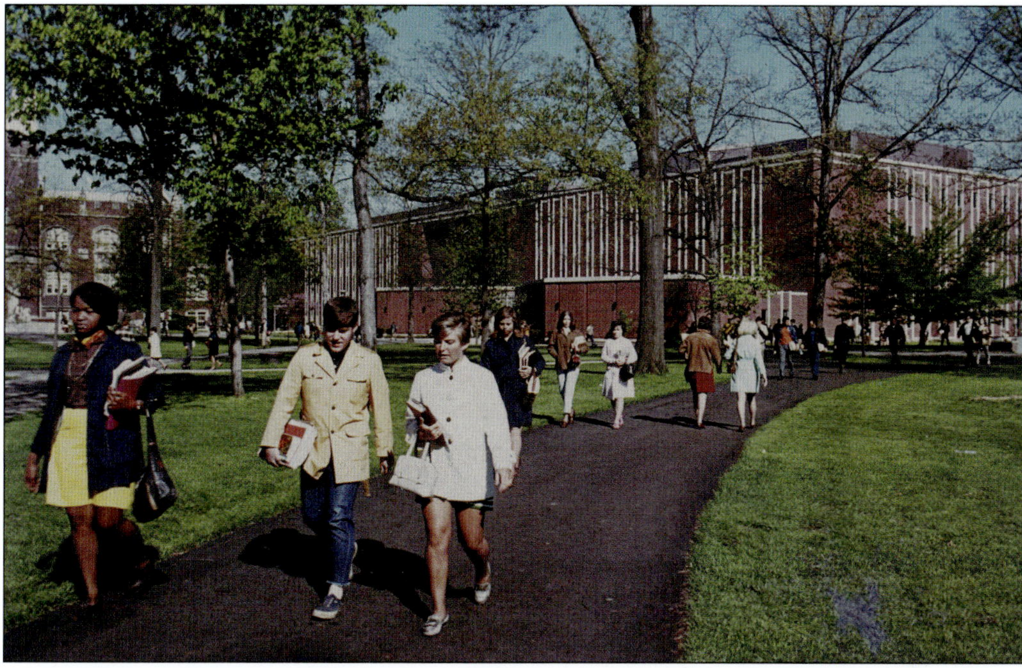

Opening in stages from 1967 to 1970, Ball State's Cooper Science Complex was a needed replacement to the aging Science Hall (now the Richard W. Burkhardt Building). The new structure provided a home for academic departments including chemistry, nursing, mathematics, biology, physics, physiology and health science, and geography/geology and included a planetarium and observatory accessible to both students and the public.

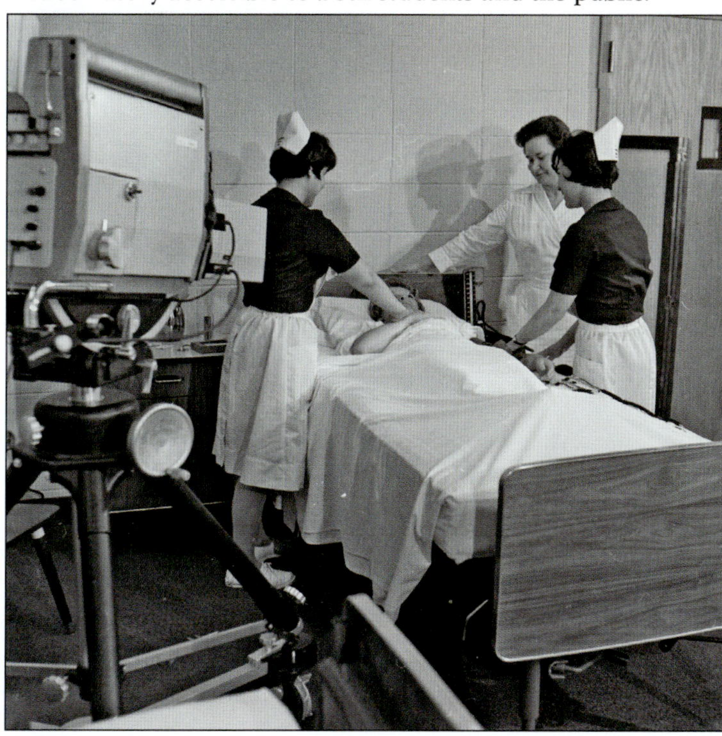

In 1963, Ball State made plans to develop a baccalaureate nursing program, subsuming the nursing training program previously overseen by Ball Memorial Hospital. The nursing program received a permanent home in 1967 with the completion of the nursing wing of the complex. Here, nursing faculty member Betty Larimer and students use the newly opened classroom facilities to tape a nursing instruction video.

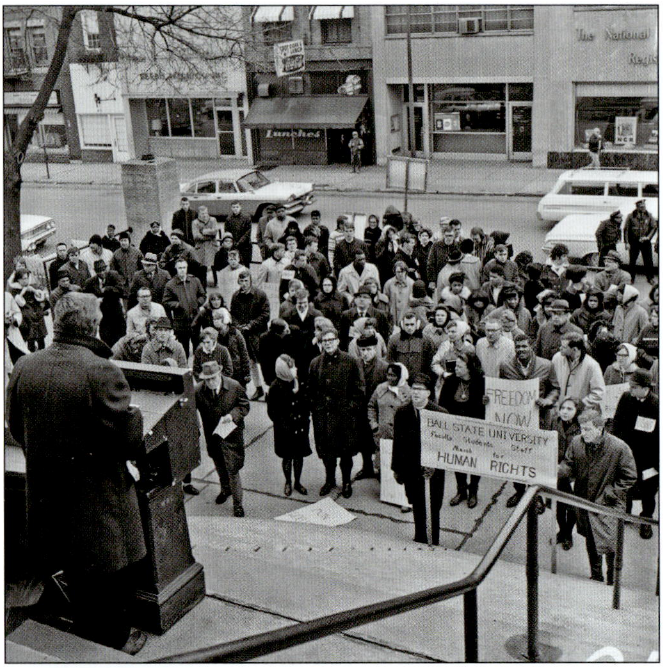

Students and faculty in the 1960s showed increasing engagement with national and global social and political issues through demonstrations, student publications, and artistic expression. On March 25, 1965, faculty and students participated in a march of affirmation to show solidarity with the Selma-to-Montgomery civil rights marches in Alabama.

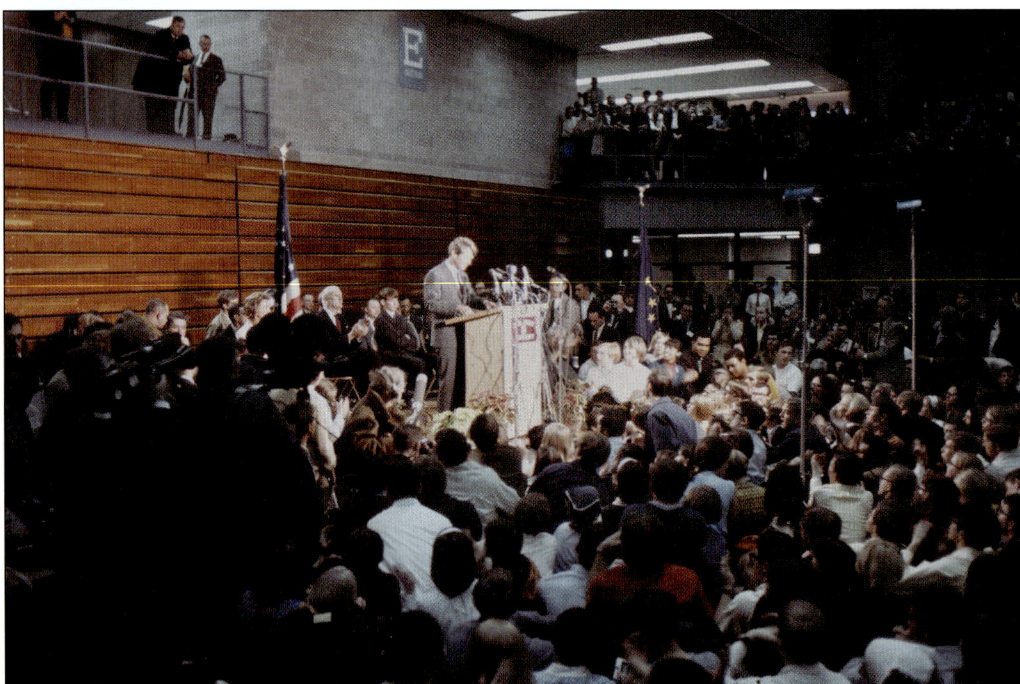

Political engagement on campus reached a high-water mark on the afternoon of April 4, 1968, when Sen. Robert F. Kennedy campaigned for the Democratic presidential nomination at Ball State's Men's Gym to a crowd of 9,000. In his hour-long speech, Kennedy discussed solutions to national and global poverty and spoke out against the Vietnam draft. On his way back to Indianapolis that evening, the senator was notified of the assassination of Martin Luther King Jr., and he delivered an impassioned and memorable plea for peace in the state's capital.

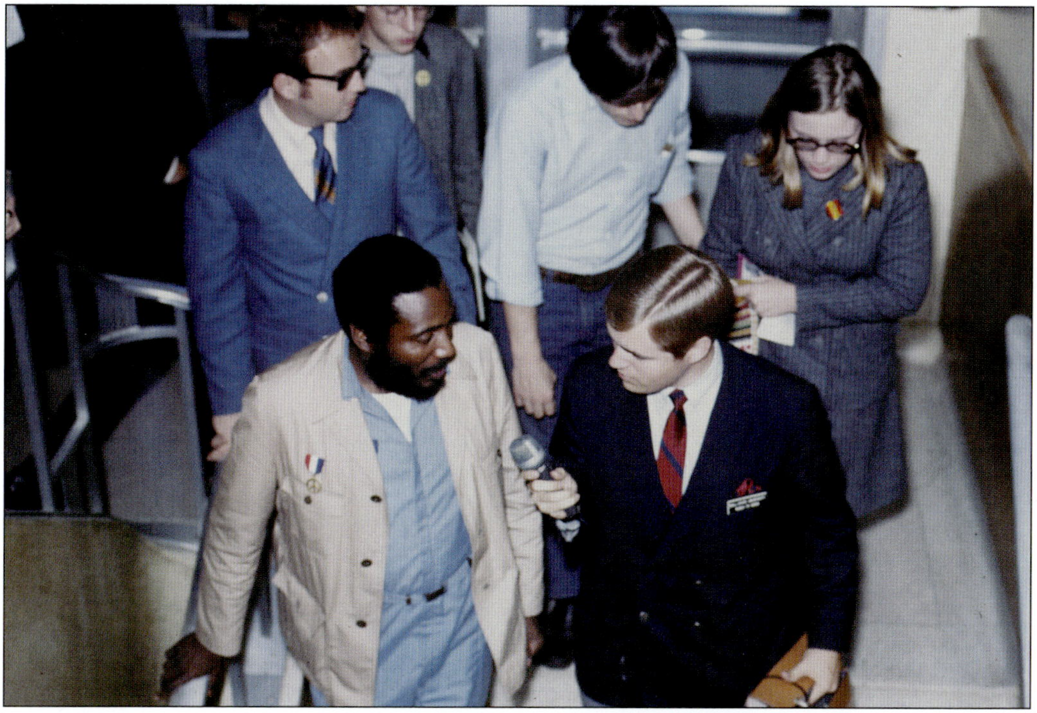

Comedian and civil rights activist Dick Gregory visited the Ball State campus in October 1968, campaigning as a write-in presidential candidate representing the Freedom and Peace Party. Gregory, a guest of the Ball State University New Politics Party student organization, is interviewed here by Al Rent, coordinator of radio and television news for Ball State.

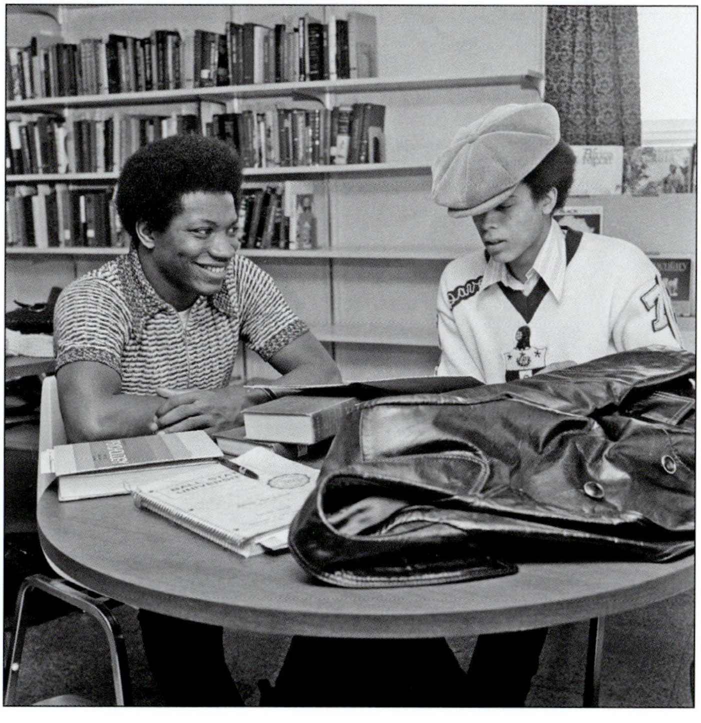

Opened during the 1970–1971 academic year, Ball State's Special Programs House (now Multicultural Center) provided the university's growing population of black students with a valuable space for social and cultural programming and events. In the decades to follow, the house would host numerous prominent African American campus visitors for lectures and conversations. Students are pictured in the center's Malcolm X Memorial Library in the winter of 1972.

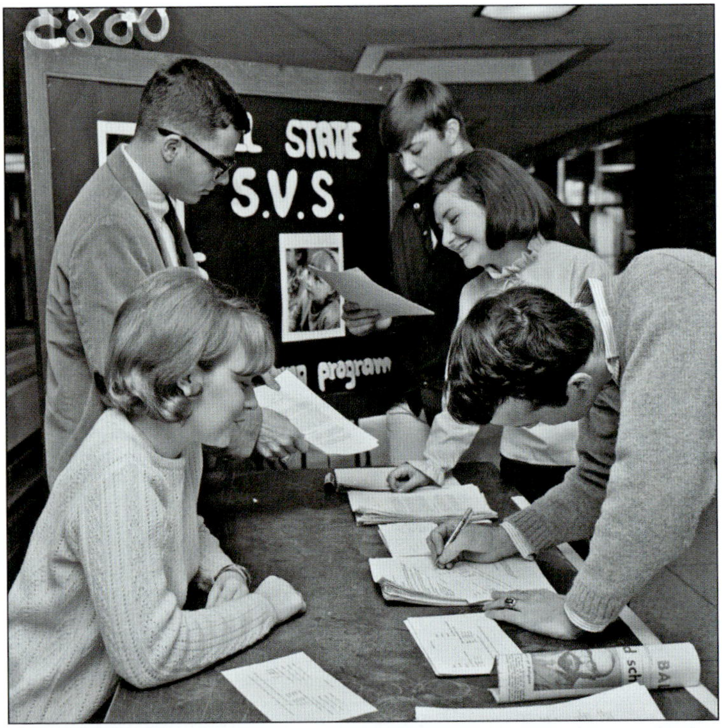

Founded in 1965, the Ball State Student Voluntary Services galvanized campus volunteerism to support community aims and charities, including involvement in tutoring programs, elder care, antipoverty initiatives, and food drives.

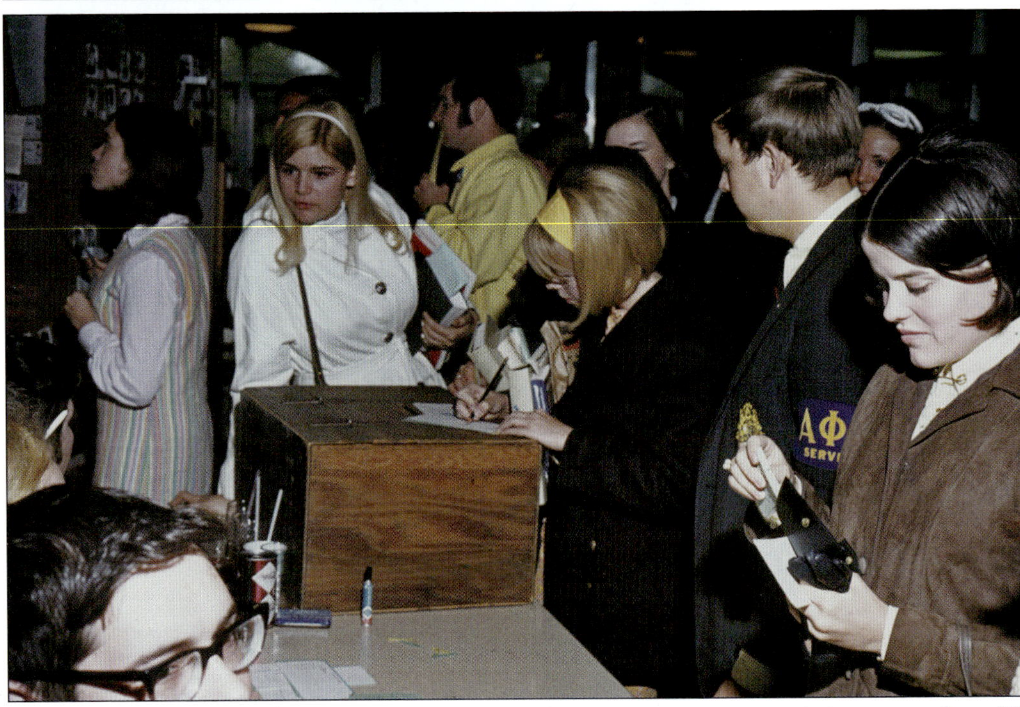

Students also began to tackle more serious and pressing issues pertaining to student life and academics through student government in the 1960s. Here, students cast their ballots at the L.A. Pittenger Student Center in May 1969 for student government officers for the 1969–1970 school year.

Coach Don Shondell, shown in 1970 with Rick Niemi, one of his players, built Ball State's volleyball program into a nationally ranked power during his tenure. The 1970 men's volleyball squad earned its first of 13 NCAA Tournament appearances with a 20-4 overall record that season. Construction of the Don Shondell Practice Facility for basketball and volleyball began in 2017.

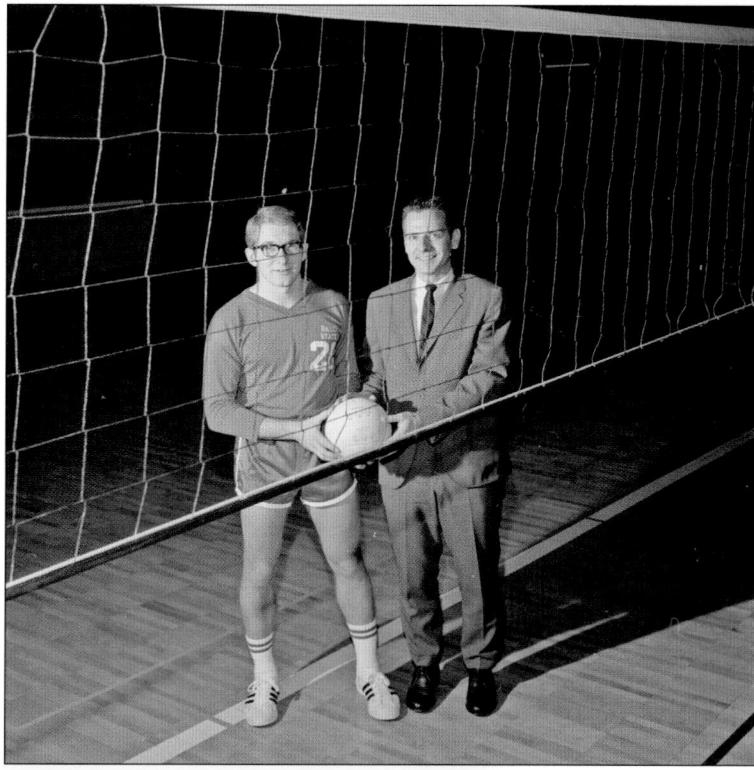

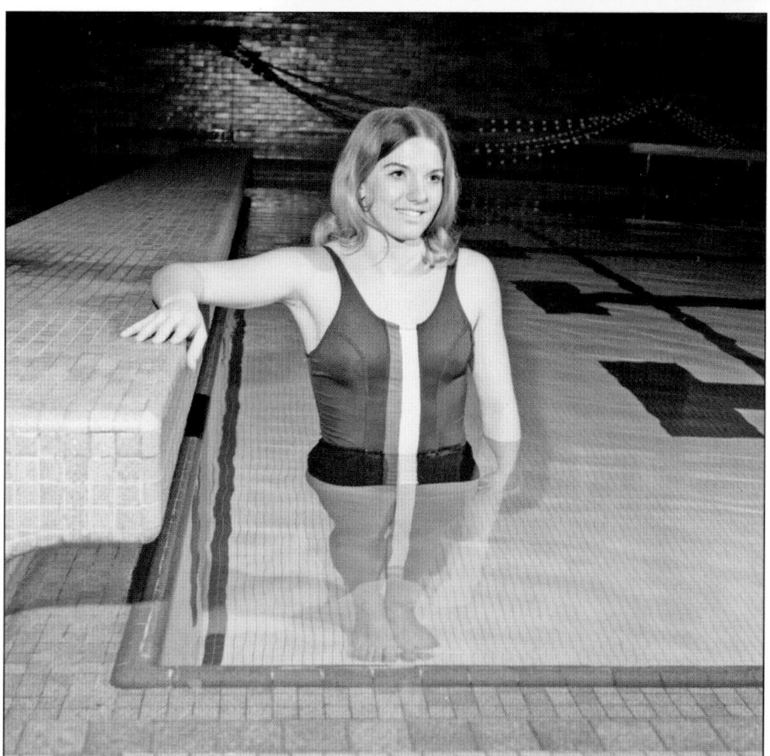

Swimmer Patricia Bergman became the first female national champion in the history of Ball State athletics when she won the 100 backstroke and 100 individual medley in 1970. In 1971, she won her third championship, defending her title in the 100 individual medley with a time of 01:30.20.

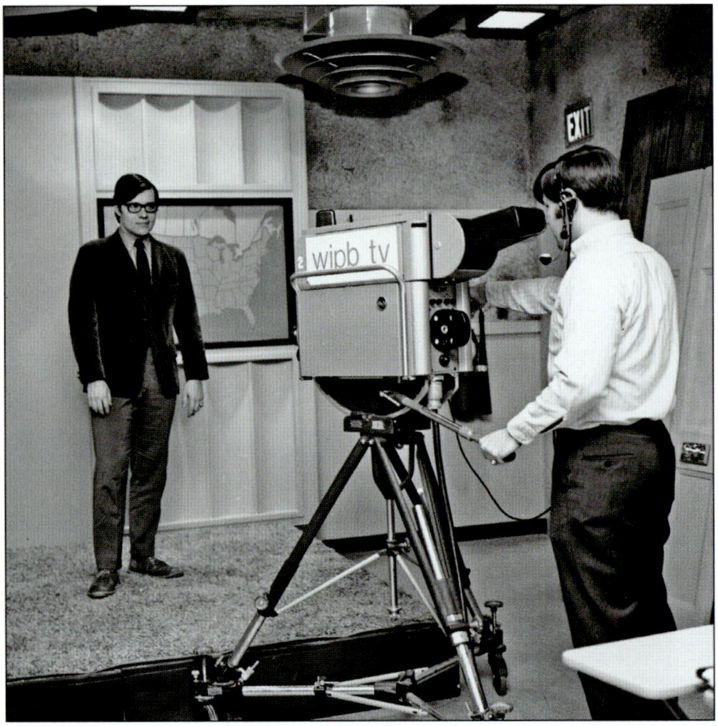

WIPB-TV, Ball State University's Public Broadcasting Service affiliate, went on the air for the first time on October 31, 1971, broadcasting on Channel 49, previously occupied by WLBC-TV. The station was founded due to the efforts of community members Gretchen Huff and Sunny Spurgeon, who formed the Eastern Indiana Community Television organization in hopes of improving access to educational television programming in the Muncie area.

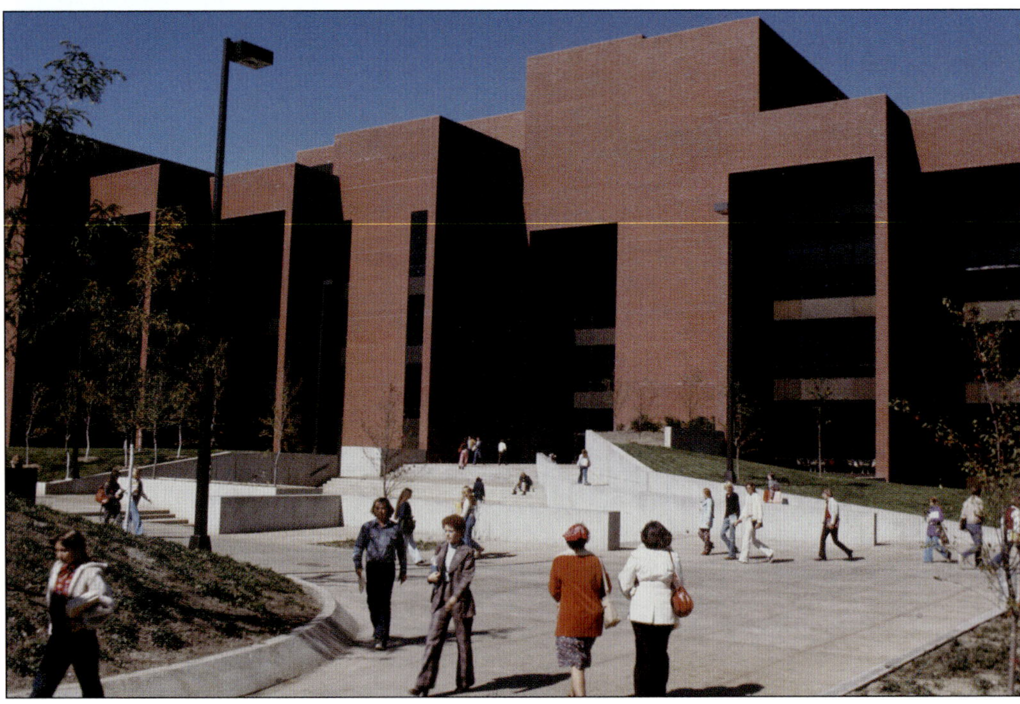

Opened in the fall of 1975 and dedicated the following spring, Bracken Library provided Ball State with a spacious, modern research library befitting a growing university. Located strategically at the center of campus, the library contained nearly 1,300 study carrels upon opening across a total footprint of roughly 320,000 square feet.

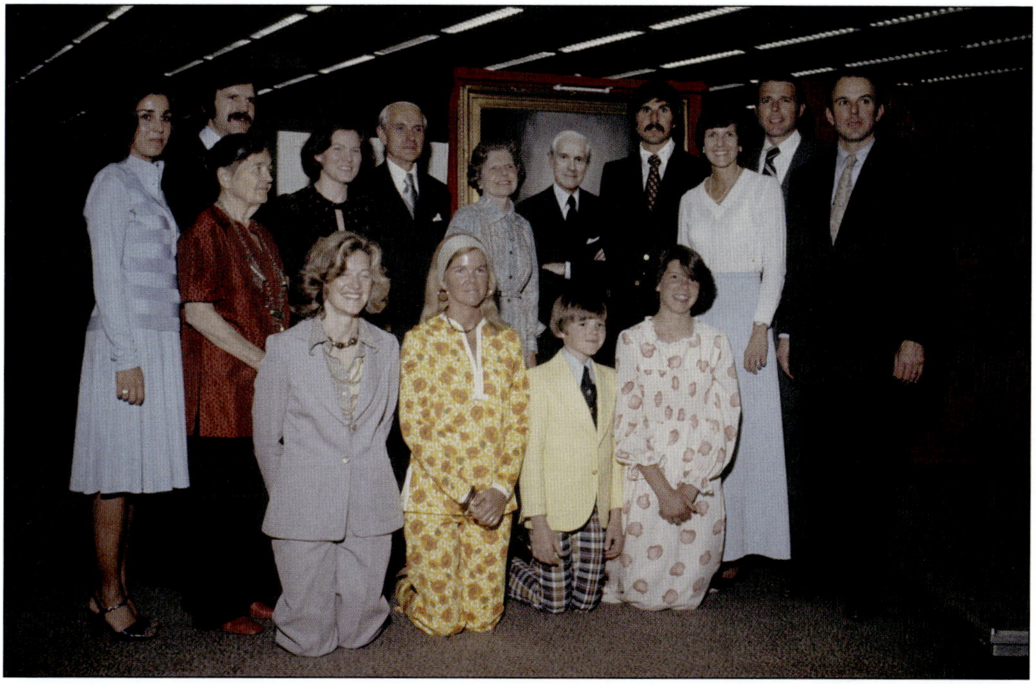

The library was named for Alexander M. Bracken, whose distinguished leadership of Ball State's board of trustees for 22 years successfully led the institution through a period of monumental growth. Pictured here are Alexander M. Bracken and his family at the dedication of the library on March 26, 1976. From left to right are (front row, kneeling) Margee Bracken, Judith Bracken, Tom Bracken, and Annie Bracken; (back row, standing) Sally Bracken, unidentified, William Bracken, Hillary Bracken, Alexander M. Bracken, Rosemary B. Bracken, Sandy Bracken, Elizabeth Bracken Wiese, Frank Bracken, and Thomas Bracken;

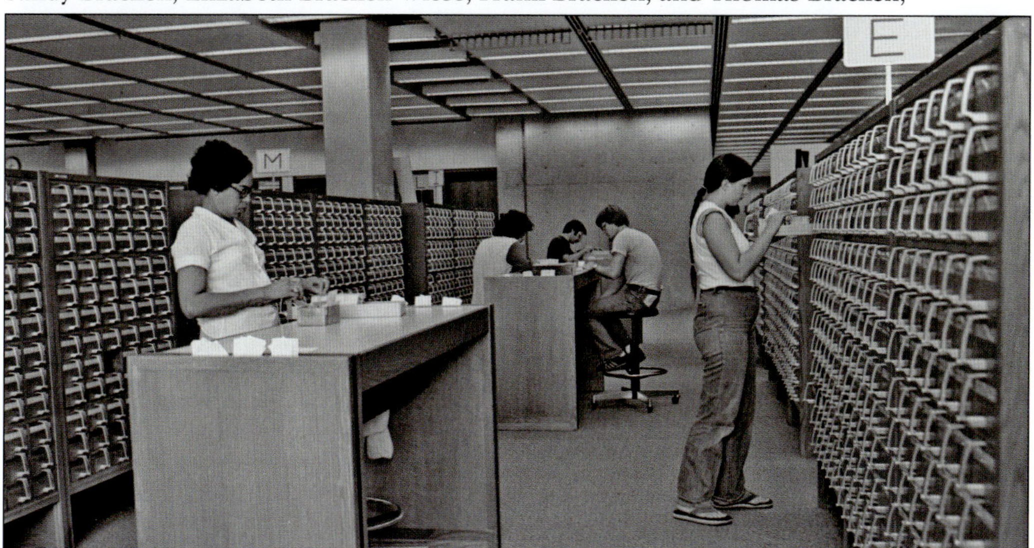

The new library facility provided students, faculty, and community members with a vast collection of accessible resources, including government publications, special collections, and educational resources.

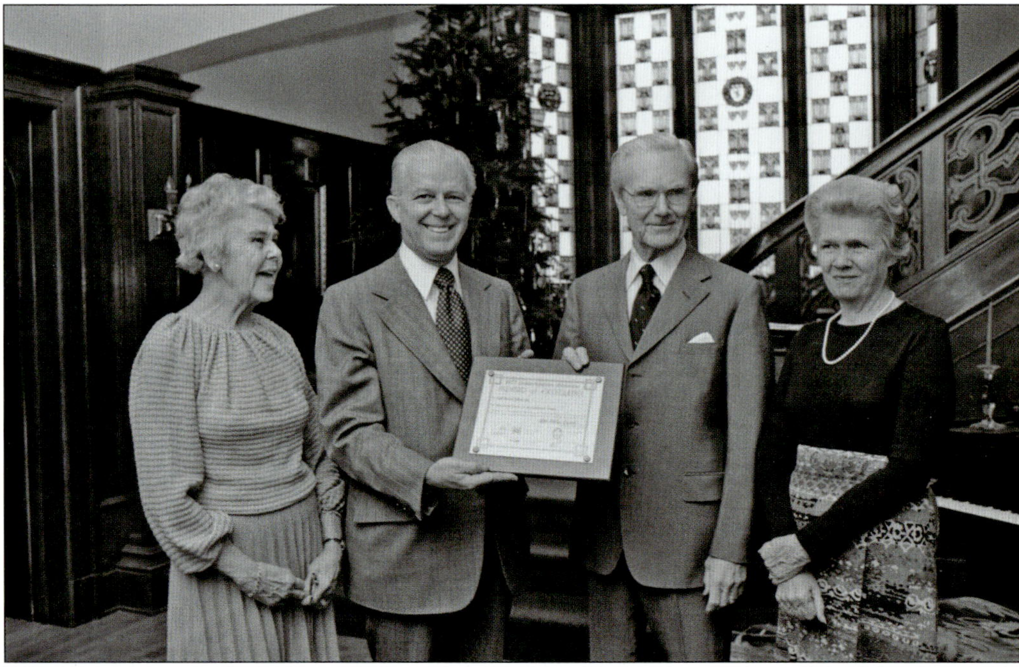

Named the E.B. and Bertha C. Ball Center in 1986, the former home of Edmund Burke and Bertha C. Ball has served as a university center for adult and community educational programming, hosting classes, seminars, workshops, and special events. Adelia Ball Morris (left), Edmund F. Ball (third from left), and Janice Ball Fisher (right), children of the building's namesakes, join John Pruis (second from left) at the dedication of the facility in 1977.

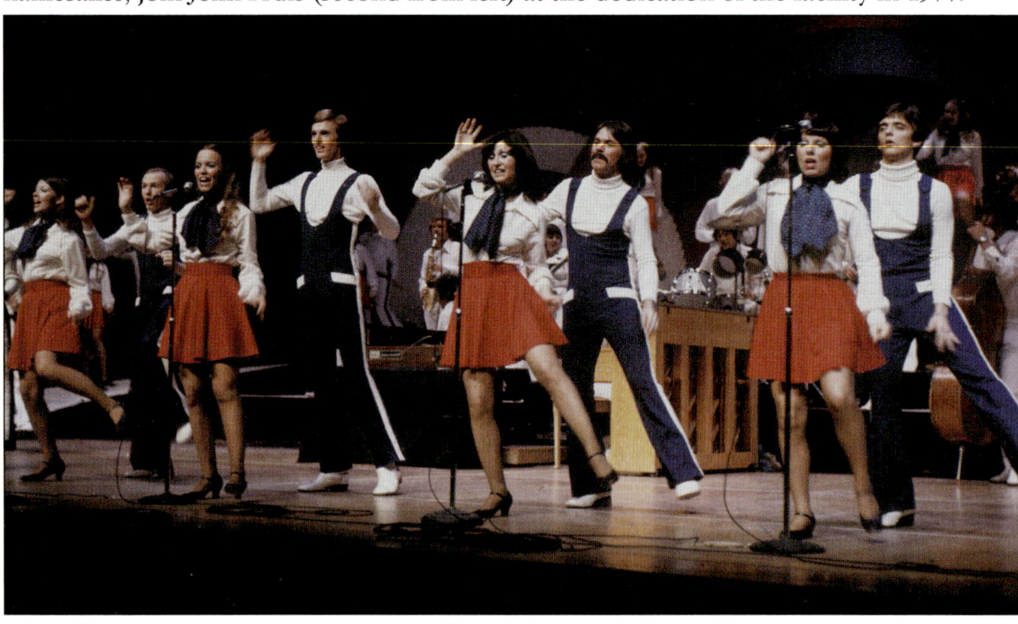

The Ball State University Singers, directed by Larry Boye, celebrated the American Bicentennial with a memorable installment of their annual *Spectacular* spring show in 1976. The show featured a special guest appearance by renowned singer William Warfield, known for his leading role in the 1952 revival of *Porgy and Bess*.

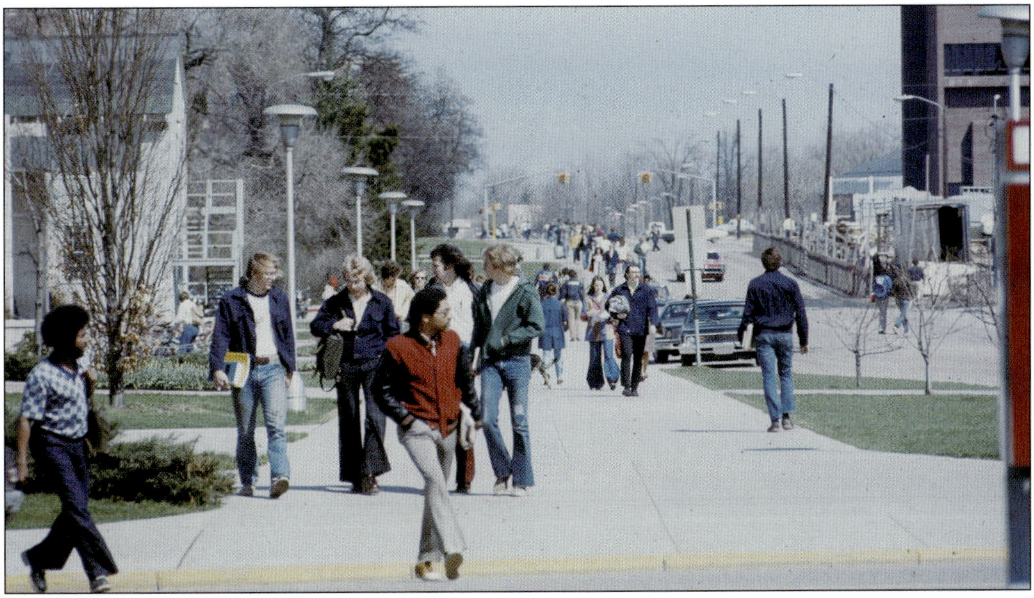

The considerable northward growth of the campus in the 1960s and 1970s established McKinley Avenue as a main campus thoroughfare for students heading from dorm rooms to classrooms and on-campus activities. This March 1974 scene shows the typical midday campus bustle from the McKinley Avenue and Riverside Avenue intersection looking north.

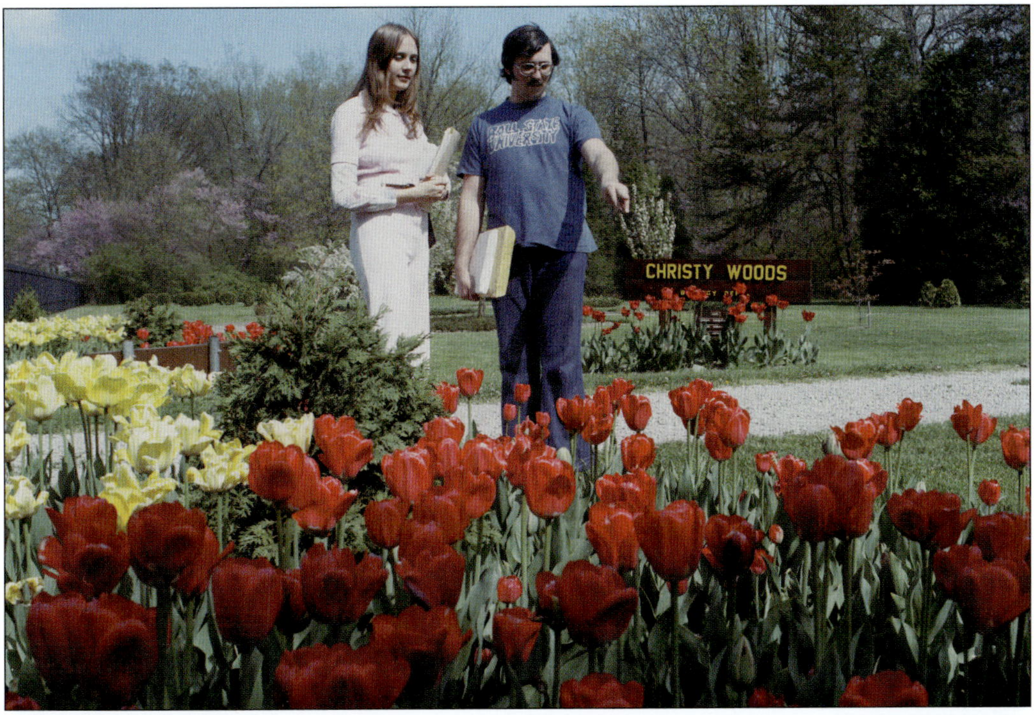

For a quieter setting, students could visit Christy Woods, pictured here in May 1975. The 17-acre outdoor teaching laboratory and nature education destination featuring multiple greenhouses was named in 1940 for Ball State biologist O.B. Christy but has been a campus institution for both education and recreation since 1919.

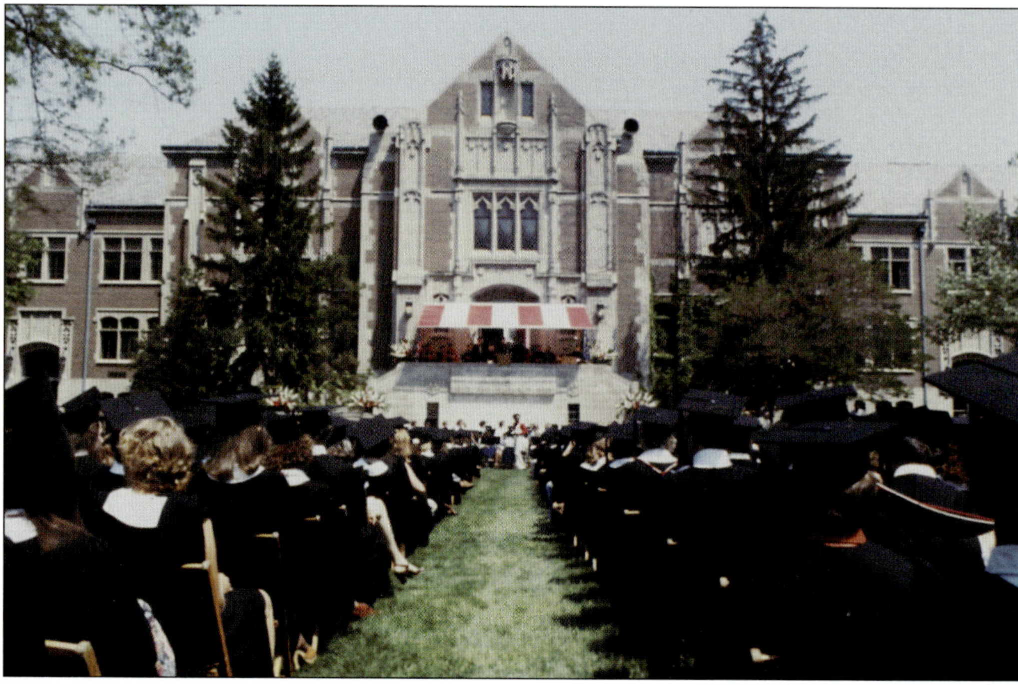

The terrace of the Arts Building has served as the traditional backdrop for spring commencements at Ball State University, weather permitting. Shown here are spring commencement exercises for the class of 1979, including over 2,800 students earning associates, baccalaureate, and graduate degrees.

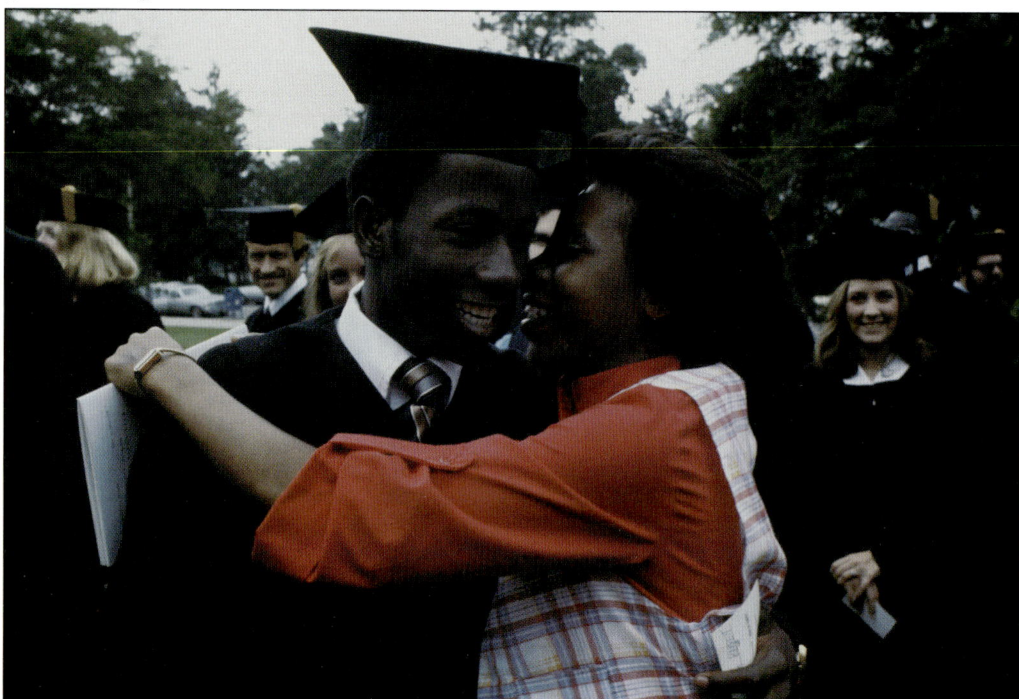

A graduate and family enjoy a celebratory moment at summer commencement in 1979.

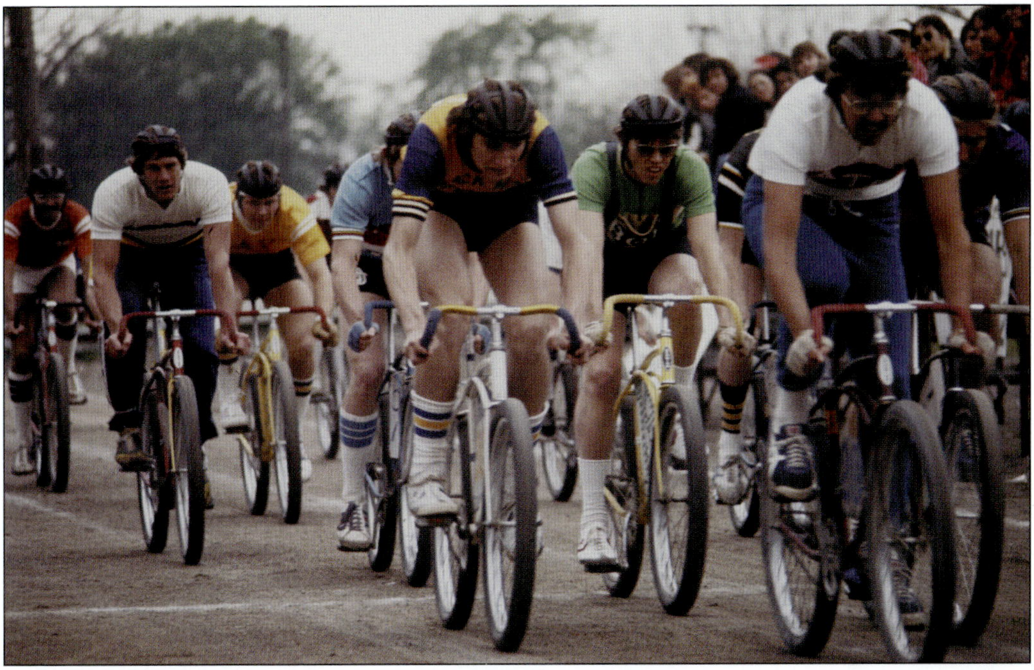

Cyclists compete in the Lambda Chi Alpha Bike-a-Thon, one of the university's most anticipated events and traditions of the era. The race's inaugural running was held in 1952 at Ball State's track and later migrated to the Delaware County Fairgrounds, the venue for the 1976 race pictured here.

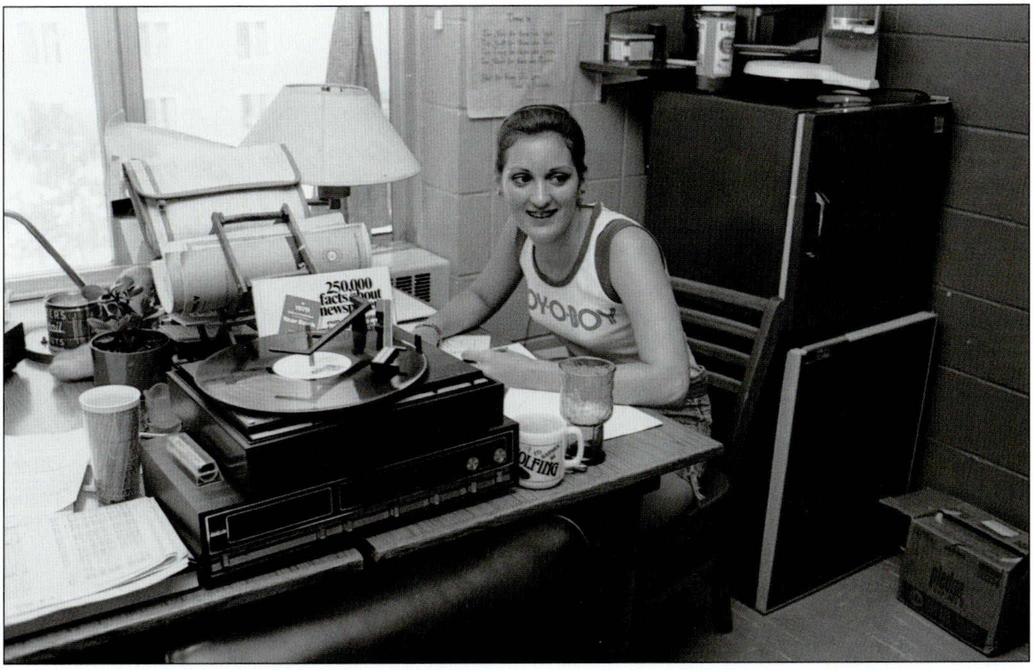

A student sits at her desk in a typical Ball State University residence in the LaFollette Complex in June 1979 with the basic necessities of the era—a course schedule, a record player, and a portable refrigerator for each roommate.

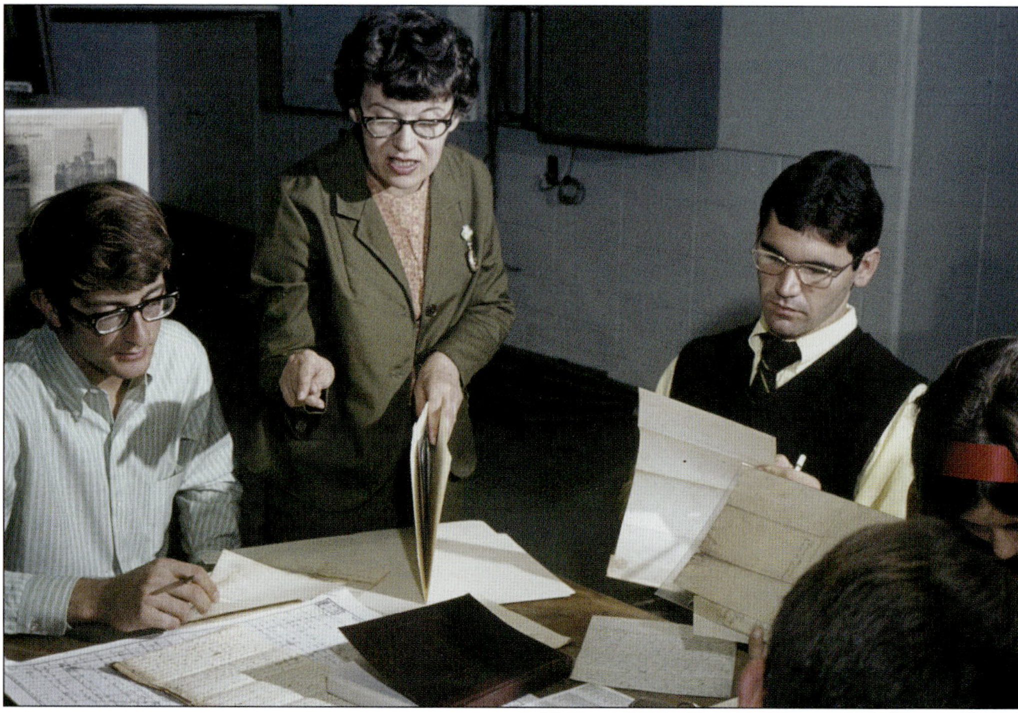

Ball State grew into its new status as a university by developing new degree programs, expanding existing ones, and exploring new methodologies and technologies to advance both undergraduate and graduate education in the 1960s and 1970s. In October 1969, Prof. Althea Stoeckel and students in the Department of History study Delaware County historical records that she rescued from Delaware County's former courthouse, demolished in 1966 and replaced by a more modern structure.

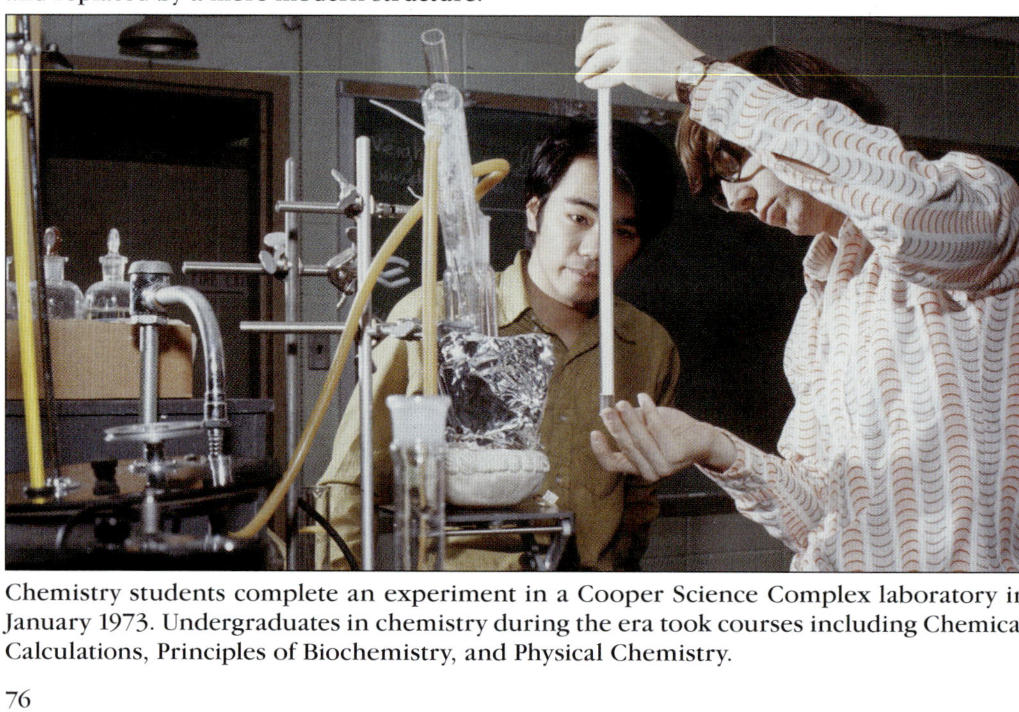

Chemistry students complete an experiment in a Cooper Science Complex laboratory in January 1973. Undergraduates in chemistry during the era took courses including Chemical Calculations, Principles of Biochemistry, and Physical Chemistry.

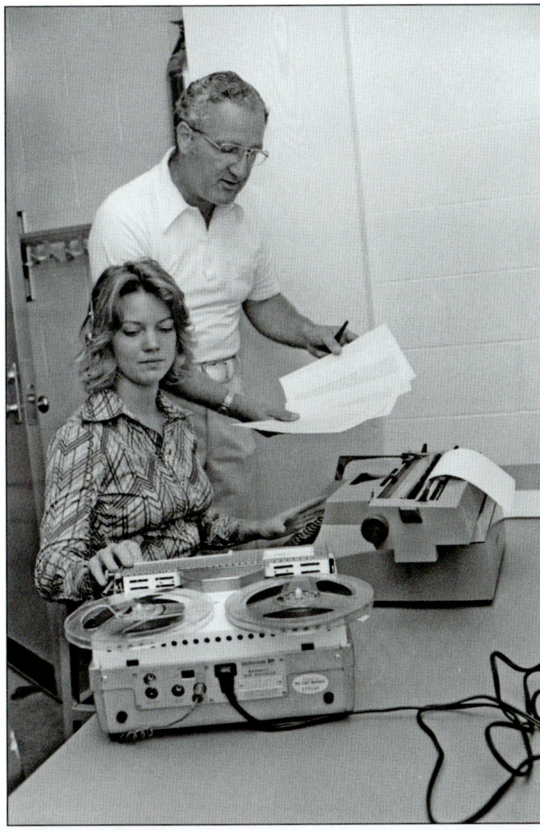

Professor of journalism Earl Conn (standing) works with a student journalist in August 1977 in the newly renovated West Quadrangle Building. Conn, whose career at Ball State spanned from 1958 to 1998, founded the Midwest Writers Workshop and was elected to the Indiana Journalism Hall of Fame in 1997.

Thomas Mertens provides instruction in a biology laboratory classroom in December 1977, guiding a student through the use of a microscope. Mertens's distinguished career on the biology faculty spanned from 1957 to 1993, during which time he established himself as a prominent educator and researcher in the field of human genetics.

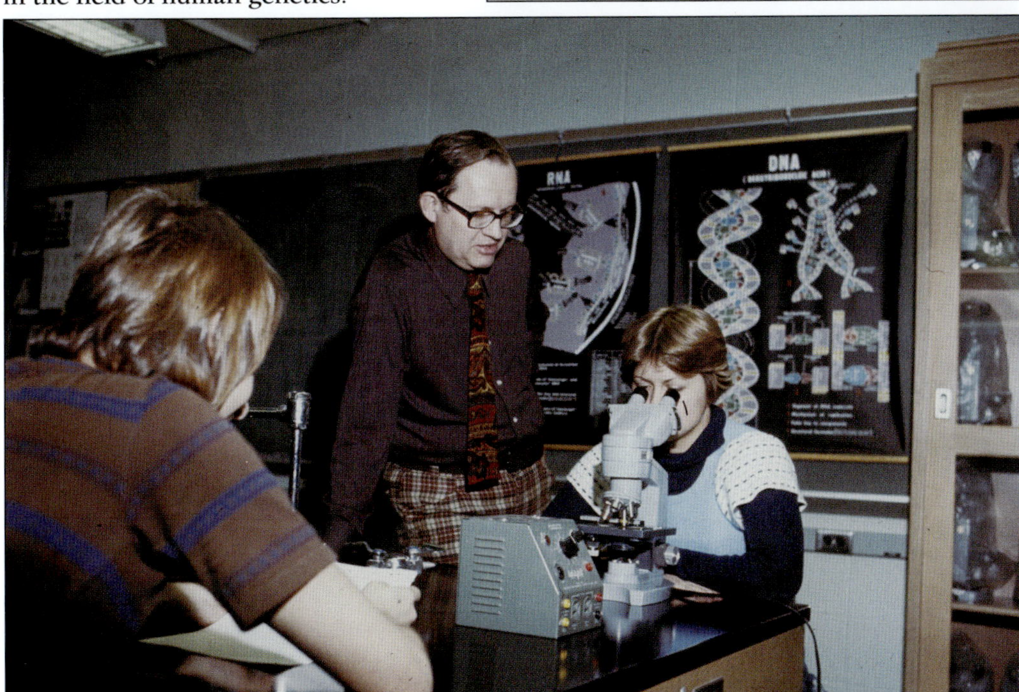

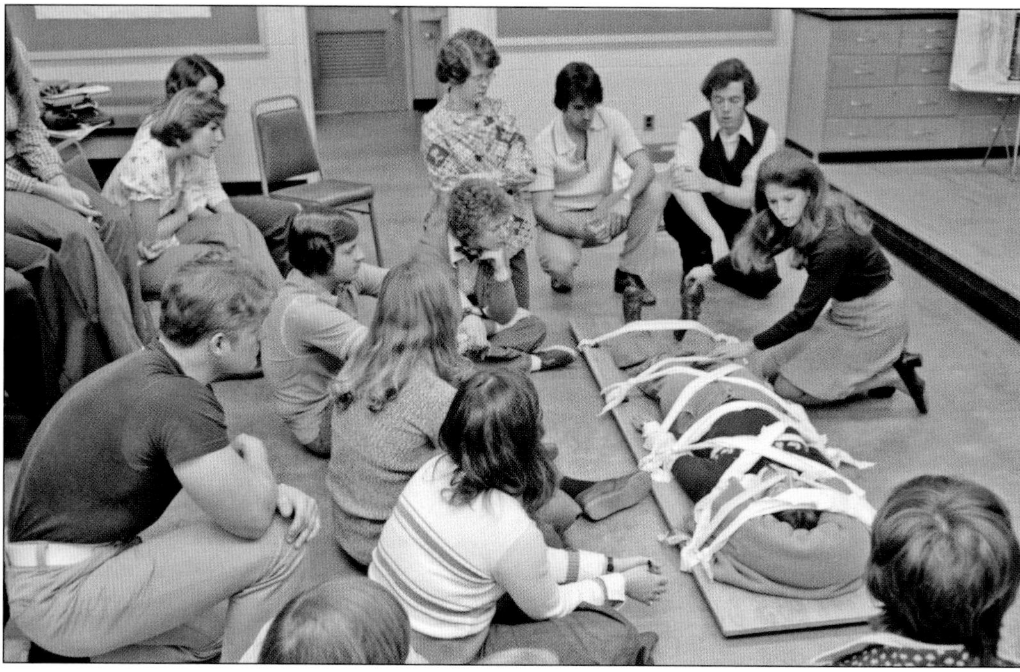

Physiology and health science became an academic program at Ball State in 1965, beginning a legacy of a strong institutional emphasis on health education. Here, students in 1975 attend a demonstration on the proper use of a stretcher.

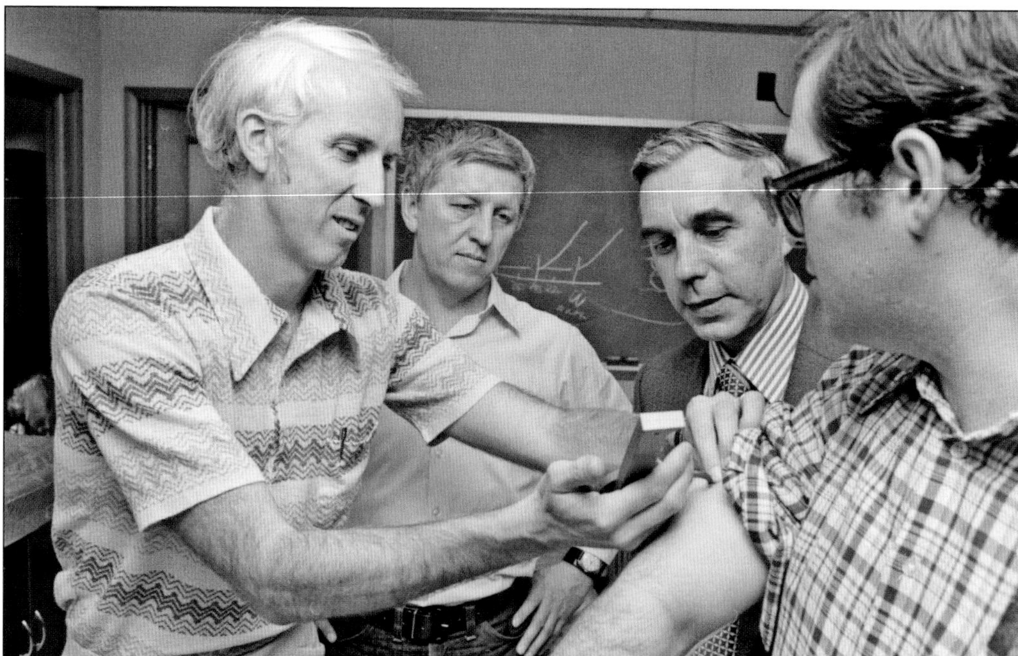

Prof. David Costill (left), director of Ball State's Human Performance Laboratory, works with his colleagues and a subject during a research project. The Human Performance Laboratory achieved national and global acclaim as a research center, having partnered with NASA to study the fitness regimen of US astronauts.

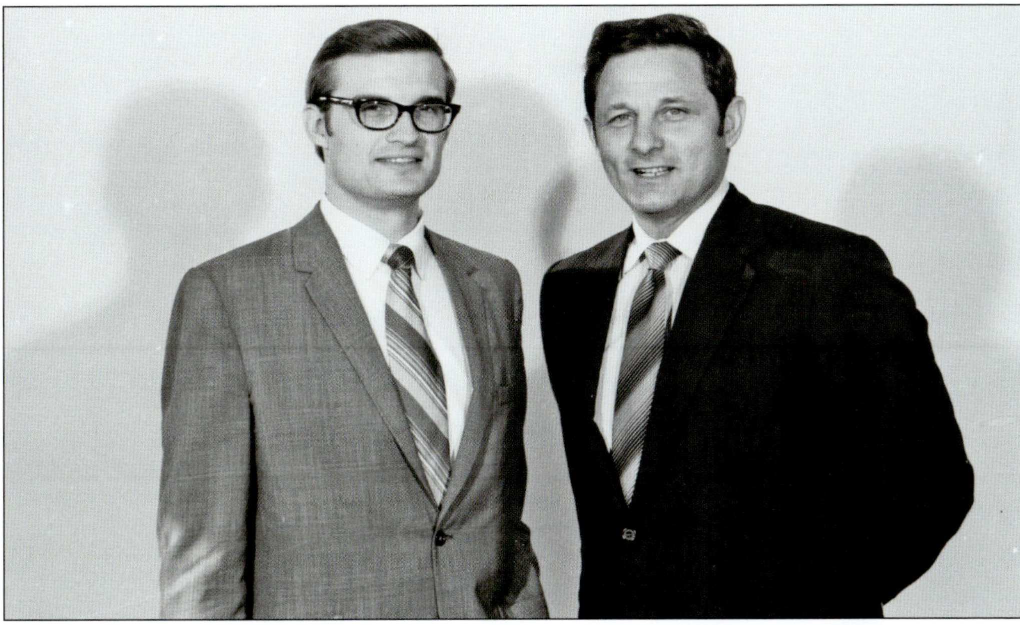

Sen. Birch Bayh of Indiana (right) was a frequent visitor to Ball State in the 1960s and 1970s. Bayh is shown during a campus appearance in 1970 visiting with Phil Sharp (left), then a professor of political science at Ball State University who would later serve for 20 years in the US House of Representatives.

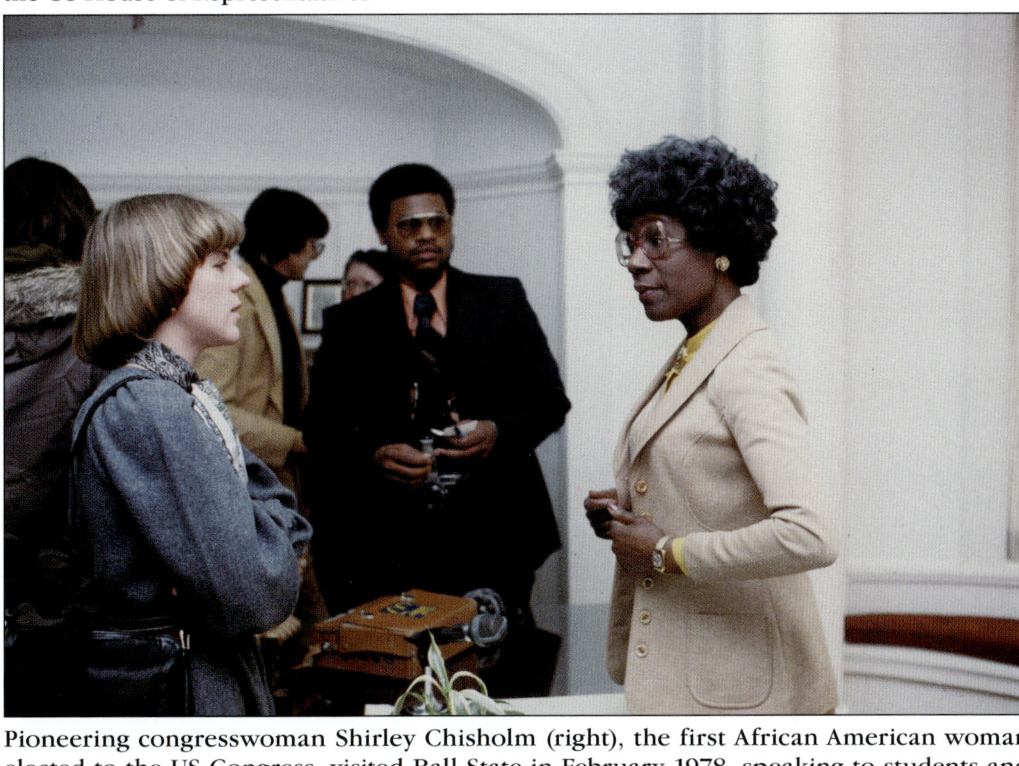

Pioneering congresswoman Shirley Chisholm (right), the first African American woman elected to the US Congress, visited Ball State in February 1978, speaking to students and community members on women's issues in American politics.

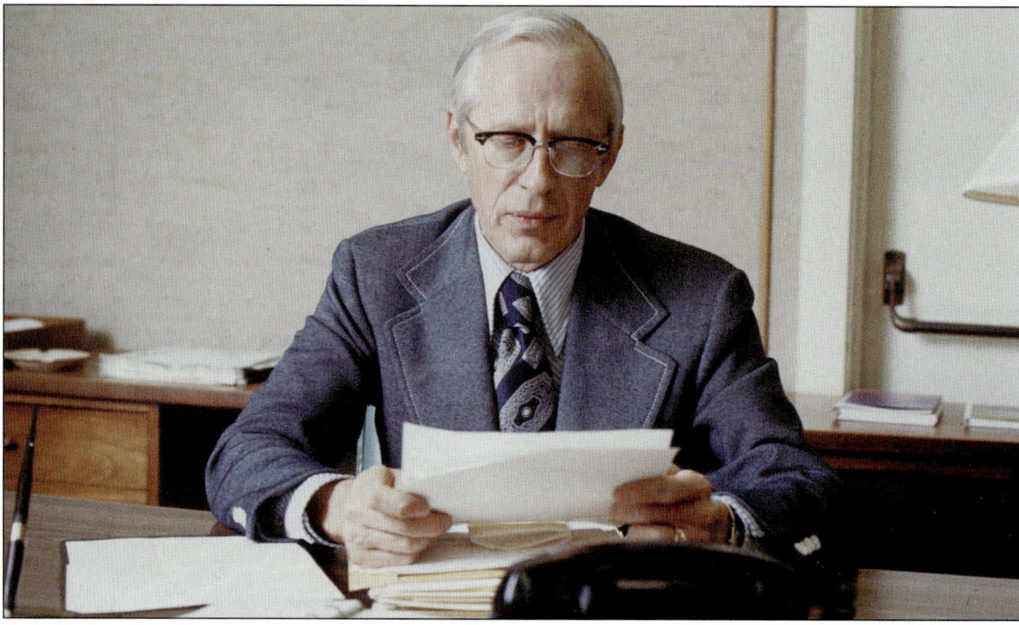

Robert P. Bell, a Ball State graduate of the class of 1940, enjoyed a distinguished career as a faculty member and administrator at the university. Bell joined the business education faculty in 1947, served as the first dean of the College of Business from 1965 to 1973, and later assumed the role of vice president for business affairs. Bell completed his distinguished Ball State career by serving as university president from 1981 to 1984.

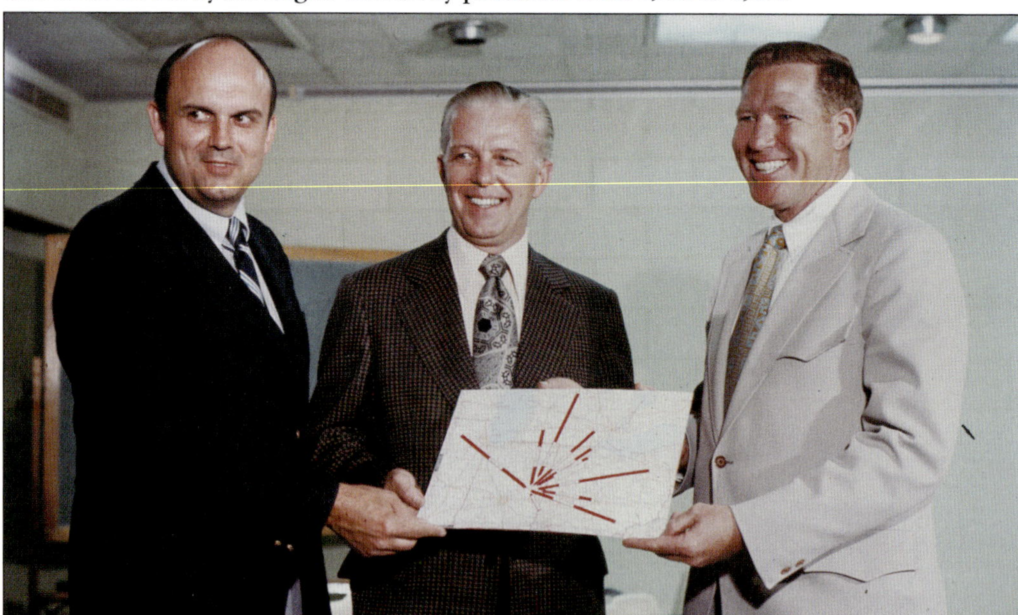

In 1973, Ball State University's athletic program joined the Mid-American Conference, a significant step in realizing Ball State's transformation from teachers college to university. Pictured here are Mid-American Conference commissioner Fred Jacoby (left), John J Pruis (center), and athletic director Ray Louthen (right) at a press conference announcing Ball State's membership in the conference.

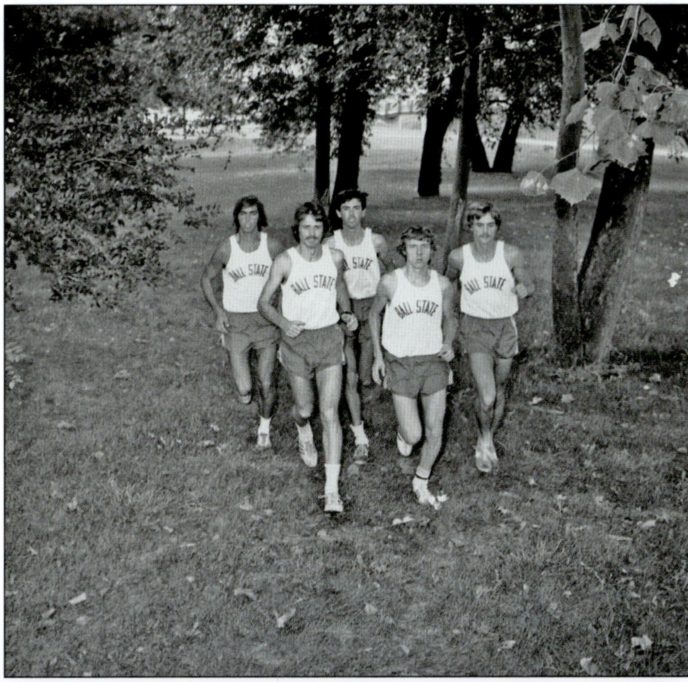

The men's cross-country team quickly became one of the most dominant Cardinal squads in the school's new conference, finishing with a 5-1 record in dual meets in the 1975–1976 season. From left to right are team members Art Becker, Bob Bowman, Jim Needler, Brian Powell, and Jeff Shoemaker.

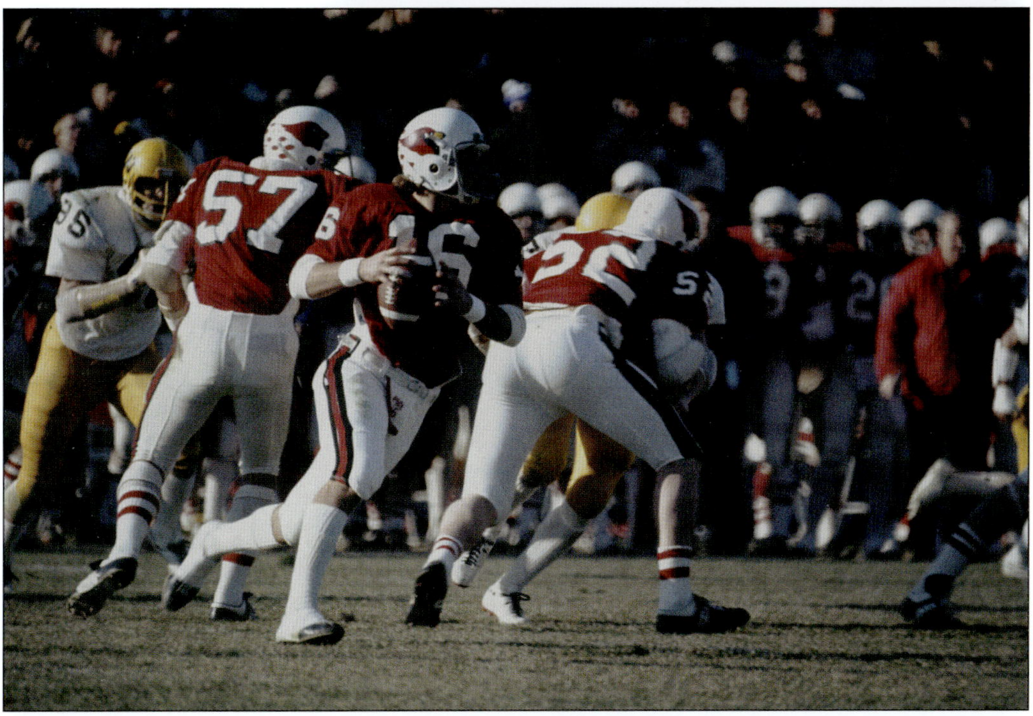

The Ball State football program also quickly ascended the ladder as a Mid-American Conference power, winning MAC championships in 1976 and 1978. On November 13, 1976, quarterback Art Yaroch (16), with blocks from Mitch Hoban (57) and Greg Mikkelsen (52), leads the Cardinals against Western Michigan. Both Yaroch and Hoban were later elected to Ball State's Athletics Hall of Fame.

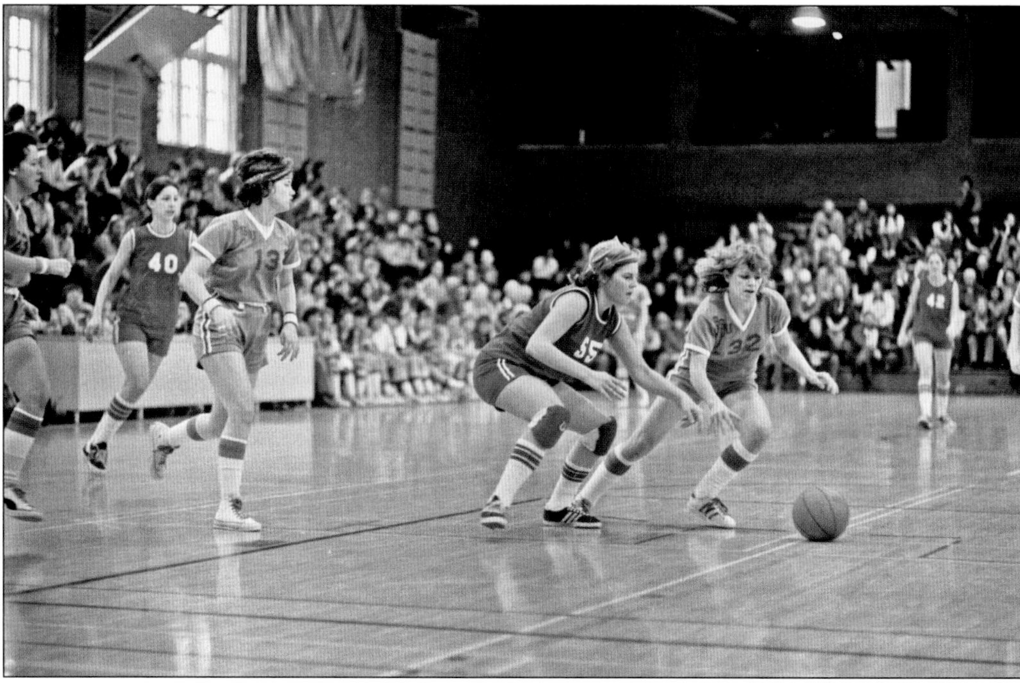

In the 1974–1975 school year, the Ball State women's basketball team completed its first season of major intercollegiate competition in the Indiana Women's Intercollegiate Sports Organization, later known as the Indiana Association of Intercollegiate Athletics for Women. Coached by Rosalie DiBrezzo, the team finished with a 17-6 overall record. Here, the Cardinals face off against Miami University on February 15, 1975.

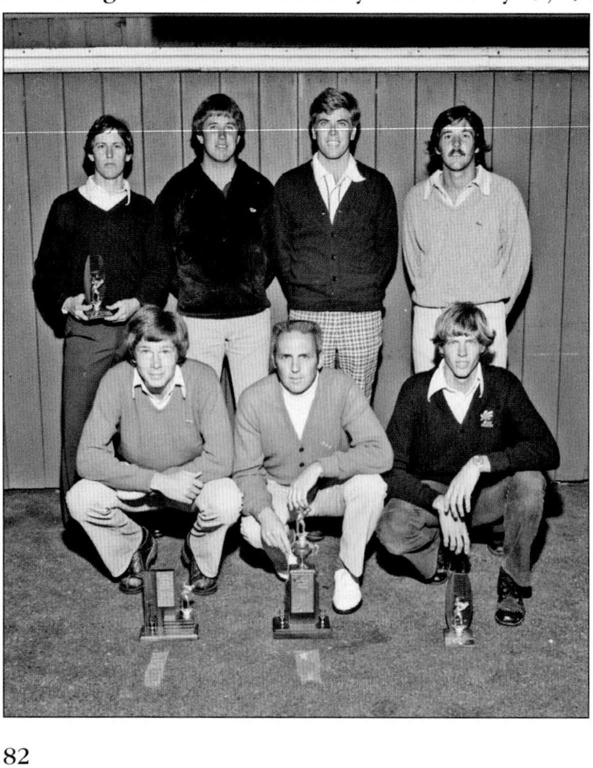

Renowned men's golf coach Earl Yestingsmeier led this Cardinals squad from 1963 to 1998 while also serving for 31 years as sports information director at Ball State. Yestingsmeier's golf teams won 107 tournament titles and earned 11 NCAA Tournament appearances, accomplishments that helped enshrine him in the Golf Coaches Association Hall of Fame. Yestingsmeier (first row, center) is pictured with the 1977 team, including golfers (first row, left) Paul Kemps (first row, right) and Kent Kahre; (second row, from left to right) Mark Porter, Scott Steger, Mike Pasquali, Cary Huntgate, Paul Kemps, and Kent Kahre. Construction began in 2017 on the Earl Yestingsmeier Golf Center, an indoor practice facility for use by the men's and women's golf teams.

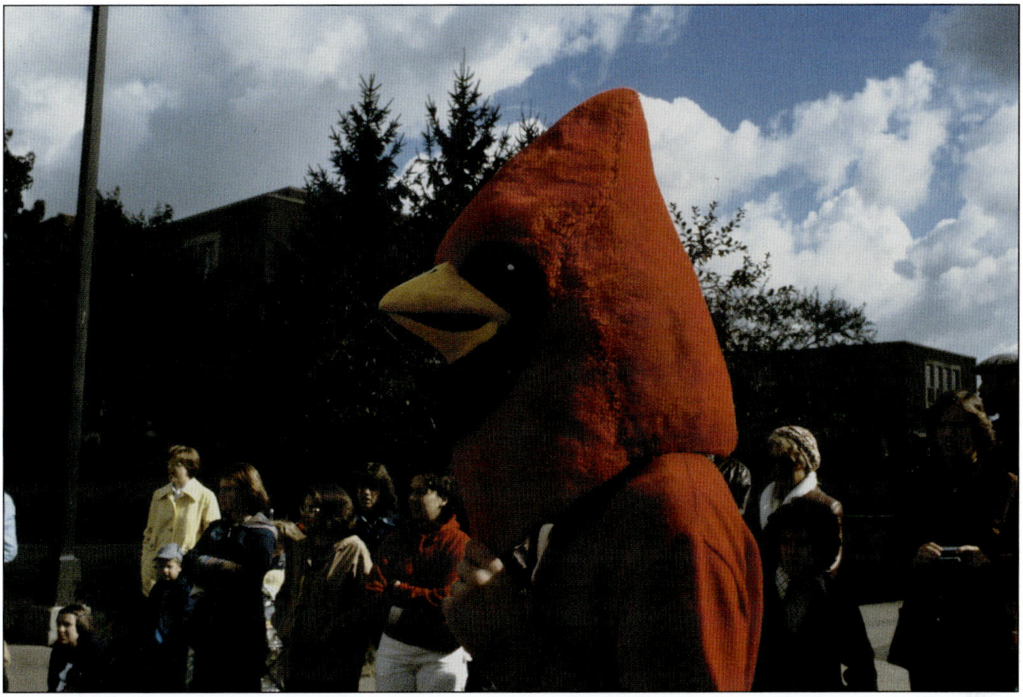

Ball State's Charlie Cardinal mascot debuted in 1968 and is seen in 1978 with a crowd of homecoming parade spectators along McKinley Avenue. Sporting a makeshift papier-mâché costume in his debut season, today's Charlie has a sleek, modern look.

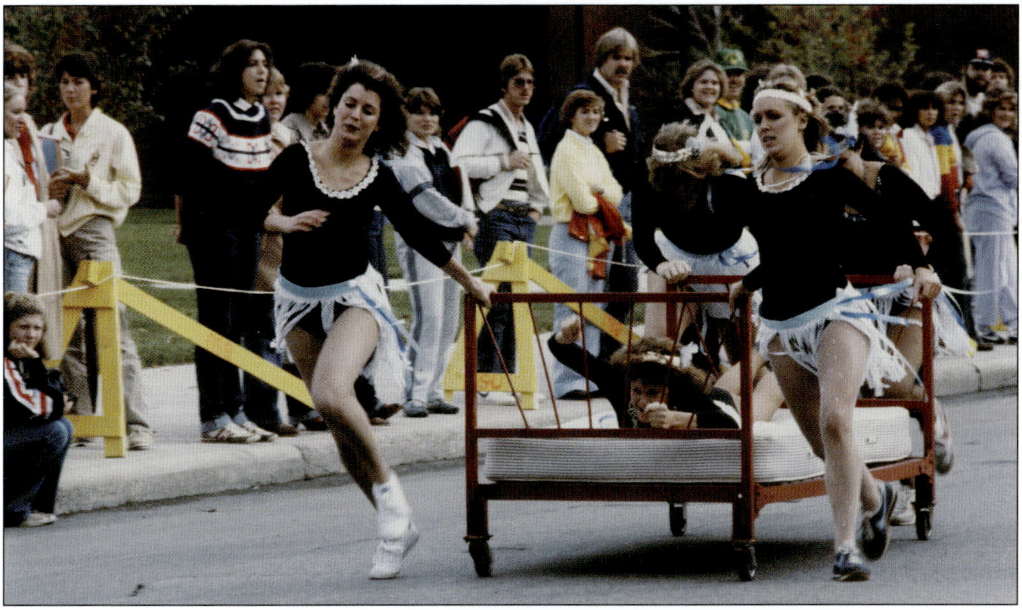

The bed race, a staple of Ball State's homecoming celebration, debuted in 1980 and quickly became a campus favorite. A quintet of bed racers dashes along a 100-yard course on McKinley Avenue in front of a crowd of over 1,000 spectators during Homecoming 1981. Clevenger Hall and Woody Hall won the main event, with Brayton Hall winning the award for best costume.

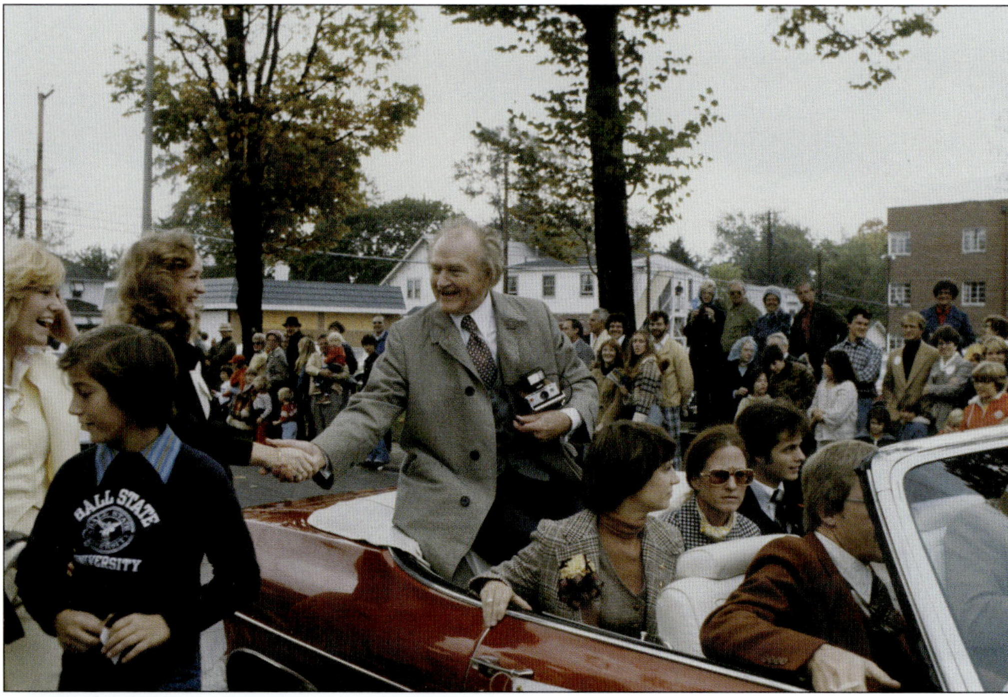

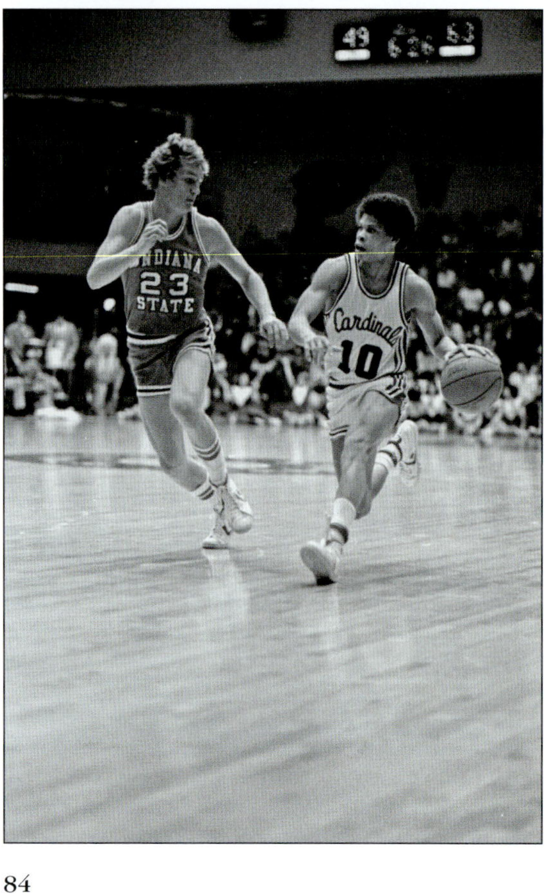

Hoosier comedian Red Skelton was a frequent visitor to the Ball State campus in his later career, earning an honorary doctorate from the university in a special ceremony in 1986. In 1977, Skelton was booked as the headline entertainment act for homecoming and was featured in the parade; he is seen here receiving enthusiastic greetings from students and alumni. So great was the demand for his show that Red agreed to perform a third show for those who were unable to get tickets for the first two sold-out performances.

Coached by Steve Yoder and led by point guard Ray McCallum, the 1980–1981 Ball State men's basketball team earned its first NCAA Tournament berth, finishing with a 20-10 record and MAC regular season and tournament championships. Here, McCallum, who finished the season as Ball State's leading scorer with 18.4 points per game, brings the ball up the court against in-state rival Indiana State University on December 13, 1980. The Cardinals won the contest, 76-60.

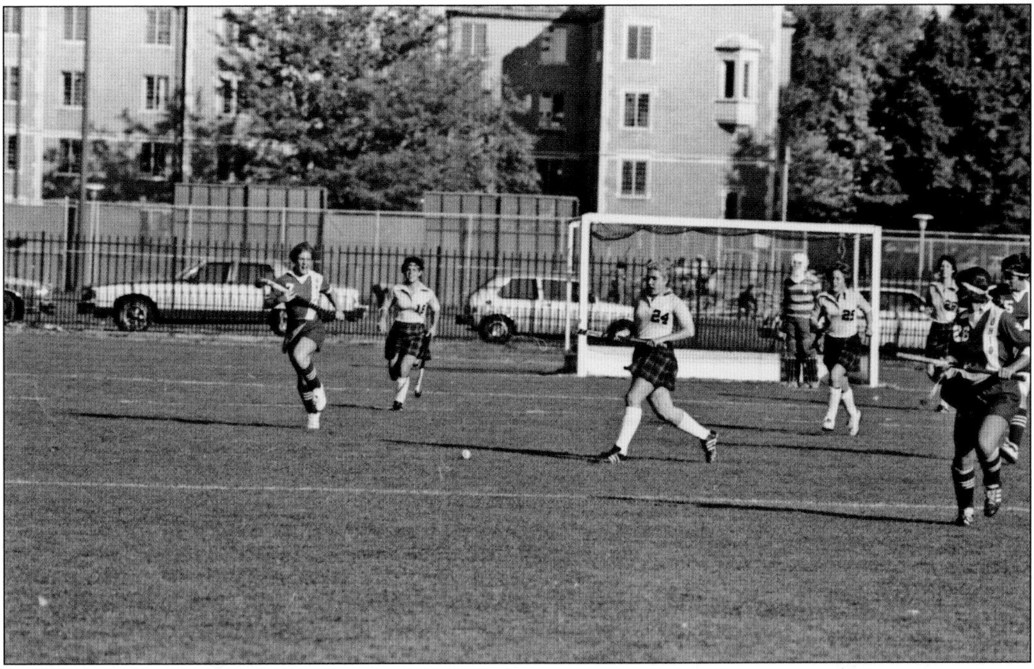

Ball State's field hockey team began a dynasty under coach Karen Fitzpatrick in the 1980s, winning nine consecutive conference championships from 1983 to 1991. The 1983 squad, pictured defeating Ohio University at home on October 7 by a score of 1-0, finished the season with a 15-5 record.

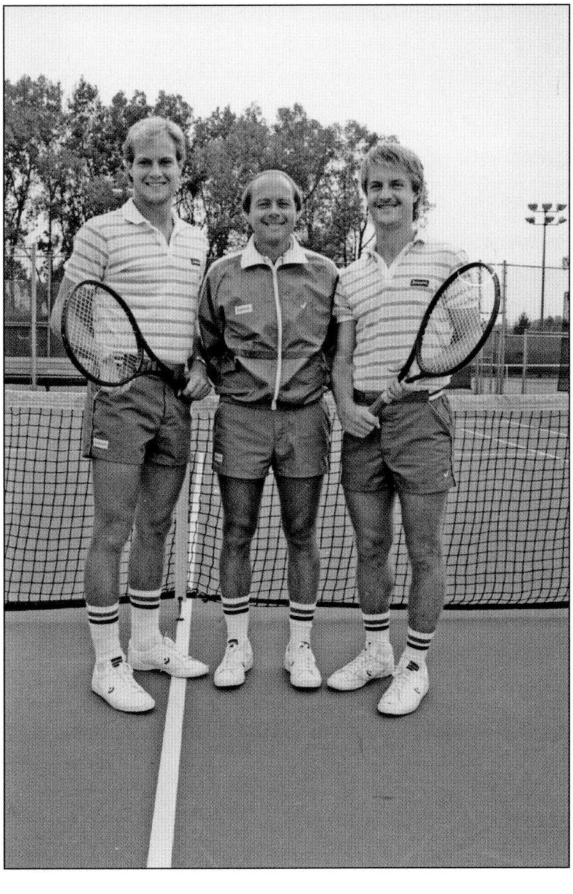

Ball State's men's tennis team, coached by Bill Richards (center), won its first of 12 consecutive MAC championships in 1984. Bill Richards is the most successful coach in Ball State history, with his teams having won 38 Mid-American Conference regular season and tournament championships. Richards is flanked by John Mermer (left) and Tom Coulton (right).

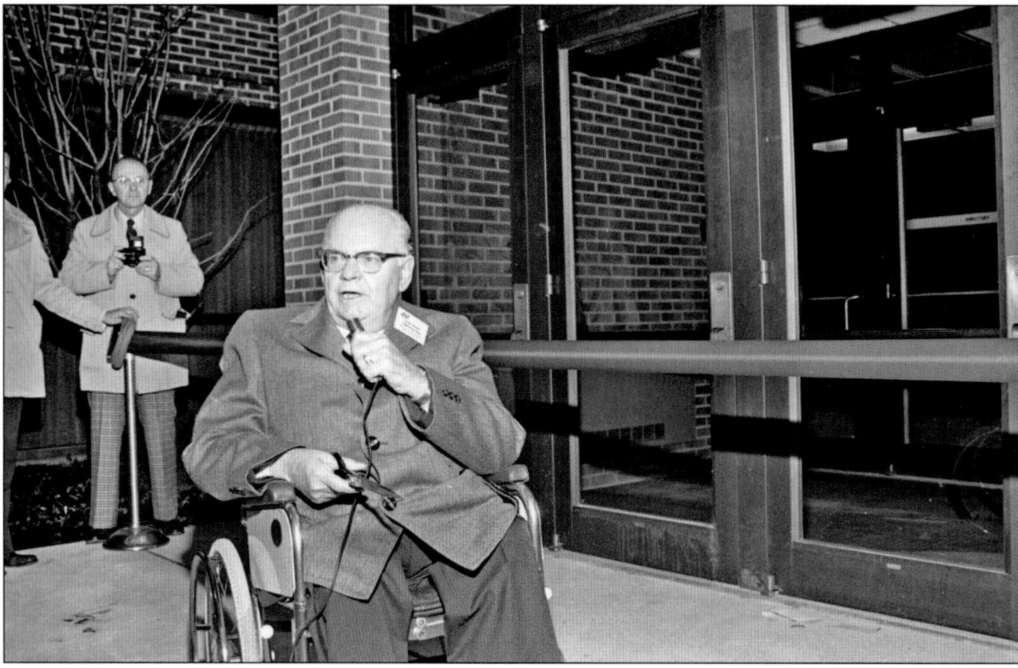

Ball State alumnus and noted benefactor Ralph Whitinger presides over the ribbon-cutting ceremony for his namesake building, the Whitinger Business Building, on November 27, 1979. Whitinger, a prominent Muncie accountant and 1929 graduate of Ball State, was a key figure in the founding of the Ball State Teachers College Foundation in 1951, later the Ball State University Foundation, and provided decades of philanthropic leadership for the university until his death in 1982.

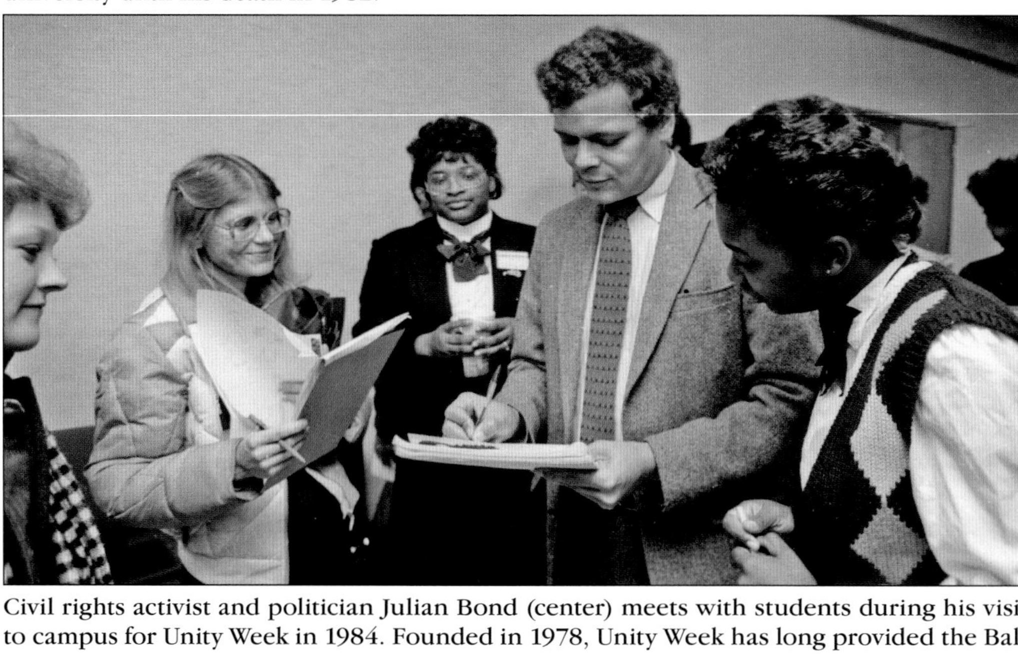

Civil rights activist and politician Julian Bond (center) meets with students during his visit to campus for Unity Week in 1984. Founded in 1978, Unity Week has long provided the Ball State community with an opportunity to engage in dialogue on diversity and inclusivity through prominent guest lecturers, cultural programming, and student activities.

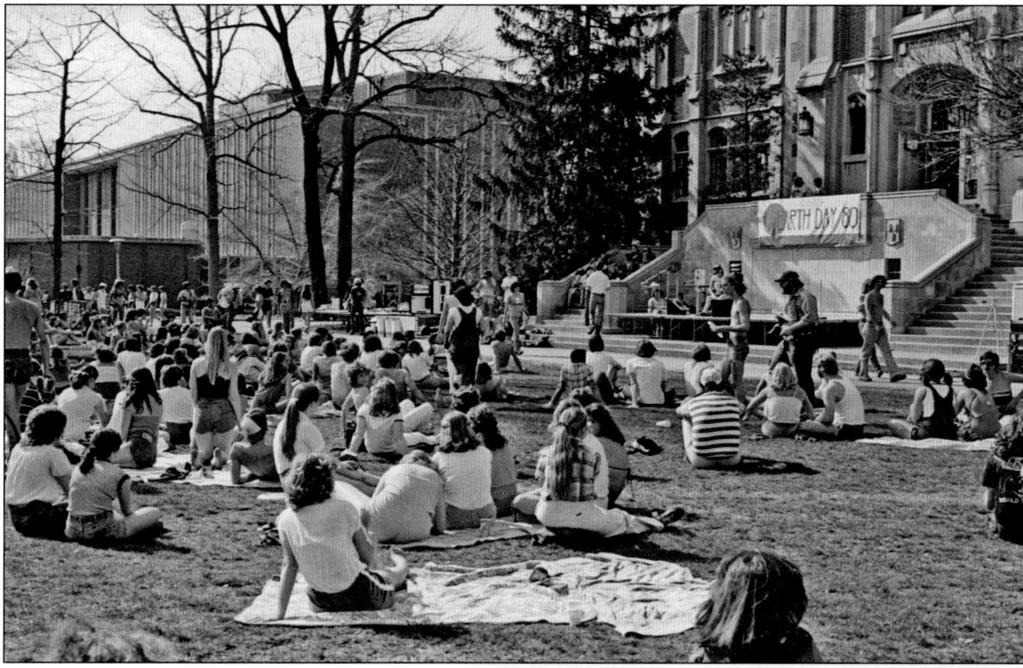

Ball State students became increasingly engaged with the issue of environmentalism during the 1970s. The university held its first Earth Day event in 1970. Earth Day events, like this one in 1980, typically featured educational booths on topics related to pollution and alternative energy sources as well as musical and theatrical performances.

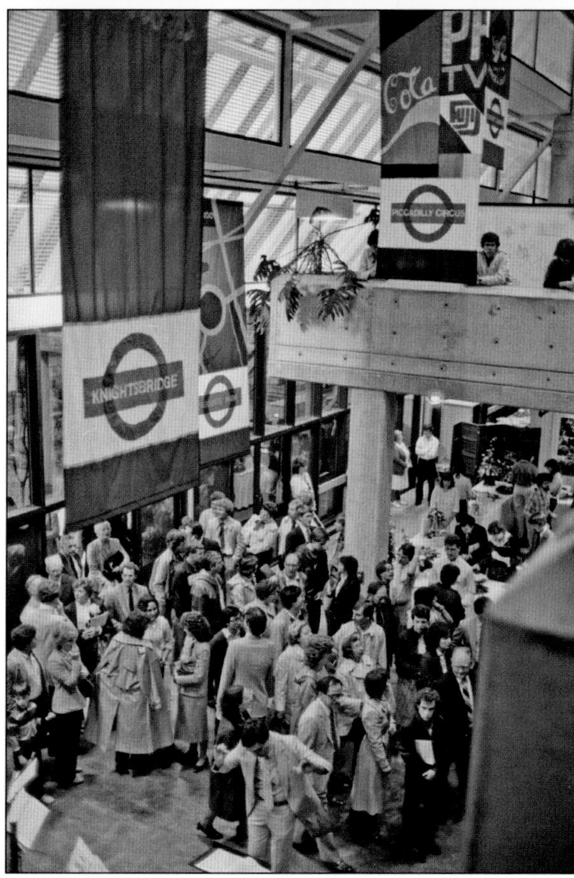

An addition to the College of Architecture and Planning was dedicated in 1983, greatly increasing the available studio space for both undergraduate and graduate students. The addition also included space for the university's Center for Energy Research/Education/Service, which serves local, state, and regional communities by exploring innovative energy use practices.

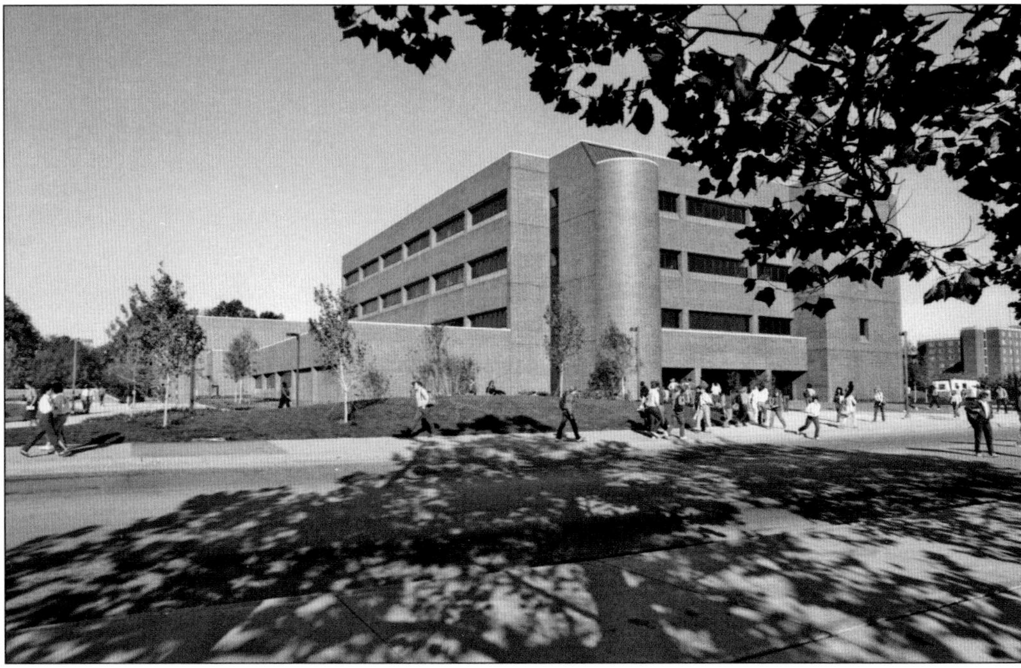

The Robert P. Bell Building, opened in 1984, expanded the footprint of the campus westward and provided a new home for Ball State University's English, mathematics, and computer science departments. The building also accommodated the university's growing computer center and included a 24-hour computer lab.

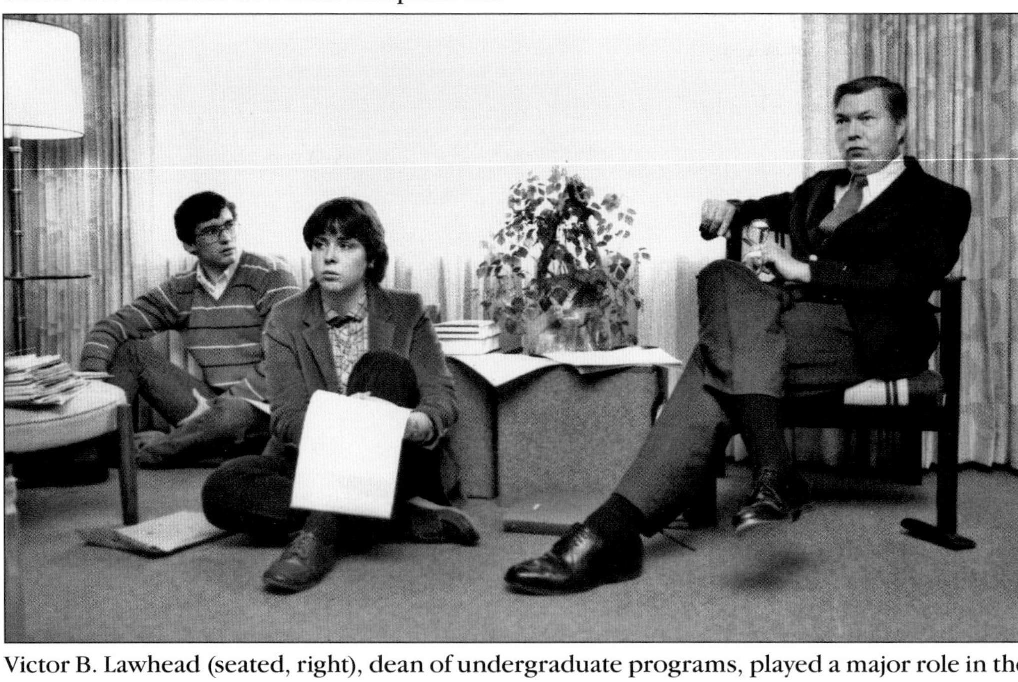

Victor B. Lawhead (seated, right), dean of undergraduate programs, played a major role in the establishment of honors education at Ball State. He regularly taught an honors colloquium dealing with contemporary issues in higher education, and students met at his home for their class meetings, like the one shown here in 1984.

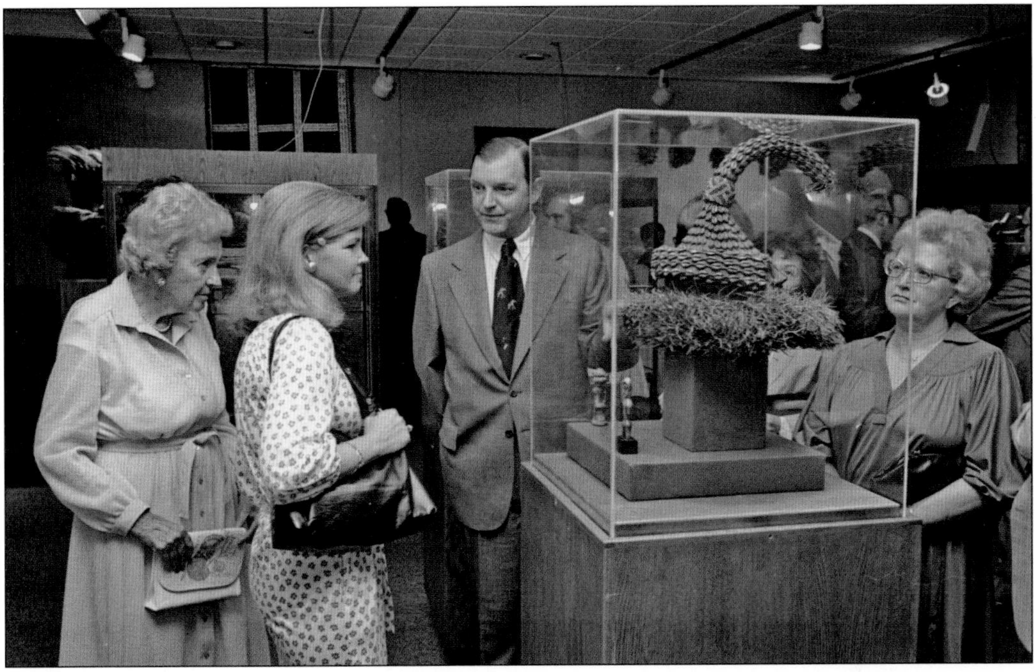

Pictured in 1979, art historian and benefactor David T. Owsley, grandson of Ball State founder Frank C. Ball, has provided unparalleled support for the ongoing growth and expansion of the Ball State Museum of Art, contributing artwork representing the Americas, Europe, Africa, China, India, Japan, Southeast Asia, and the Pacific Islands. In 2011, the Ball State Museum of Art was renamed the David Owsley Museum of Art to honor his contributions and philanthropy.

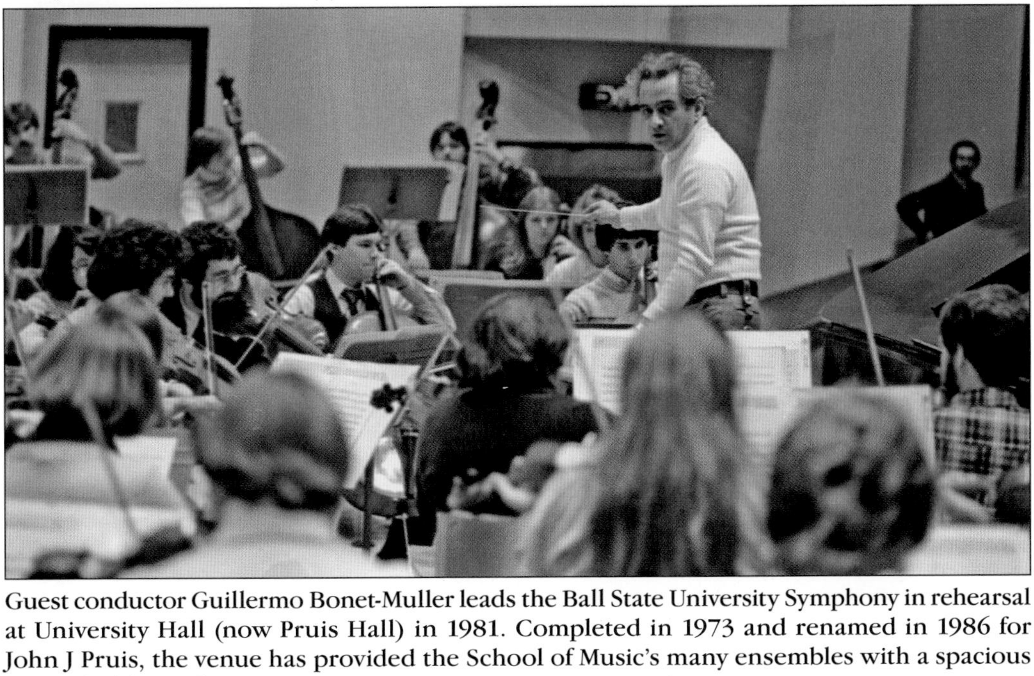

Guest conductor Guillermo Bonet-Muller leads the Ball State University Symphony in rehearsal at University Hall (now Pruis Hall) in 1981. Completed in 1973 and renamed in 1986 for John J Pruis, the venue has provided the School of Music's many ensembles with a spacious and valuable performance space.

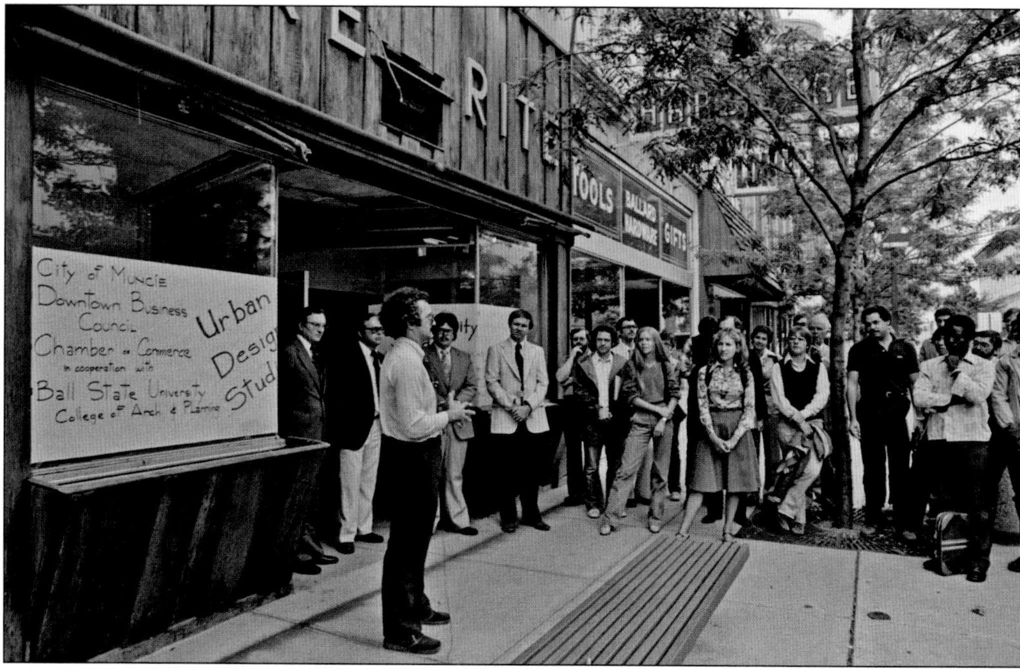

Ball State's College of Architecture and Planning opened its campus-community Urban Design Studio in downtown Muncie in 1980. In this photograph, architecture professor Anthony Costello (front left) speaks at the opening of the center.

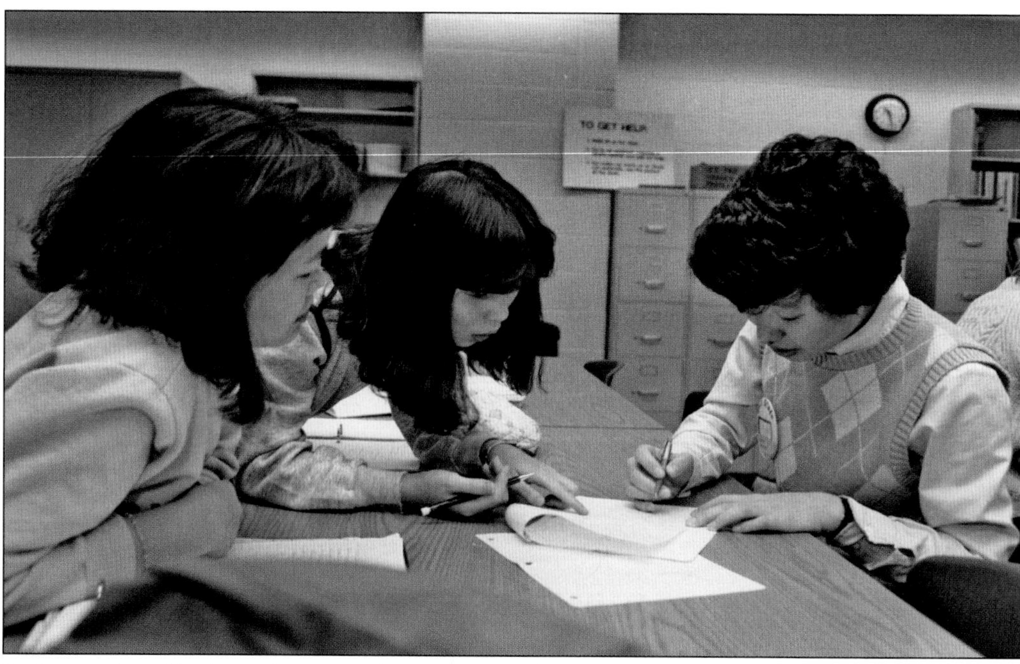

In December 1984, mathematical sciences students convene to review their calculations. In addition to a traditional mathematics curriculum, students in the mid-1980s could also pursue emphases in secondary mathematics education and actuarial science.

Five

A Premier Teaching University 1984–2000

In 1984, John E. Worthen became the president of Ball State University, succeeding Robert P. Bell, who served in the office from 1981 to 1984. Worthen held Ball State's presidency until 2000, providing some much-needed stability to the senior leadership and, in the process, instituting some new emphases that became permanent features.

During the Worthen years, student enrollment stabilized in the range of 17,500, and a new program called Freshman Connections helped incoming freshmen adjust more smoothly to campus life. Funded initially by a three-year grant from the Lilly Endowment, Freshman Connections soon became a hallmark at Ball State and helped make the university nationally recognized for the effectiveness of its first-year experience. Ball State also successfully completed its first capital campaign, Wings for the Future, raising $44.1 million between 1988 and 1992. Ball State's athletic teams continued to be successful, winning MAC championships in football, women's field hockey, and men's basketball. The most successful of all the teams was the men's tennis team, which won 12 consecutive MAC championships between 1984 and 1996.

In the early 1980s, as increasingly scarcer resources were granted to Indiana's public universities, it became clear that Ball State needed to redefine its focus. For example, what should be the primary focus of the professoriate: teaching or research? The answer soon became clear as Ball State emulated what became known as the teacher-scholar model, with teaching being the primary emphasis but with faculty members also pursuing an active research agenda. In that respect, Ball State aspired to be Indiana's premier teaching university, which also meant the application of the latest developments in educational technology, such as computerization and multimedia, into the teaching-learning process. Under Worthen's leadership, Ball State invested heavily in the technology of fiber optics to provide access to technology in the university's classrooms.

By the end of the century, Ball State had acquired a new identity. It was to fill the niche between the large, research-oriented public university and the small, private liberal arts college. "Quality education at reasonable cost" became the message that Ball State was sending to the people of Indiana as the 20th century came to a close.

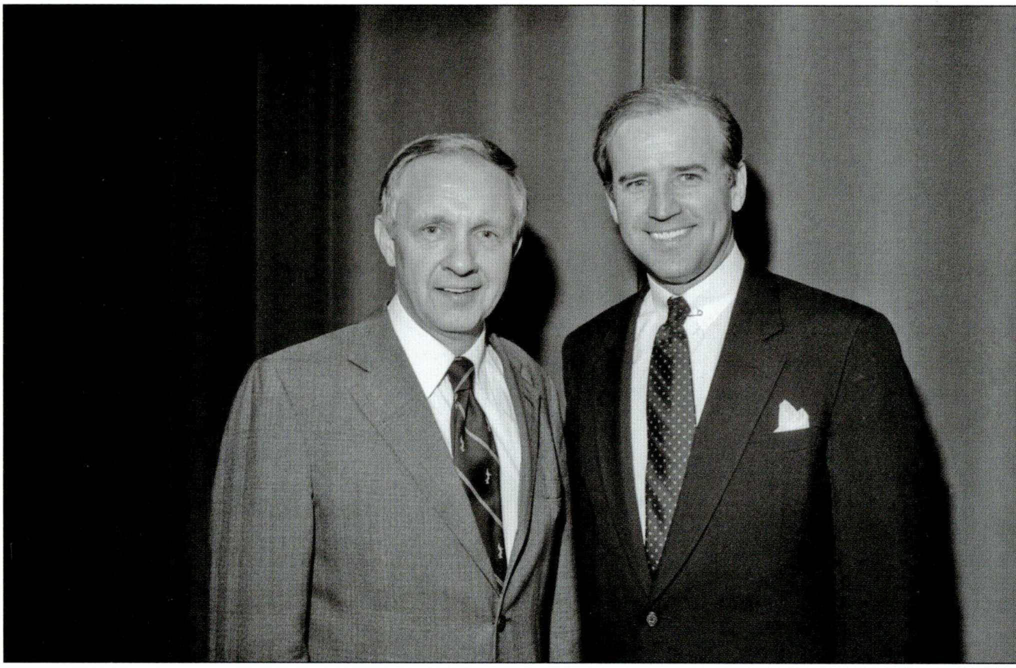

Pres. John Worthen led Ball State through a period of valuable administrative stability from 1984 to his retirement in 2000, overseeing significant campus modernization and growth in prestige of the university's academic programs. Worthen (left) is pictured in 1986 with campus guest speaker Joseph Biden, future US vice president and then-senator from Delaware.

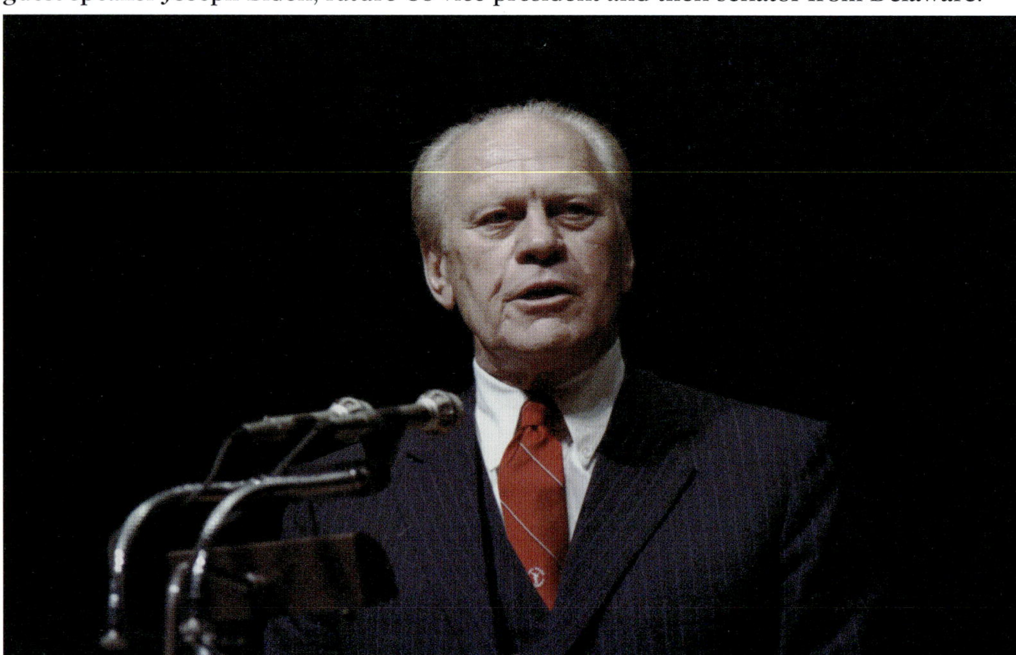

Spring 1985 saw former US president Gerald R. Ford visiting the Ball State campus in an event sponsored by the Student Association and the Provost's Lecture Series. Ford spoke to a crowd of roughly 3,200 at Emens Auditorium with a speech titled "Issues of the Next Presidency."

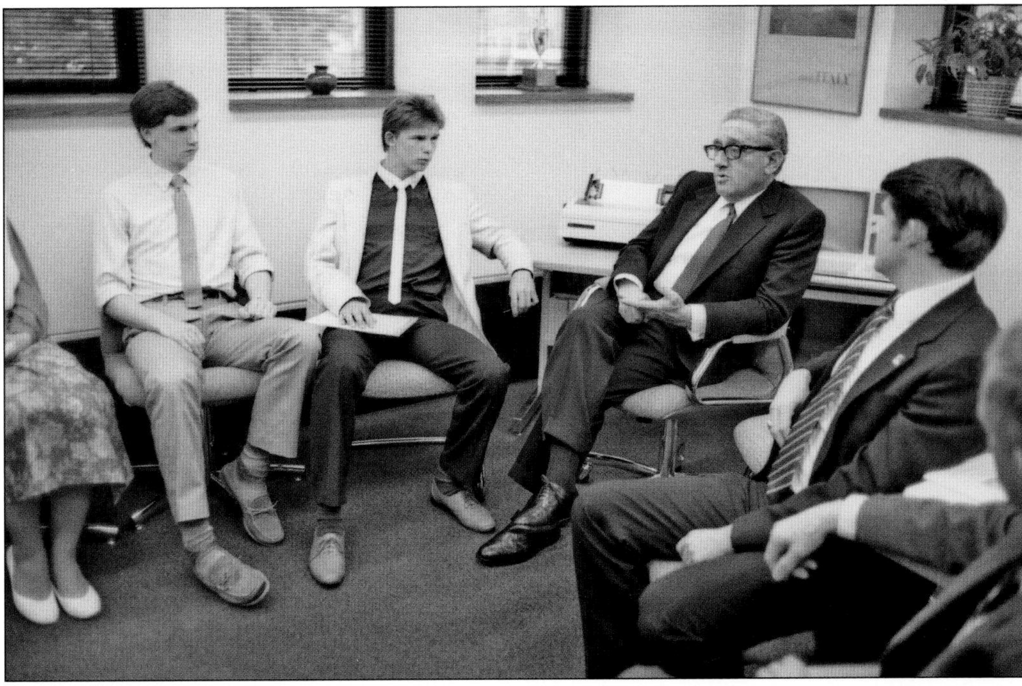

Diplomat and former secretary of state Henry Kissinger was a guest on Ball State's campus in April 1987, giving a talk to a full house at Emens Auditorium, meeting with students in a discussion group as shown here, and giving an interview for WIPB-TV's *Ball State Today* program.

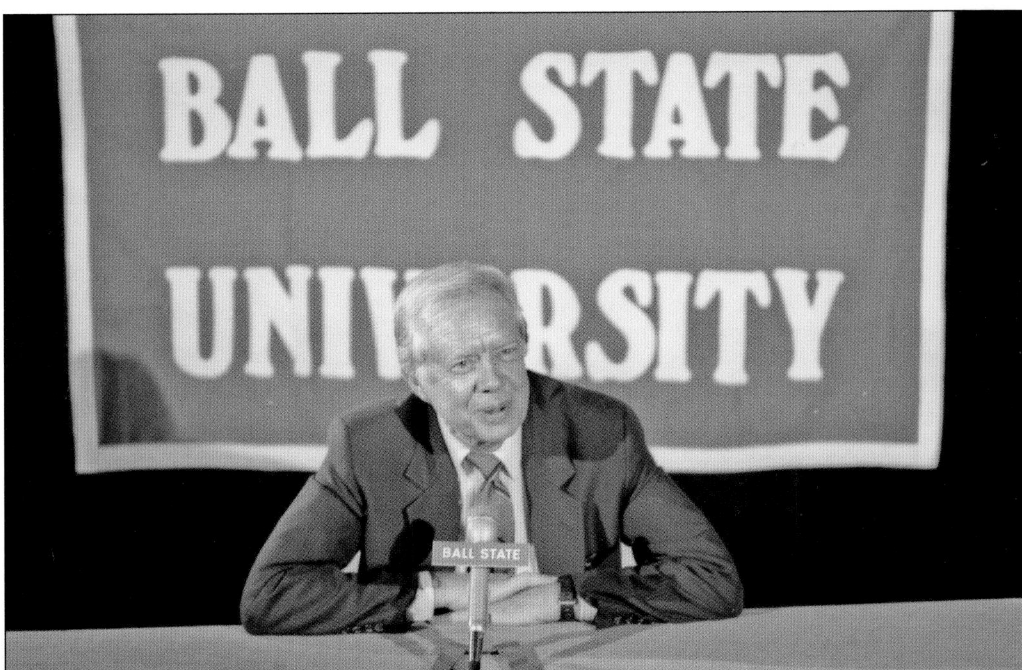

In 1988, former president Jimmy Carter visited campus, giving a speech on US foreign policy in Central America and in the Middle East as well as the 1988 presidential election.

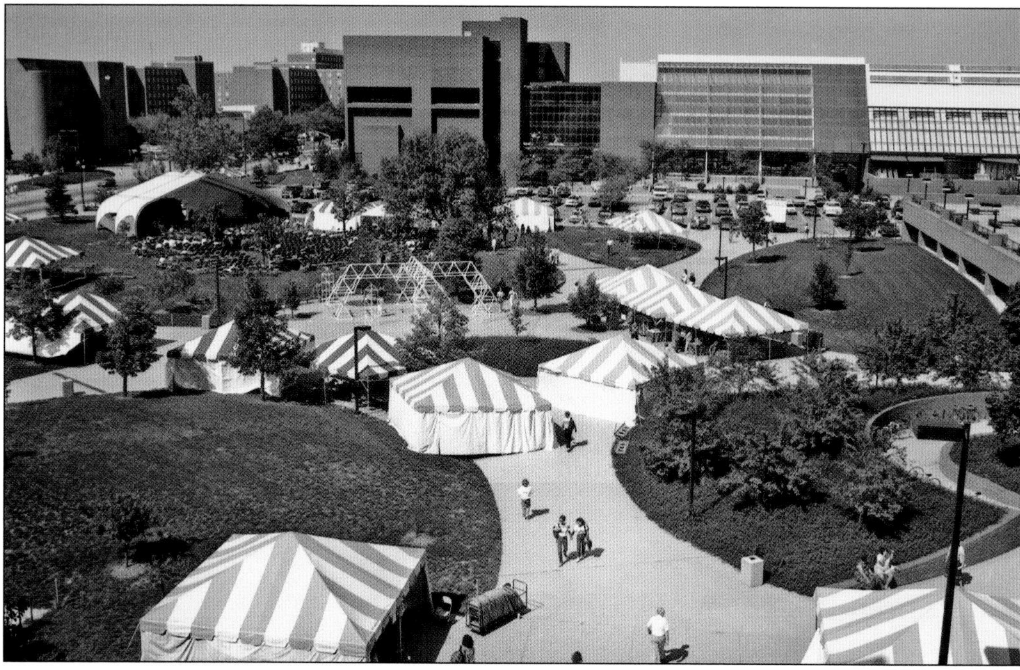

In 1988, Ball State organized the first of a series of multiday UniverCity campus/community celebrations. It featured cultural programming, including talks and lectures given by scholars, artists, advocates, and other speakers, as well as artistic performances, cultural demonstrations, and panel discussions. The success of the 1988 event encouraged four additional reprisals of UniverCity in 1990, 1992, 2000, and 2002, bringing luminaries to campus including James Burke, Cornel West, Elie Wiesel, and Sally Ride.

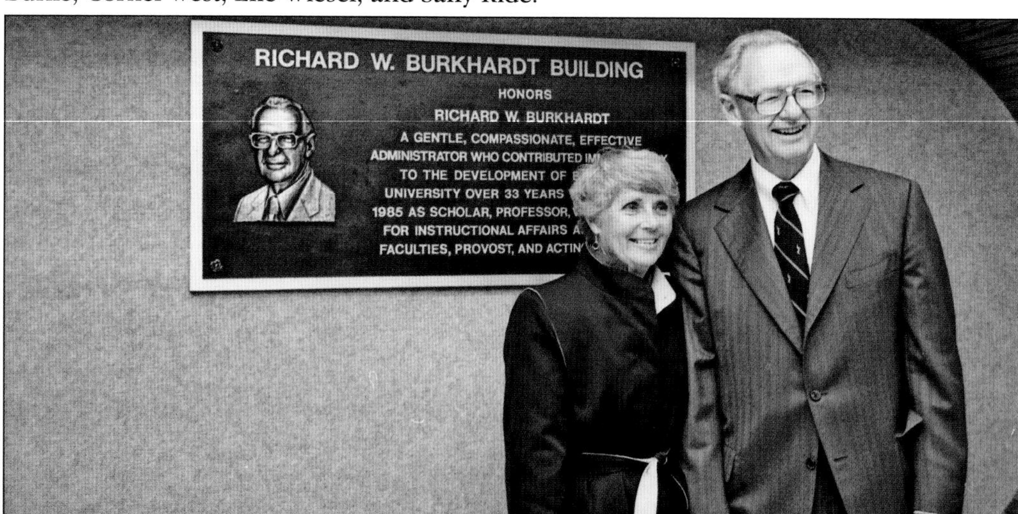

Once Science Hall and subsequently East Quad, Ball State's second oldest current structure was dedicated as the Burkhardt Building in 1986 in honor of Richard W. Burkhardt (pictured with wife Dorothy Burkhardt), who had retired the previous year after an illustrious tenure as an administrator, teacher, and acting president. The newly renovated building included classrooms, offices, and conference rooms to accommodate the history and anthropology departments, the university's anthropology museum, the Honors College, and the London Center.

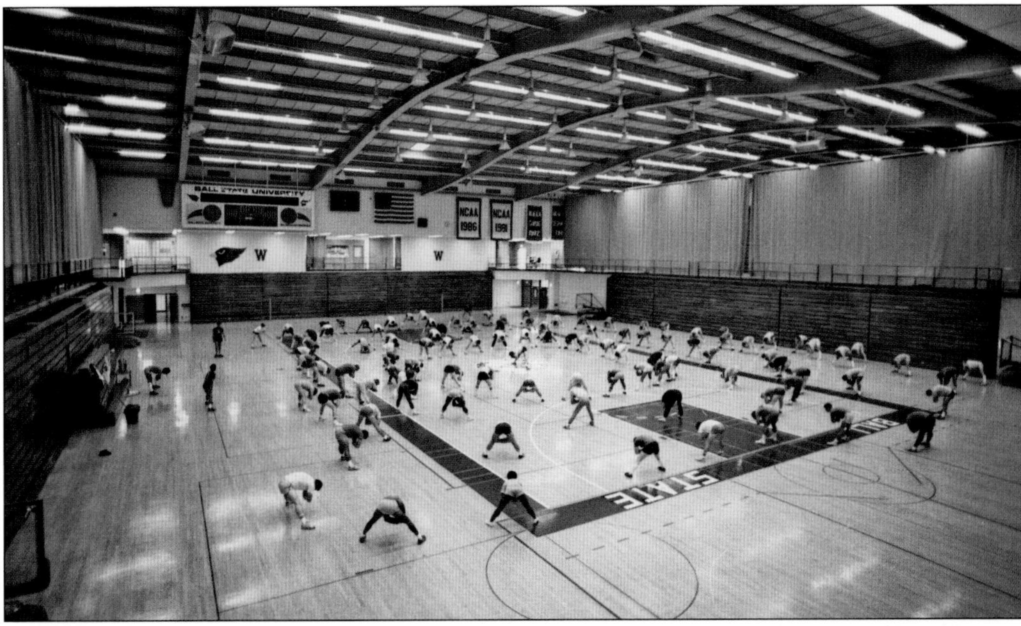

Seven years after the closing of the Air Force ROTC program, military training returned to campus with the establishment of an Army ROTC program in 1978 and the hiring of military science faculty shortly thereafter. Seen in 1987, Army ROTC cadets work through exercises in University Gym.

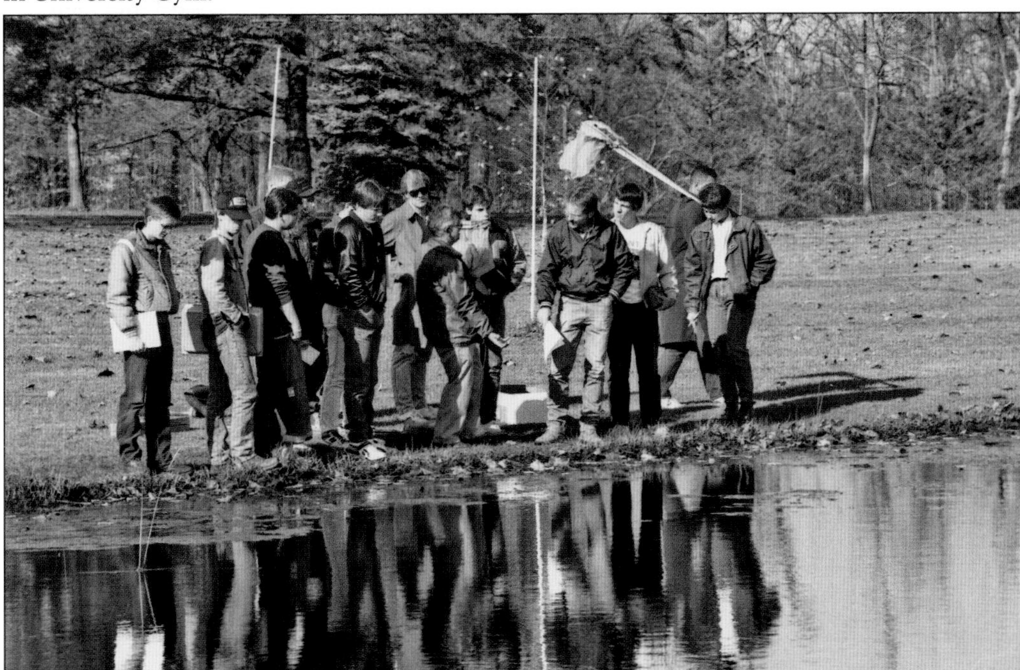

In 1989, faculty and students in the Department of Natural Resources investigate a freshwater habitat during a field study expedition. Course offerings of the era provided students with training in subjects such as land resource management, environmental protection, soil science, and outdoor recreation management.

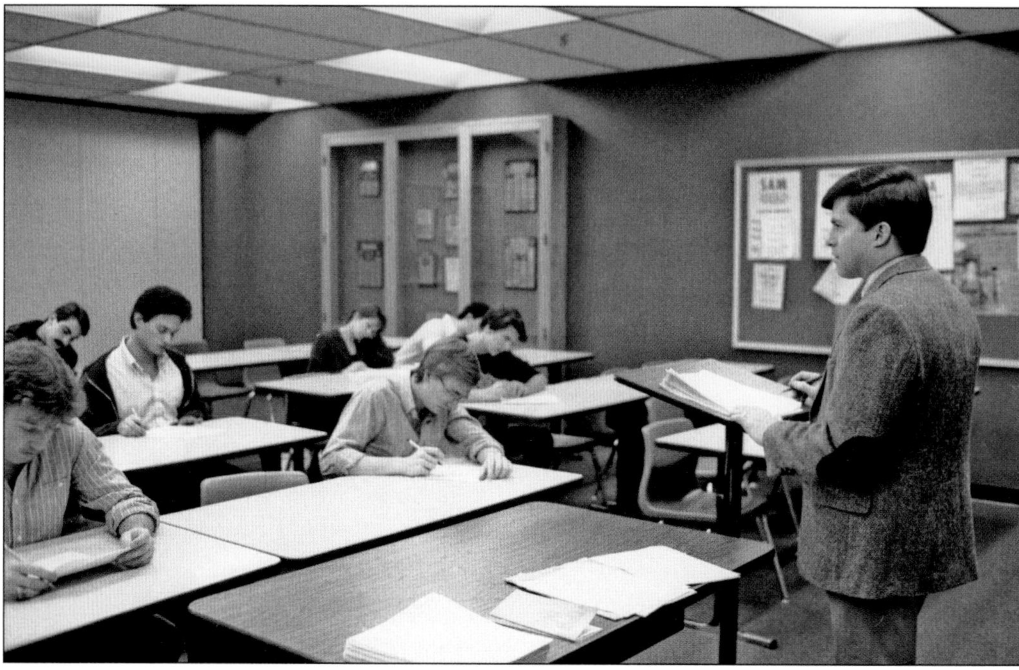

Ball State University's College of Business, named the Miller College of Business in 2003, blazed a trail in the field of entrepreneurship education, providing a highly rigorous course of study for would-be leaders of business ventures big and small. Donald F. Kuratko, pictured leading a class of entrepreneurship students in 1987, founded the program in 1983 and served on the faculty until 2004.

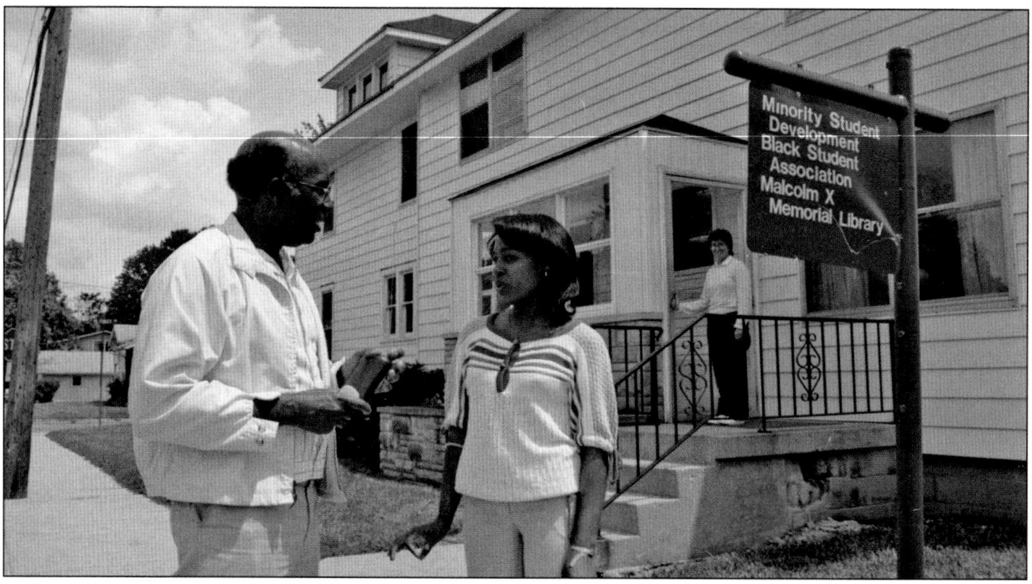

Retiring in 1986 after an 18-year career at Ball State University, Robert O. Foster served as an invaluable community builder for racial and ethnic minority students on campus. Originally hired as director of special programs, Foster headed up the Office of Multicultural Affairs beginning in 1970, developing and organizing numerous cultural programs, events, and activities celebrating diversity and multiculturalism.

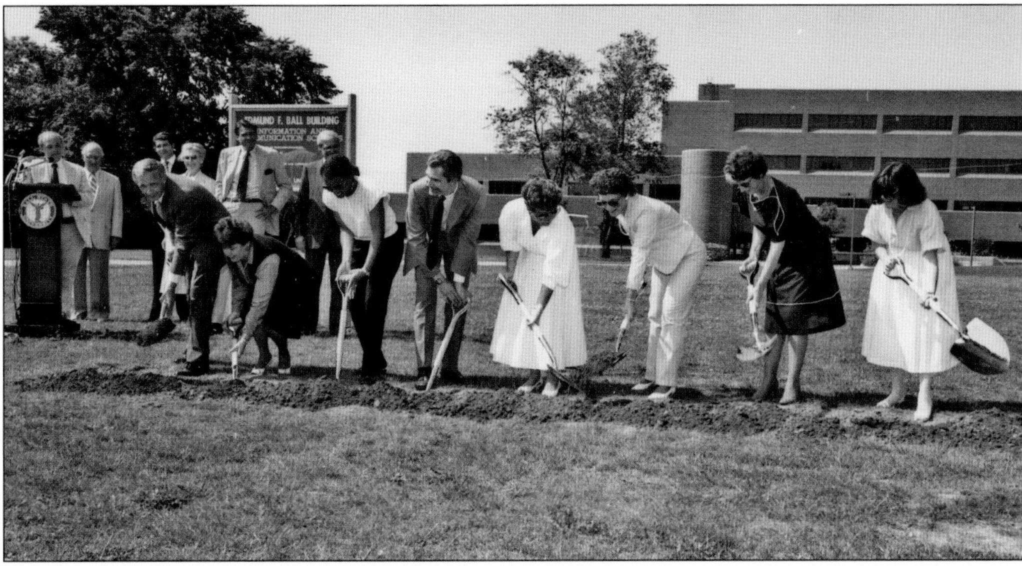

After completion of the Robert P. Bell Building, development of the campus west of McKinley Avenue continued with the construction of the Edmund F. Ball Communications Building. The building, for which ground was broken on June 20, 1986, and which was completed two years later, provided much-needed space for the university's growing communications programs and a home for WBST-FM and WIPB-TV.

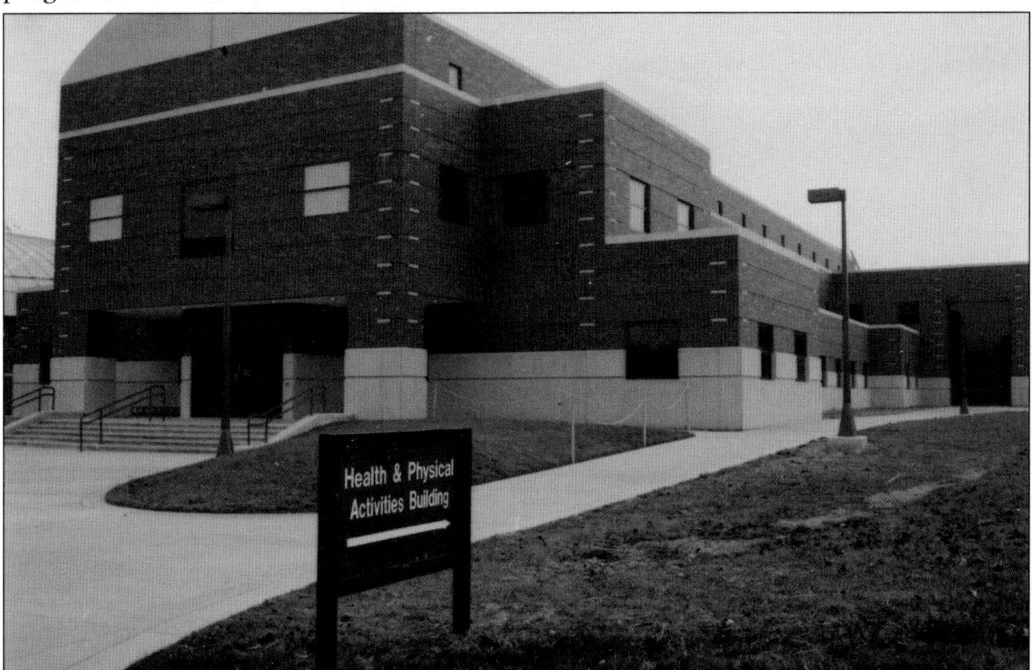

Shown in November 1990, Ball State's new Health & Physical Activities Building provided greatly expanded space to accommodate the research program of the Human Performance Laboratory and for teaching in the School of Physical Education, including programs dedicated to exercise science, sport biomechanics, sport management, physical education teacher education, and human bioenergetics.

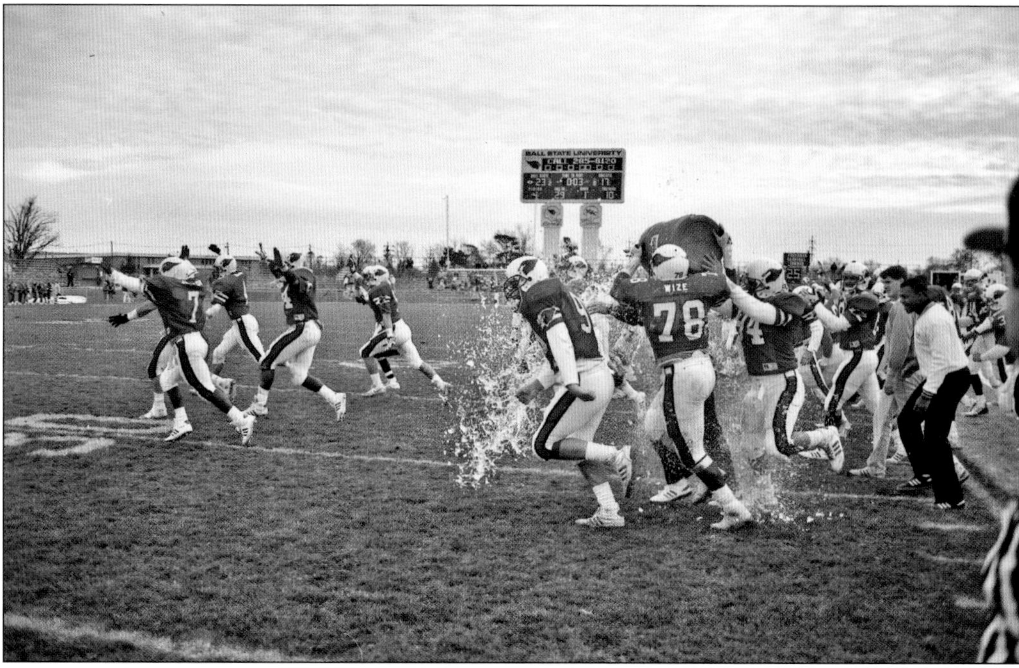

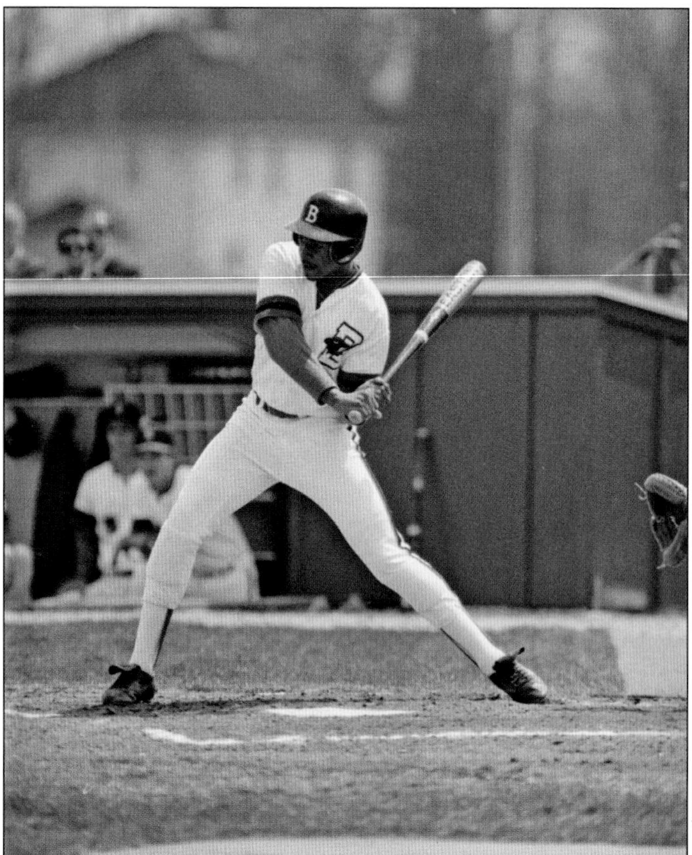

The Cardinals football squad returned to the top of the MAC with a conference title in 1989, earning an invitation to the California Raisin Bowl, the first NCAA Division I bowl game in program history. Here, teammates Ralph Wize (78) and Steve Martin (94) give coach Paul Schudel a Gatorade bath after Ball State's 23-17 win over Eastern Michigan on November 11, 1989, at Ball State Stadium, clinching a conference championship.

Multisport star Thomas Howard was best known for his prowess on the baseball field, batting .448 in his final season as a Cardinal in 1986. A first-round pick in the 1986 draft, Howard enjoyed an 11-year career in Major League Baseball.

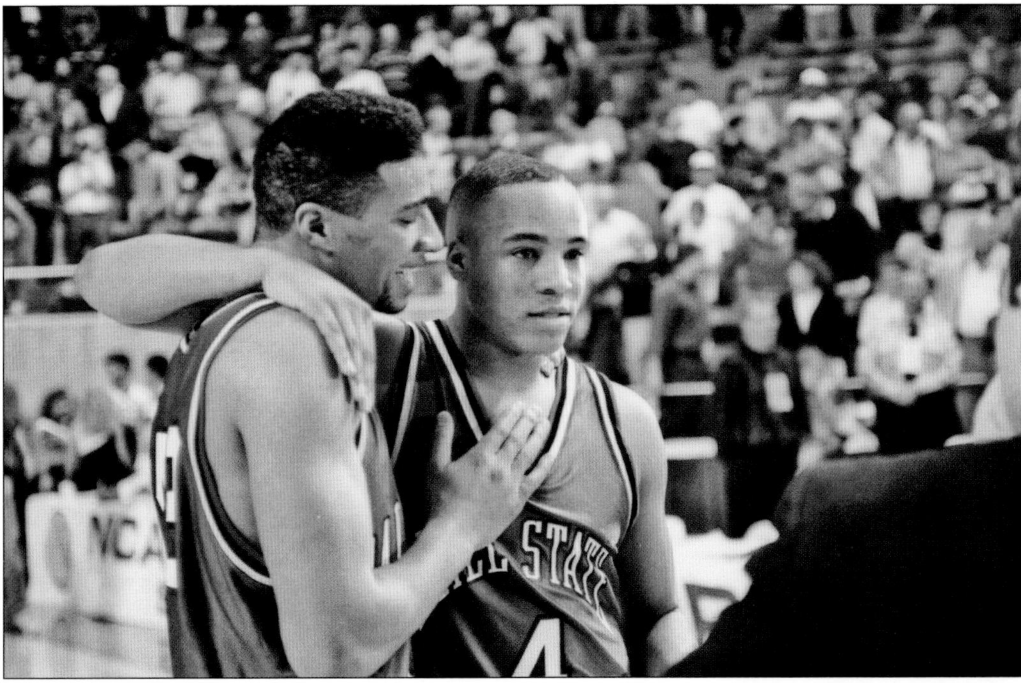

In 1989–1990, the men's basketball team enjoyed a Cinderella season, finishing with a 26-7 record and a Sweet Sixteen appearance in the NCAA Tournament with dramatic upset wins over Oregon State and Louisville. Here, team leaders Paris McCurdy (left) and Chandler Thompson (right) celebrate after their 62-60 victory over Louisville in Salt Lake City, Utah.

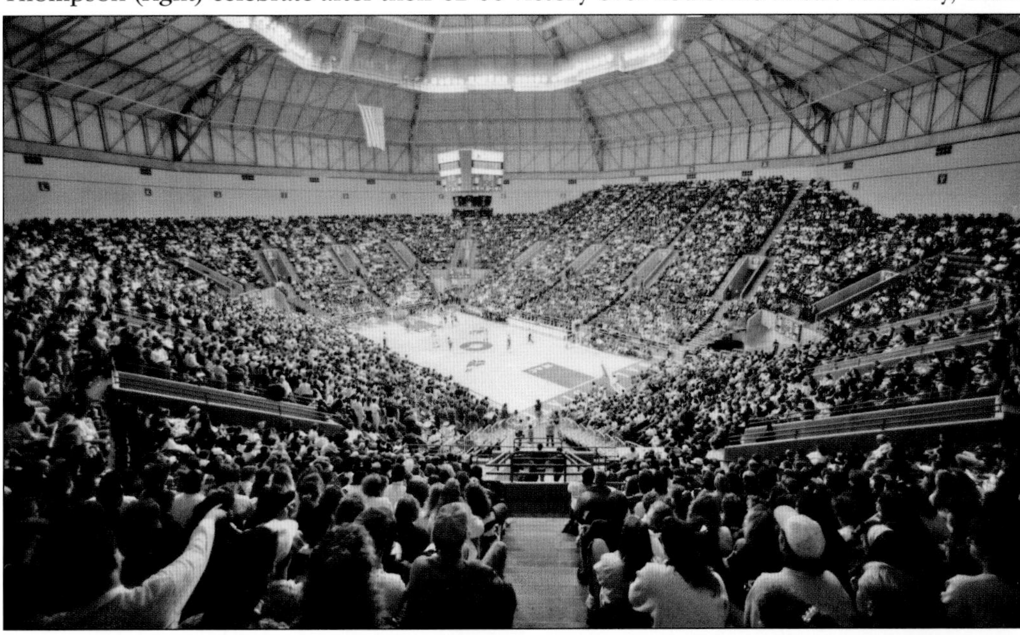

Replacing Irving Gymnasium, Ball State University's new arena opened with men's and women's basketball games against Miami University on January 15, 1992, in front of a capacity crowd of 11,500 fans. The facility was named John E. Worthen Arena in 2000 to honor Worthen's 16-year tenure as Ball State University's president.

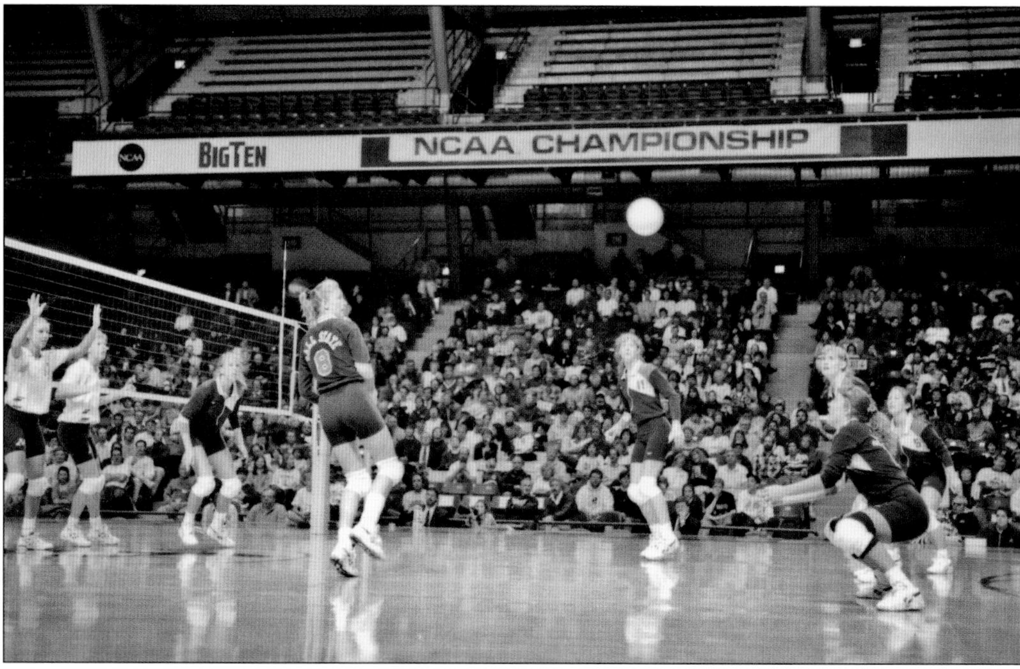

The Ball State women's volleyball team dominated the competition in the early to mid-1990s, earning four straight NCAA Tournament appearances from 1992 to 1995. The 1993 team, shown here against Minnesota in the first round of the NCAA Tournament, boasted a 26-5 overall record and went undefeated in conference play.

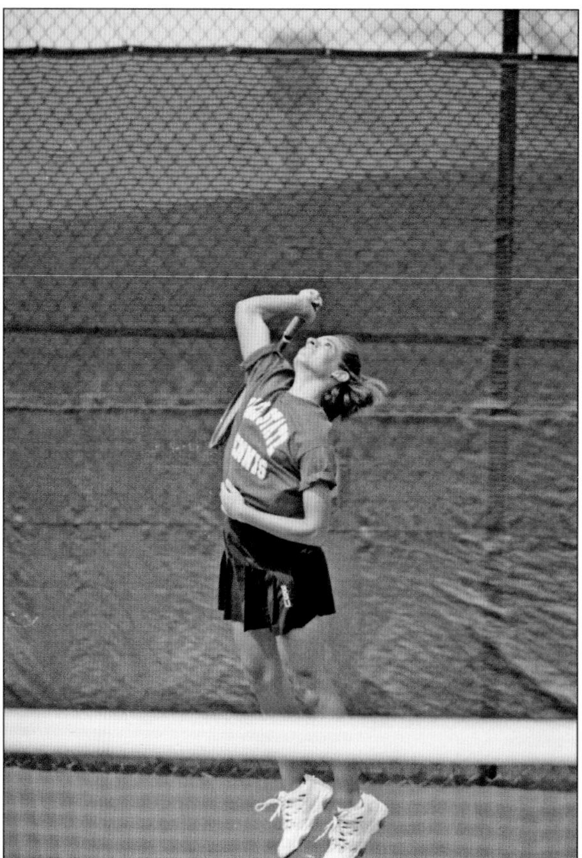

A star on the women's tennis team during the mid-1990s, Lisa Drewitt finished her career as the school record holder for both singles wins (overall record of 98-58) and doubles wins (overall record of 102-40).

Between 1990 and 1994, Dave Keener earned All-MAC and All-American honors as a diver on the men's swimming and diving team, coached by Bob Thomas. At the conclusion of his career, Keener held every one of Ball State's records in diving as well as five of the six MAC records.

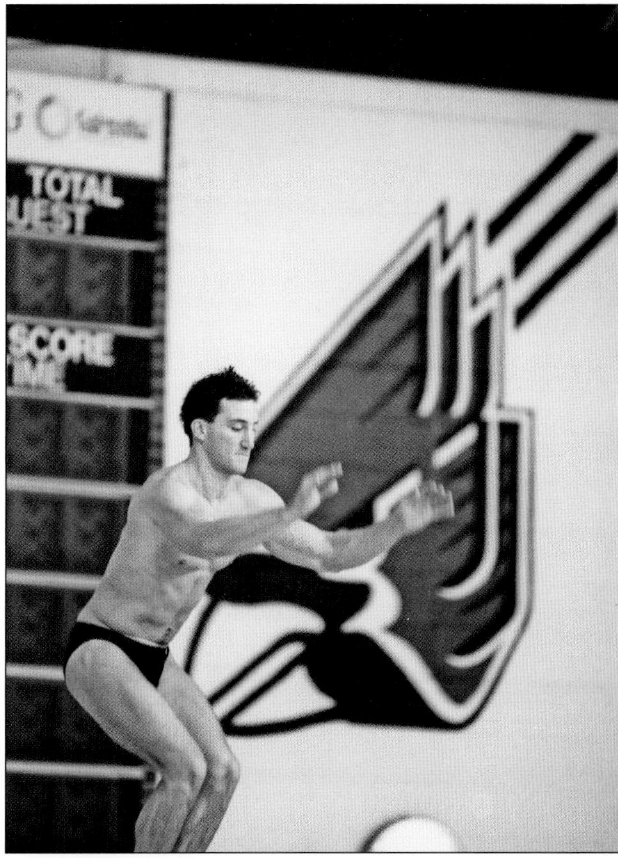

Ball State football recaptured conference titles in 1993 under coach Paul Schudel and in 1996 under coach Bill Lynch, appearing in the Las Vegas Bowl in December of both years. Pictured here, the 1993 team celebrates clinching the conference title after a victory over Kent State. From left to right are men's athletic director Don Purvis, coach Paul Schudel, and players Jose Muñoz (71), Mike Neu (14), Jermaine Daniels (45), and Malawi Hills (21).

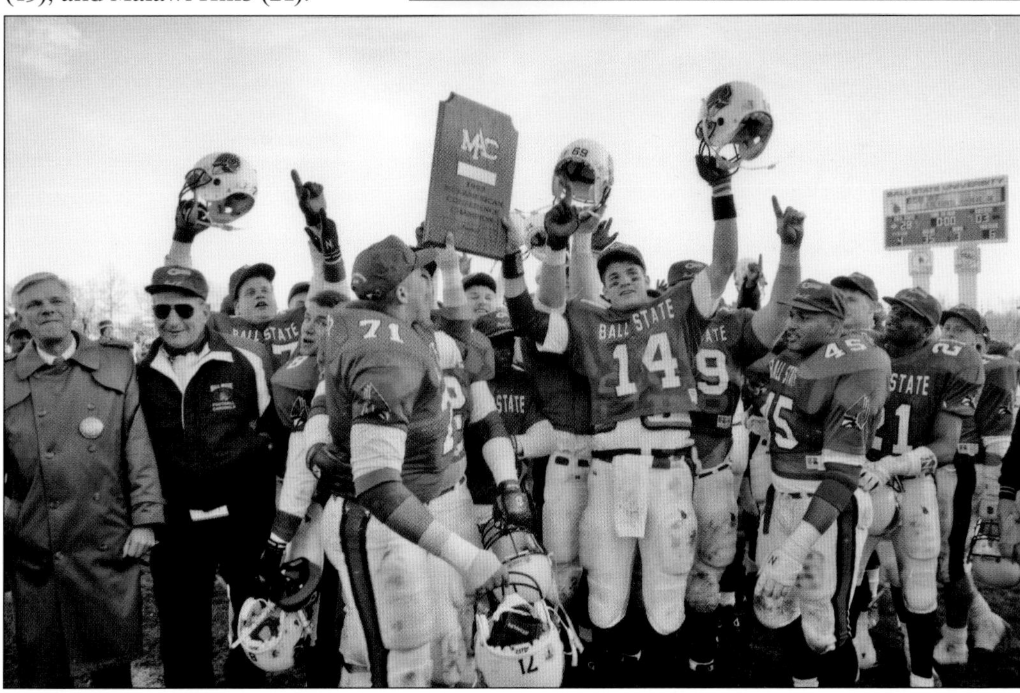

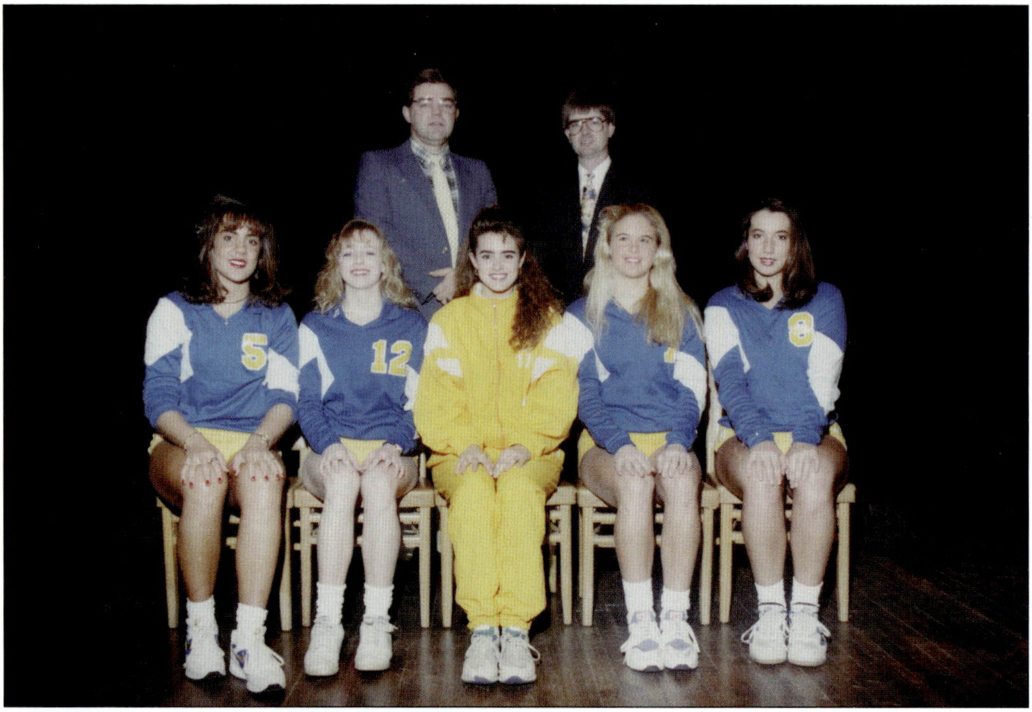

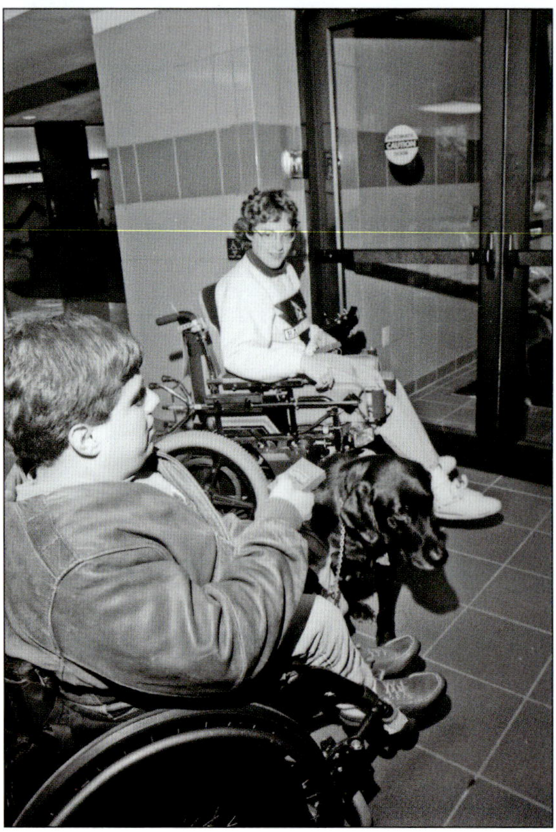

The Burris Laboratory School's girls' volleyball team built a dynasty under coach Steve Shondell, amassing 21 state championships in the 1980s, 1990s, and 2000s. Shondell (top right), who coached at Burris from 1976 to 2009 with an overall record of 1,183 wins and 95 losses, is pictured with members of the 1993 championship team.

Ball State's Office of Disability Services, founded in 1973 as Handicapped Services and led by director Richard Harris, has championed the needs and rights of disabled students on campus, vastly improving the accessibility of Ball State services and resources by improving physical spaces, learning technologies, and general campus awareness. Seen in 1991, students take advantage of automatic doors in the L.A. Pittenger Student Center.

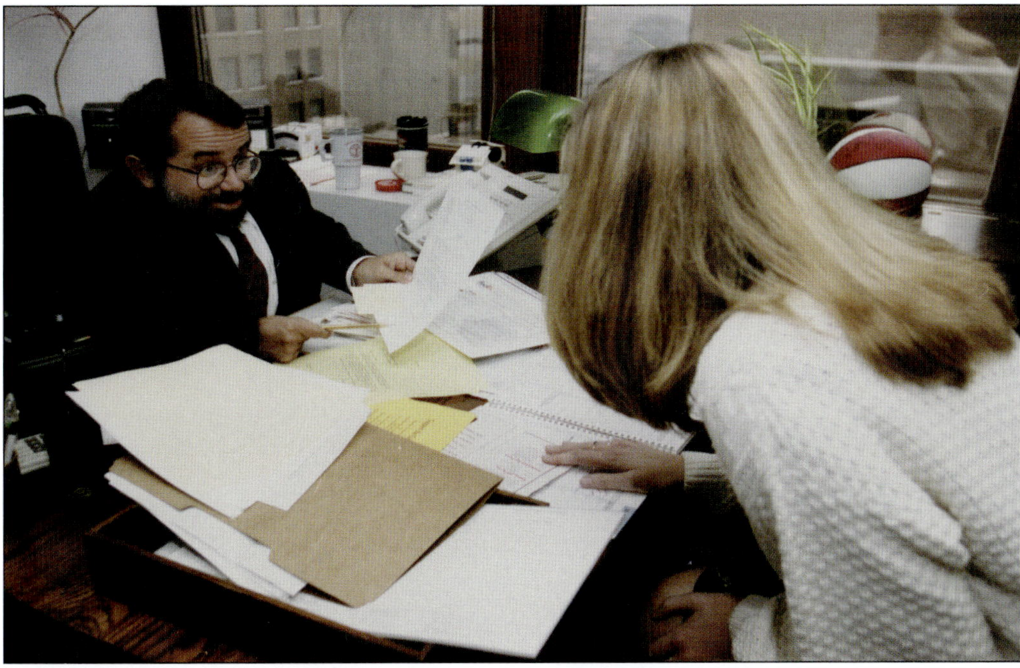

Greg "G" Fehribach graduated from Ball State in 1981 with a bachelor's degree and in 1983 with a master's degree. A student leader during his time on campus, Greg went on to earn a law degree and became a practicing attorney in Indianapolis. He played a major role in establishing the Office of Disability Affairs in Indianapolis and also served as a member of the Ball State Board of Trustees from 2004 to 2007.

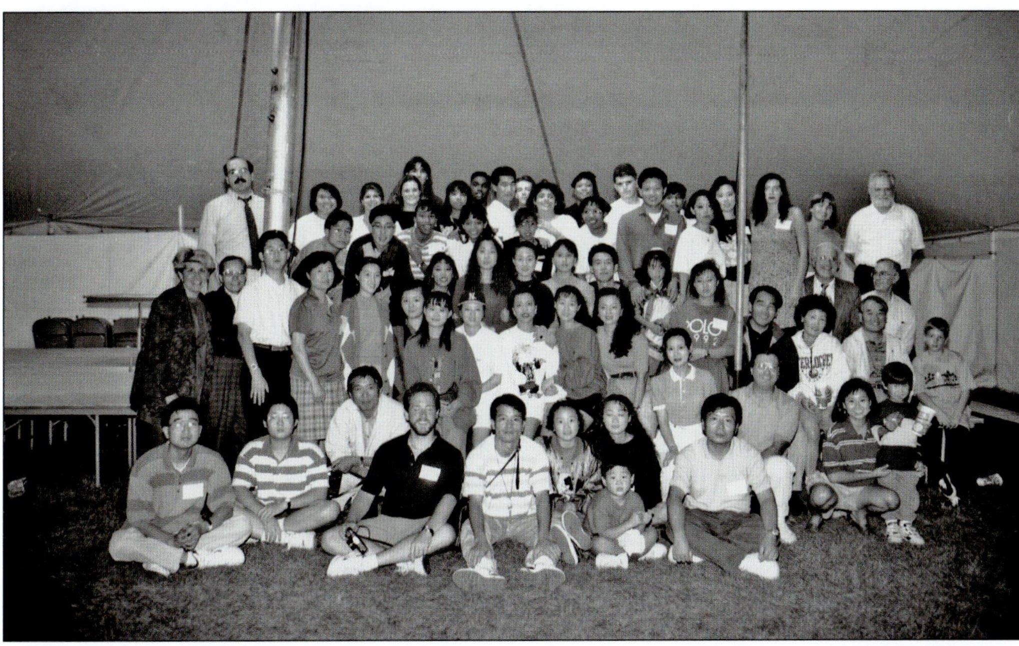

International exchange programs to support learning and research thrived at Ball State during the 1980s and 1990s. Here, students, faculty, and staff gather in 1992 to celebrate the 25th anniversary of Ball State's exchange program with Yeungnam University in South Korea.

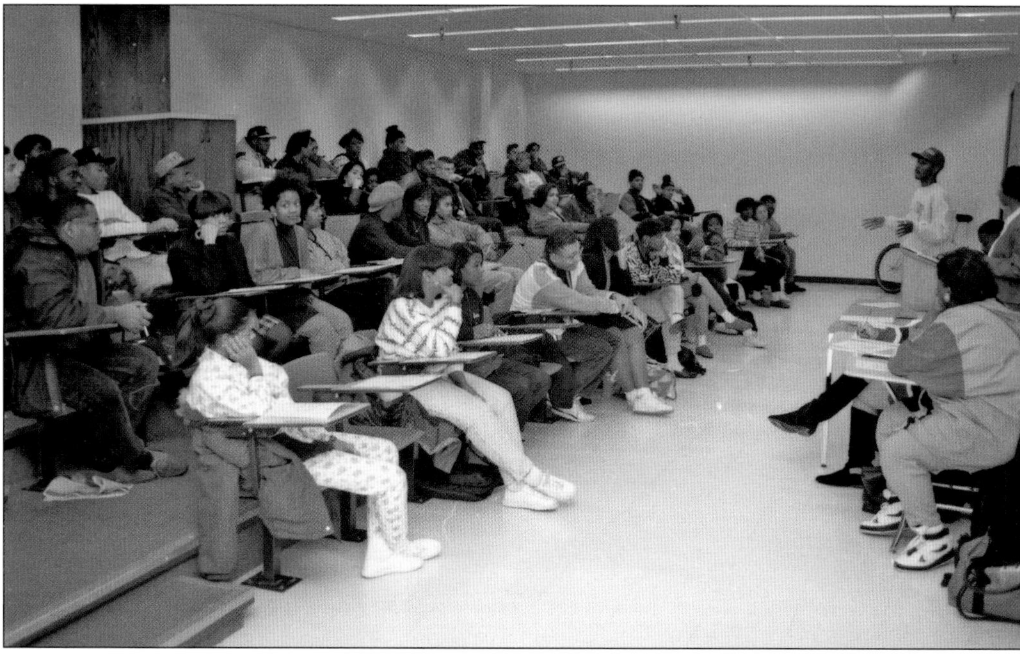

Ball State's Black Student Association, formed in the spring of 1969, has long served as a leader of organized on-campus student life and cultural activity, participating in community outreach activities while planning major programming on campus. The organization is seen here meeting in December 1992.

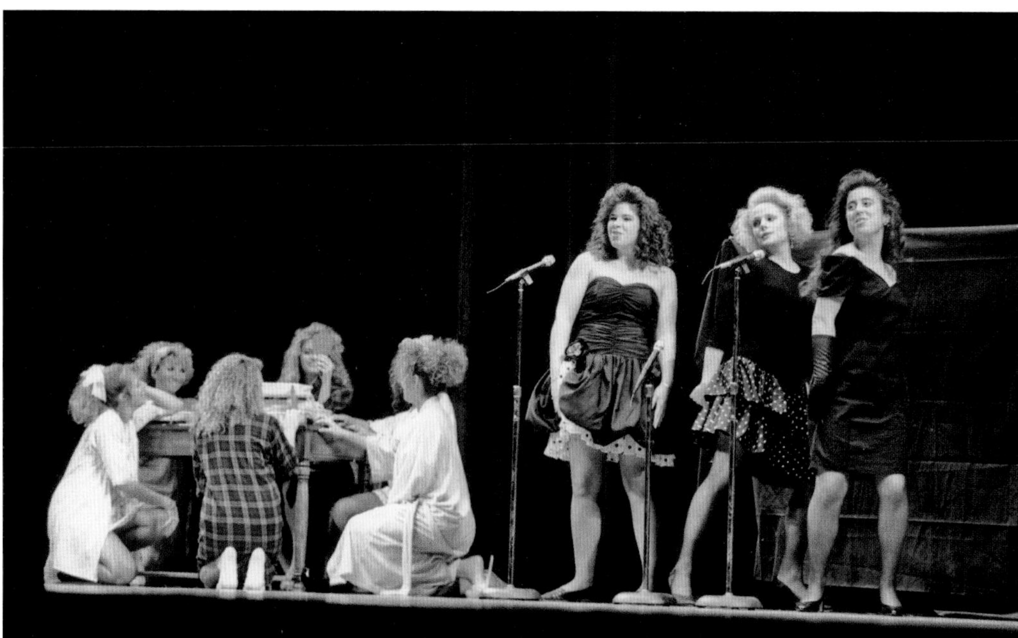

One of Ball State's newer and most popular homecoming traditions is the lip sync contest known as Air Jam, pictured here in 1991. This event was won by men and women from the Sigma Pi fraternity and Delta Delta Delta sorority with a Disney-themed performance.

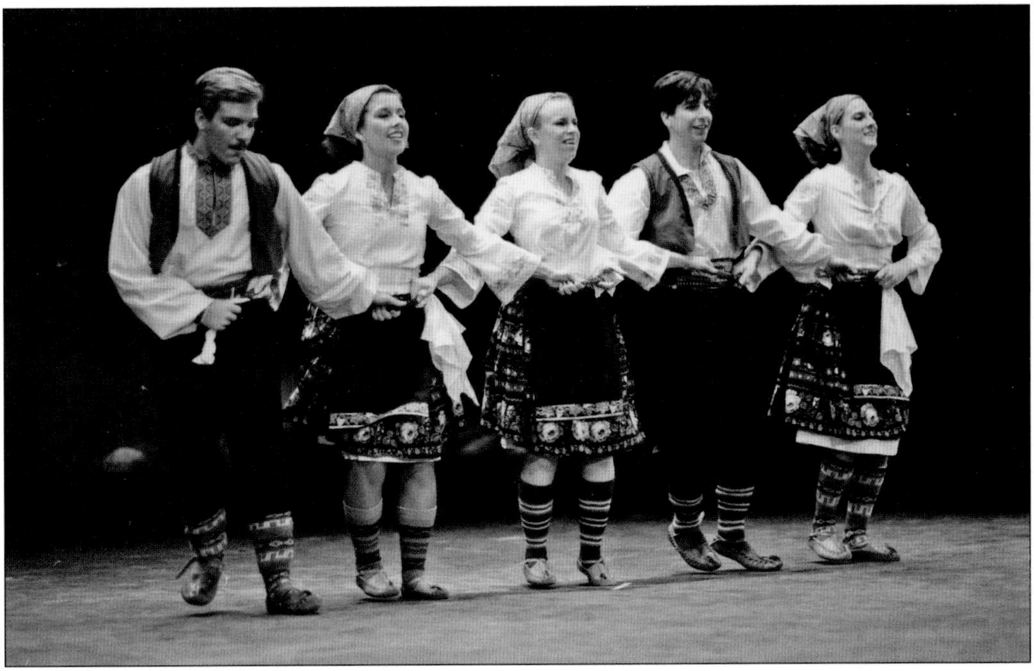

The Banevolks dance troupe was a popular draw both on campus and off with its creative and authentic international folk dance performances. Founded in the early 1970s, the group flourished under the direction of dance faculty members Ya'akov Eden and Greg Lund and includes international tours and performances on its résumé.

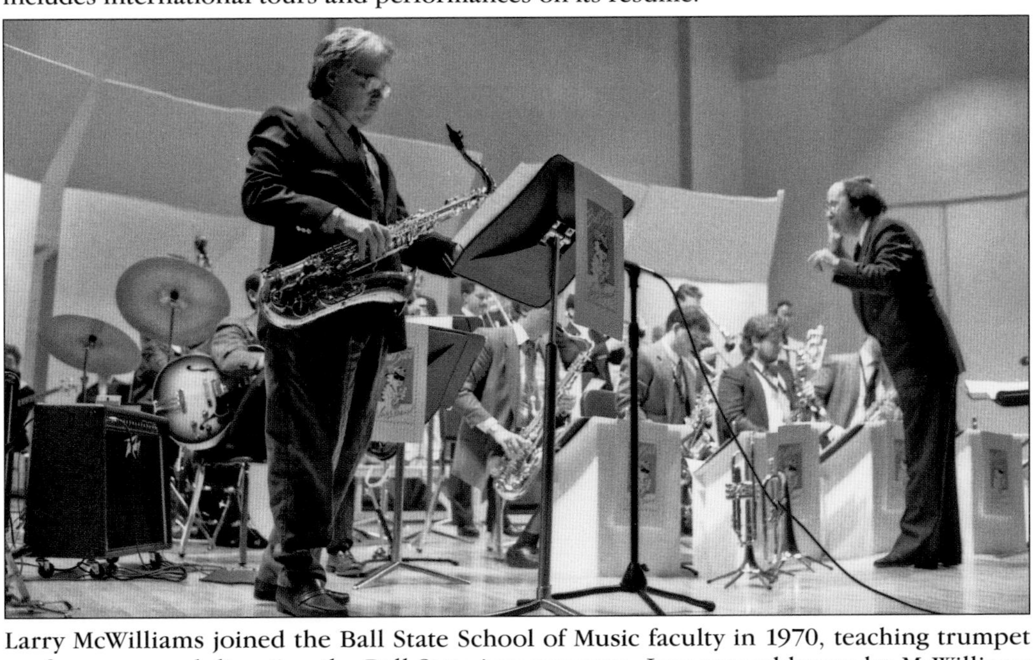

Larry McWilliams joined the Ball State School of Music faculty in 1970, teaching trumpet performance and directing the Ball State jazz program. Jazz ensembles under McWilliams thrived, earning invitations to perform at the famed Montreux Jazz Festival in Switzerland. Shown in 1990, the jazz ensemble with McWilliams conducting is joined by guest saxophonist Ralston "Morgy" Craig.

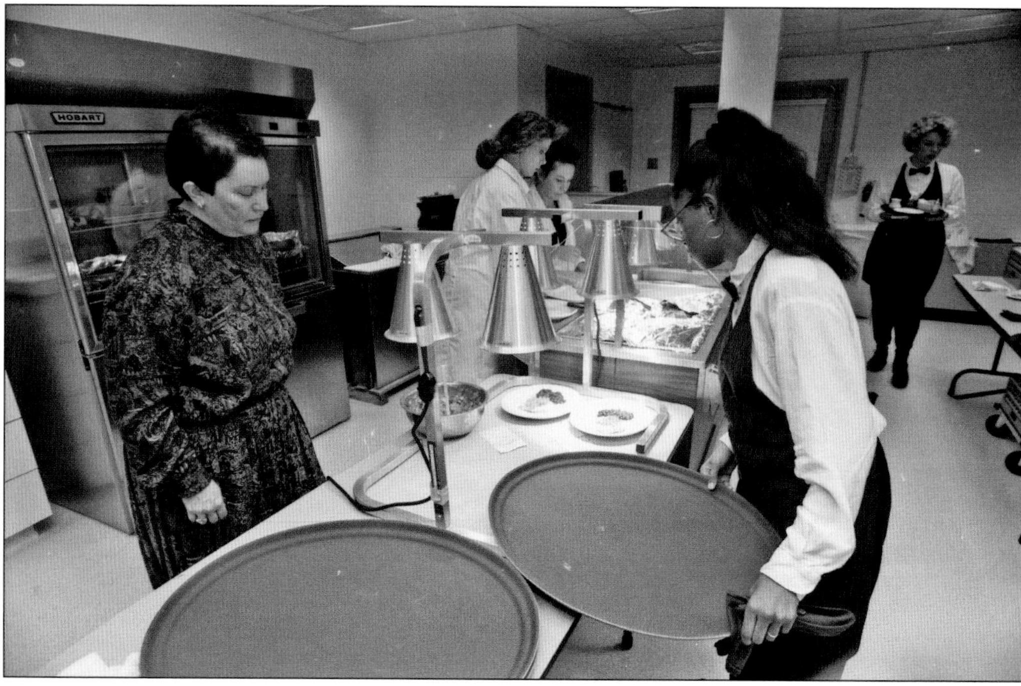

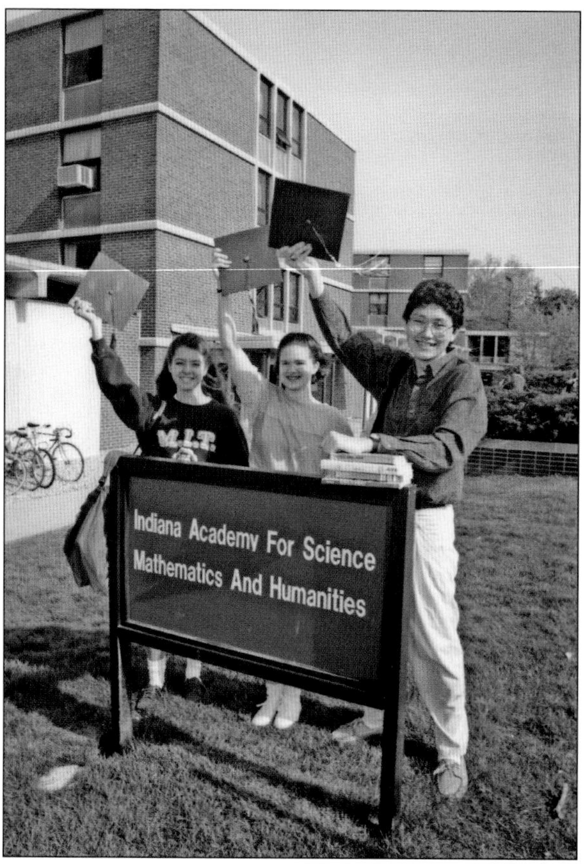

Allègre, Ball State University's student-run restaurant, opened its doors in 1991 on the first floor of the Practical Arts Building, allowing family and consumer science students in hospitality and food management to gain practical experience in their field.

The Indiana Academy for Science, Mathematics, and Humanities, a residential high school administered by Ball State University, opened its doors in 1991 to gifted and talented high school students from around Indiana. Seen in the spring of 1992 are some of the first graduates of the academy posing at Wagoner Hall, a former Ball State residence hall repurposed to house academy students.

Ball State University's Teachers College has included some of the institution's most robust research and graduate teaching programs. Renowned neuropsychology researcher Raymond Dean, seen here with a student in 1990, served as the George and Frances Ball Distinguished Professor of Neuropsychology and director of the Neuropsychology Laboratory at Ball State from 1984 until his passing in 2015.

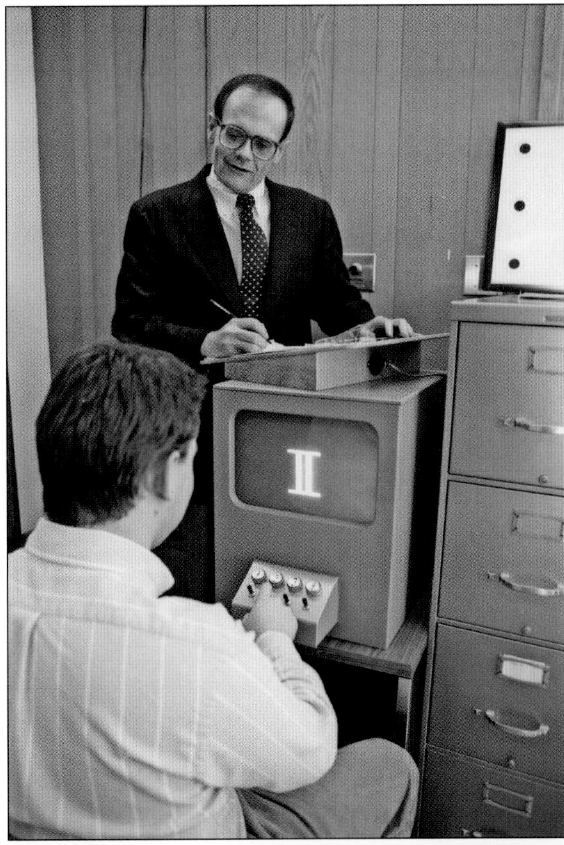

Beginning in the 1960s, Ball State proactively provided distance education offerings via television broadcasts to connect and deliver education content to students throughout Indiana. Here, secondary education students in the Teachers College interact with students remotely via television.

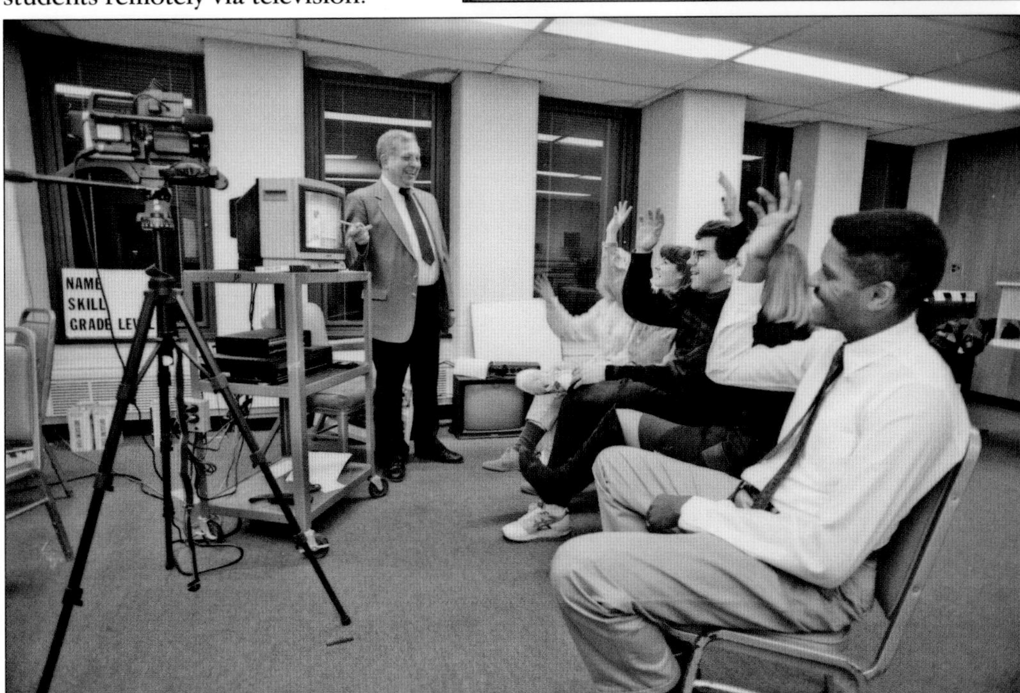

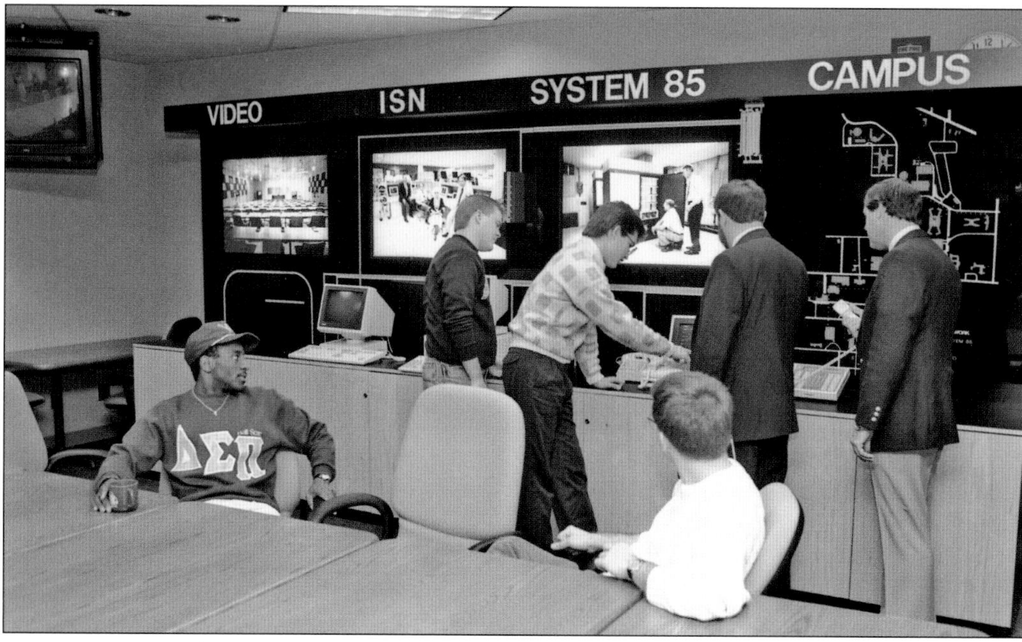

Founded in 1986, Ball State's Center for Information and Communication Science has offered master's degrees to students seeking competitive job placement in informational and communication management fields. Pictured in 1989, faculty and graduate students operate the controls of the university's telecommunications network.

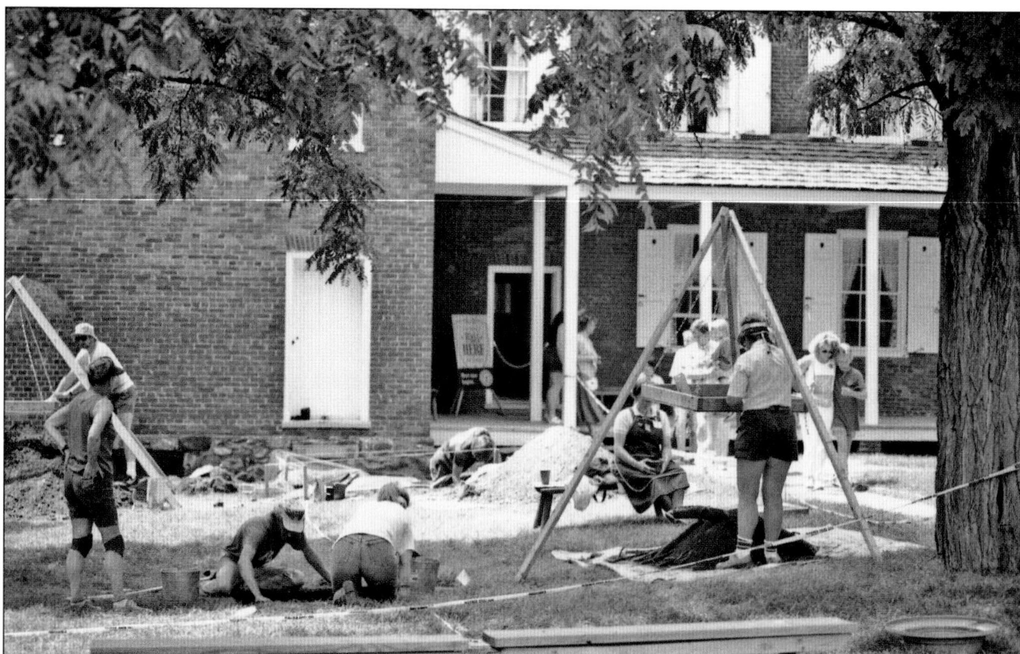

Here, Ball State University students participate in an archaeology excavation sponsored by the Department of Anthropology in the summer of 1990. Anthropology students could participate in a number of cultural field schools regionally, nationally, and internationally, providing broad exposure to varied archaeological fieldwork.

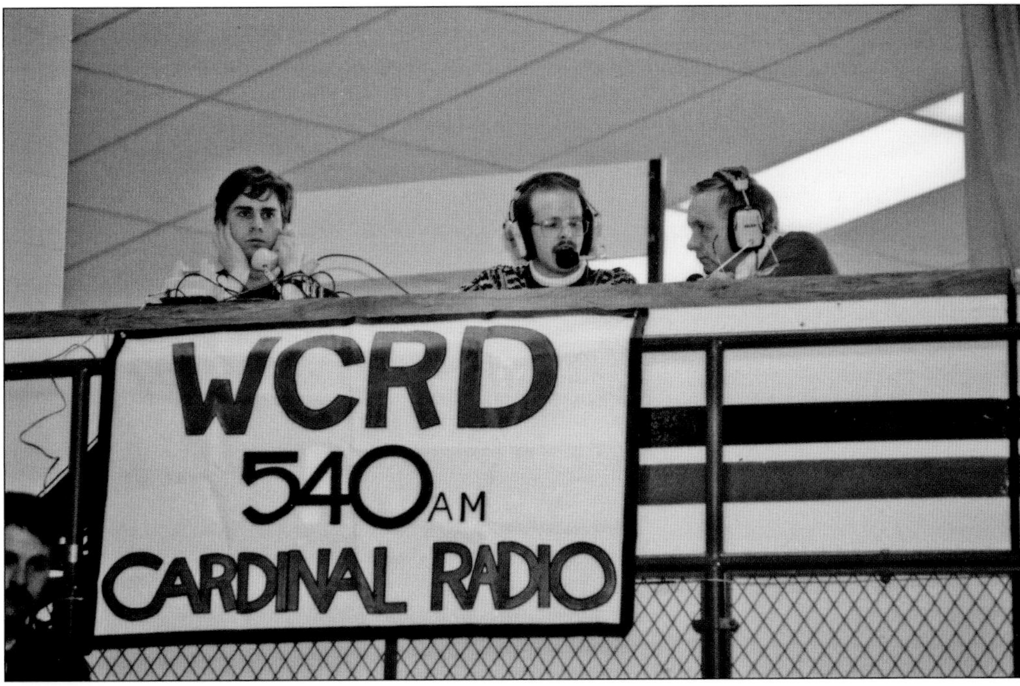

Ball State's student radio station, WCRD, began broadcasting music, talk, and sports programming on 540 AM in March 1989, supported by a $60,000 grant from Ball State alumnus and talk show host David Letterman. Covering a basketball game from University Gymnasium in the winter of 1990, student broadcasters interview Ball State president John Worthen during a break in the action.

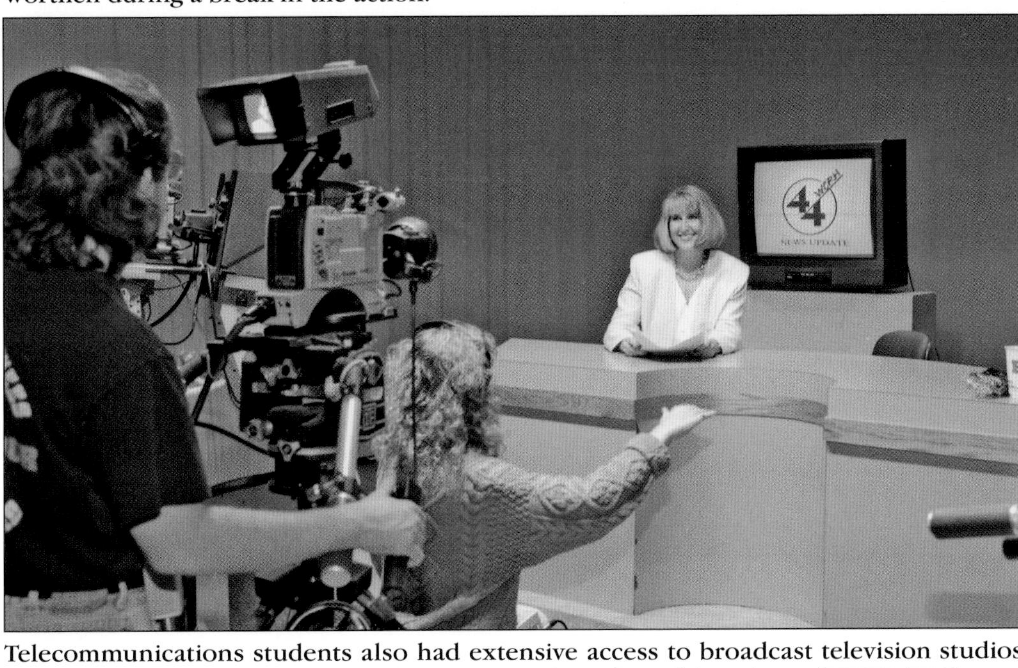

Telecommunications students also had extensive access to broadcast television studios, equipment, and opportunities. Seen here is an October 26, 1994, broadcast of WCHR-TV Channel 44's *News Update* program with the student director, camera operator, and newscaster.

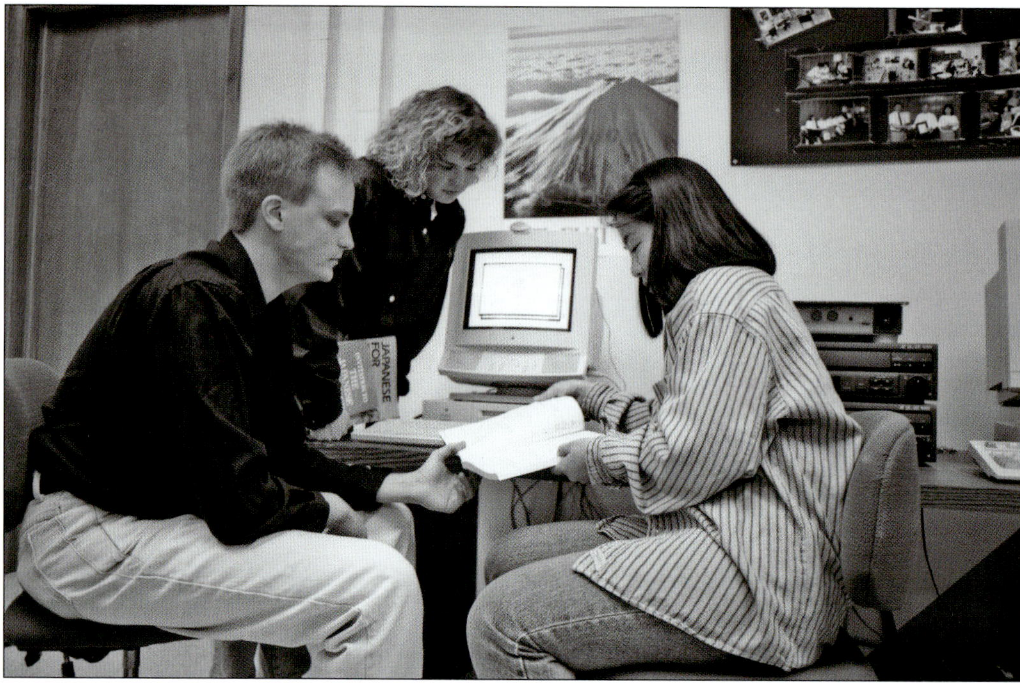

Technology was widely adopted in humanities classrooms on the Ball State campus as well as in more applied disciplines. Here, modern and classical languages students explore a computer program to learn Japanese vocabulary and phrases in 1990.

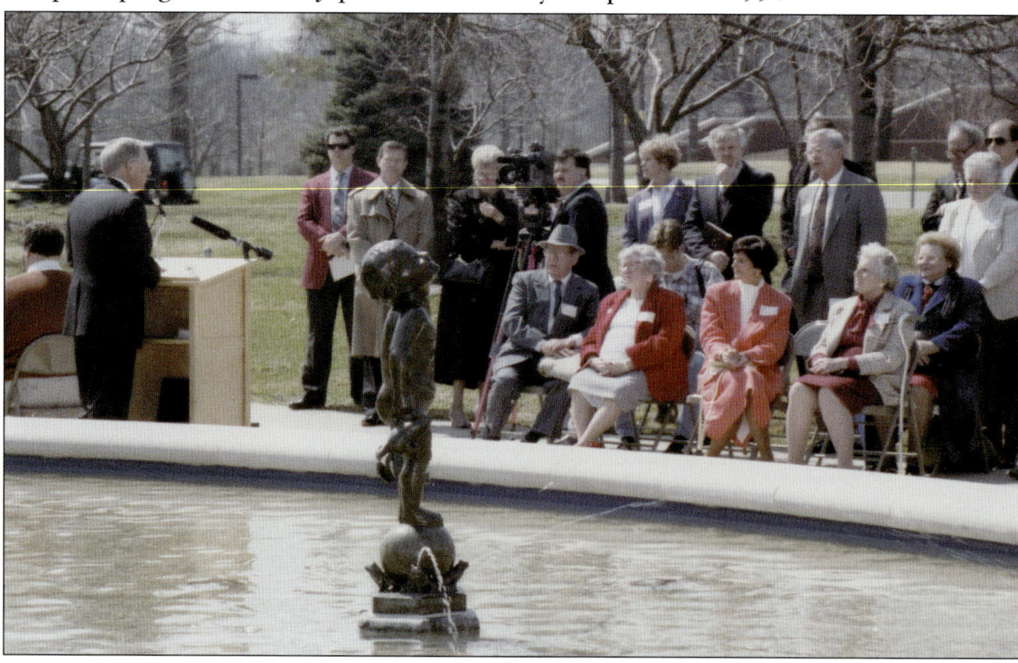

The *Frog Baby* statue was given a new home in the Bracken Garden adjacent to Bracken Library, dedicated on April 1, 1994. Already an iconic part of campus culture in its former location in the Ball State Museum of Art, the relocated *Frog Baby* helped beautify the campus's northern green spaces.

The new Alumni Center soon became one of the crown jewels of the campus, boasting over 50,000 square feet of space for offices, meeting rooms, and reception areas for hosting alumni programming and major conferences. Designed by renowned architects Pei, Cobb, Freed & Partners, the building opened during the 1997–1998 academic year.

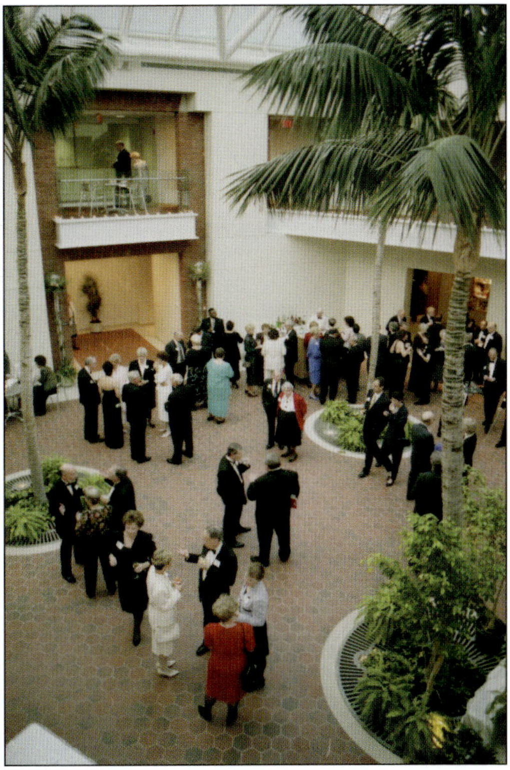

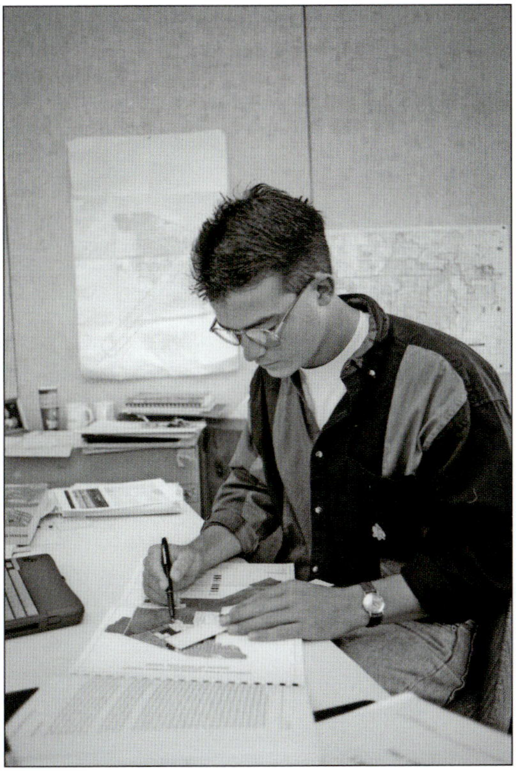

Pictured in October 1994, an urban planning student in the College of Architecture and Planning completes a neighborhood profile report. Through combining scholarship, research, and community engagement, Ball State's urban planning program provides students with hands-on experience aimed toward improving quality of life in the region.

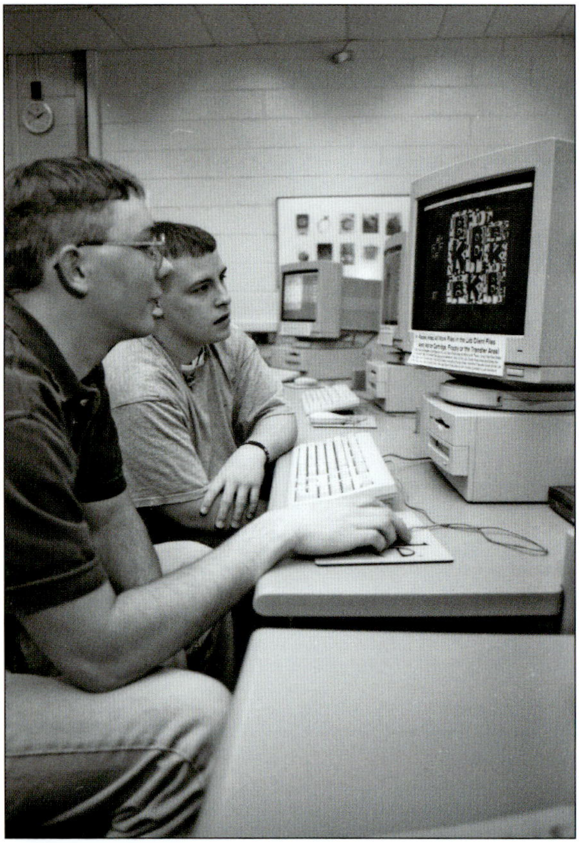

A computer laboratory in the Robert P. Bell Building is shown in 1997 occupied by computer science students exploring programming and digital art.

In 1997, Ball State founded the College of Communication, Information, and Media, bringing together the telecommunications, journalism, and speech communication departments as well as the Center for Information and Communication Sciences program. Earl Conn, the first dean of the college, is shown speaking at a ceremony for the founding of the college alongside (from left to right) Provost Warren Vander Hill, Trustee Jeffrey Smulyan, and Pres. John Worthen.

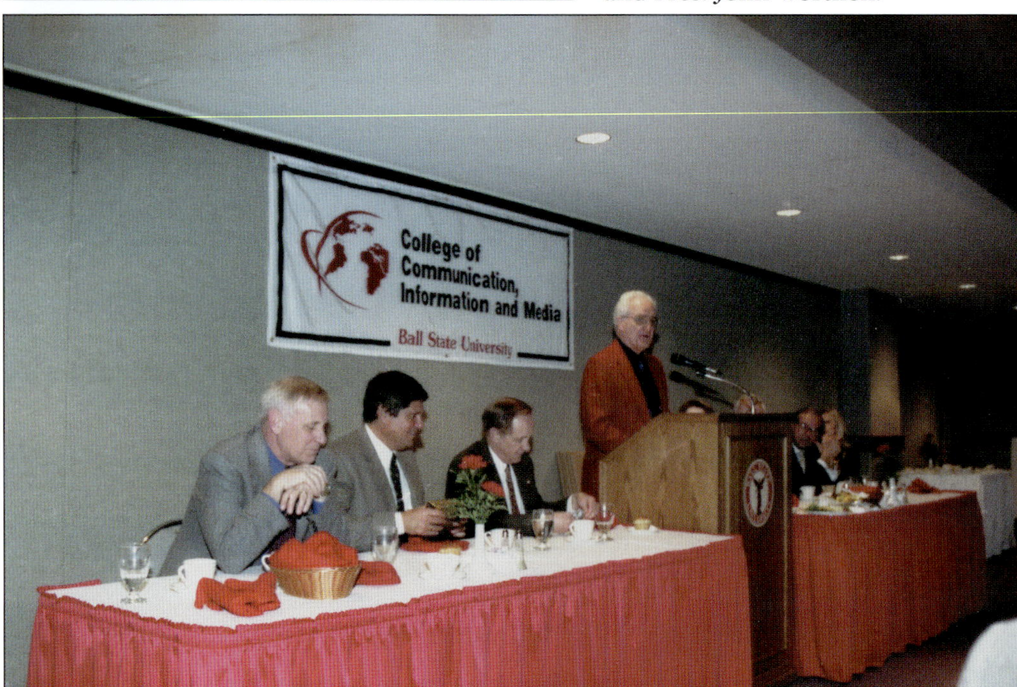

Gymnast Sarah Mikrut, elected to the Ball State Athletics Hall of Fame during the 2007–2008 school year, enjoyed a decorated career as a Cardinal. Mikrut scored the first perfect 10 in any gymnastics event in university history, earning this mark on the vault against Kent State in 1997. She also holds the distinction of being the only female gymnast at Ball State to compete in the NCAA Championships.

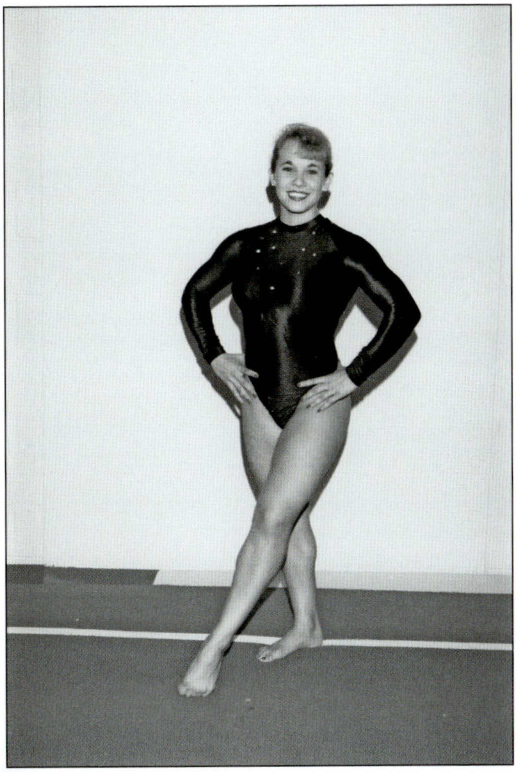

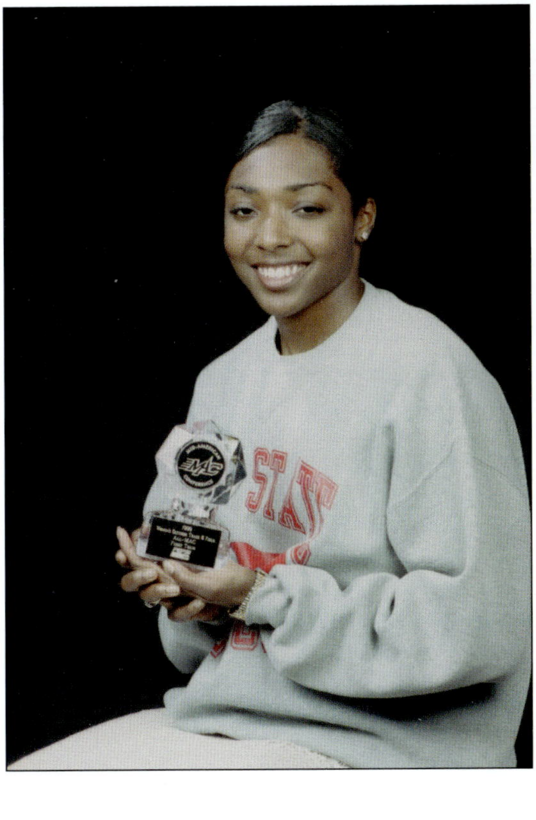

Latasha Jenkins was an outstanding performer in track and field for the Cardinals. In 1999, she won Ball State's first individual title in the NCAA Championships when she ran to victory in the 200-meter dash. She is shown as the recipient of the 1999 First Team All-MAC women's outdoor track and field honor.

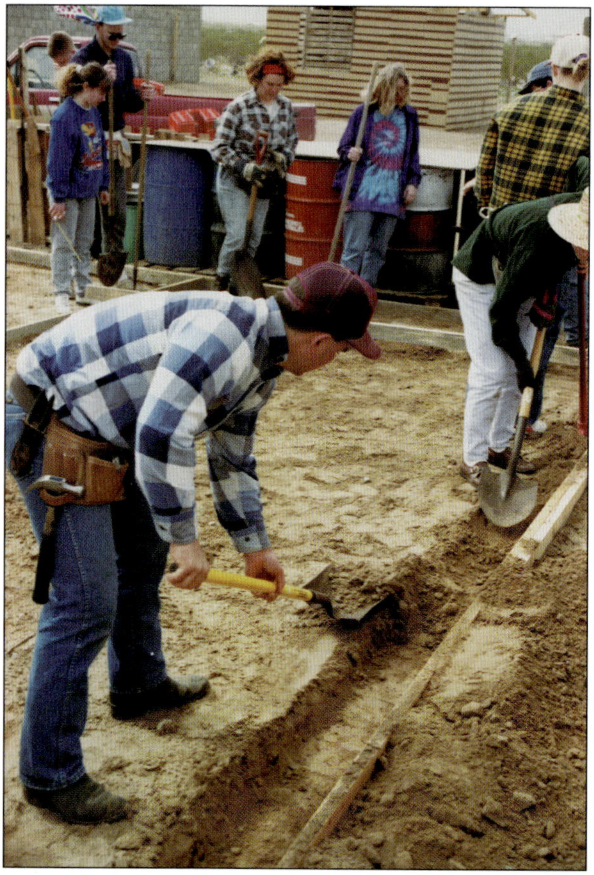

Ball State students, faculty, and staff during the era continued the university's proud tradition of contributing to local volunteer and charity efforts. Shown here in March 1995, students participate in the construction of a Habitat for Humanity house.

Bracken House, the former home of Alexander M. and Rosemary Bracken, was constructed in 1937 in Muncie's historic Westwood neighborhood. It was bequeathed to the university in 1998. The home was later renovated and established as a home for Ball State University's president and family.

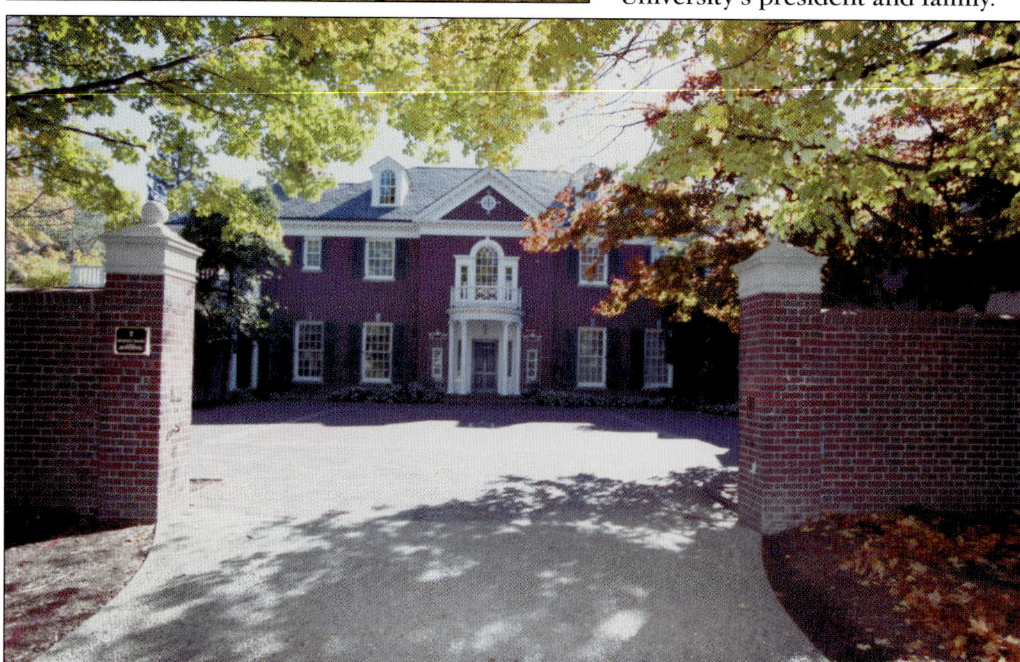

Six

The Entrepreneurial University

2000–Present

Ball State University entered the 21st century with positive momentum. Everywhere one looked, change was taking place. Students and faculty used the internet and smartphones to communicate with each other instead of making local and long-distance telephone calls. Laptop computers became valuable tools that were appearing in classrooms and meeting rooms across campus. Ball State's physical assets also changed dramatically, as two new residence halls (Park Hall and Kinghorn Hall), the Student Fitness and Wellness Center, and a geothermal heating and cooling system were constructed on campus.

In the 21st century, Ball State embraced the concept of the entrepreneurial university, in the sense that risk-taking and innovation became the new signposts. The trend toward entrepreneurialism found visibility in three new initiatives between 2000 and 2017: a renewed emphasis on internationalizing the campus; the widespread adoption of immersive learning as a new form of pedagogy; and the introduction of online education.

First, a renewed emphasis on internationalization began during the tenure of Blaine A. Brownell, Ball State's president from 2000 to 2004. By 2014, there were 800 international students from 79 countries enrolled on campus. Students from China, South Korea, India, Saudi Arabia, and Turkey comprised the largest groups of internationals.

Second, the concept of immersive learning began at Ball State with the creation of the Virginia B. Ball Center for Creative Inquiry in 2001. Participants in this program formed faculty-student teams that solved "real world" problems and featured a community dimension. Immersive learning became a hallmark of the leadership of Jo Ann M. Gora, Ball State's president from 2004 to 2014, and the university adopted the "Education Redefined" tagline in 2006 to signify the value of these community-engaged experiences to Ball State's identity. By 2013, more than 16,000 students had participated in 1,000 immersive learning projects.

Third, Ball State embraced the nationwide trend toward online learning. Ball State began offering online courses in 2005. Within a decade, more than 500 faculty members at Ball State offered online instruction. Ball State scheduled more than 700 courses that used this modality.

Over the first two decades of the 21st century, Ball State became a truly modern university. Through its academic programs, athletics events, and cultural attractions, Ball State was firmly embedded in the fabric of community life in Indiana.

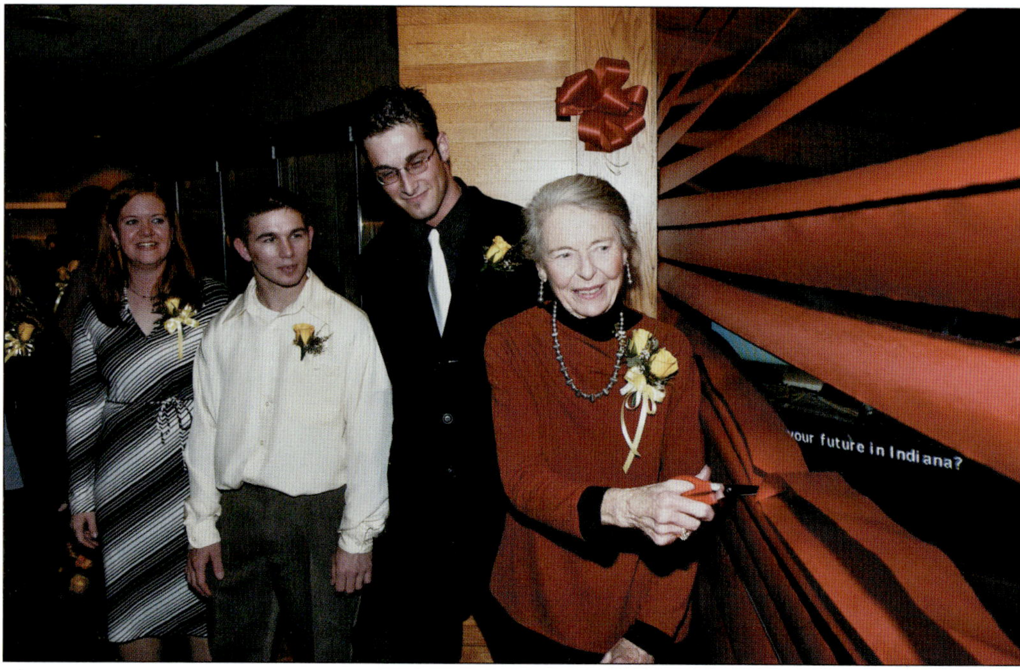

The Virginia B. Ball Center for Creative Inquiry was established in 2001 to foster immersive learning projects at Ball State. Virginia Ball, wife of Edmund F. Ball, was a graduate of Baylor University and held a lifelong interest in the humanities. In this photograph, Virginia Ball cuts the ribbon on a student seminar at the Minnetrista Cultural Center.

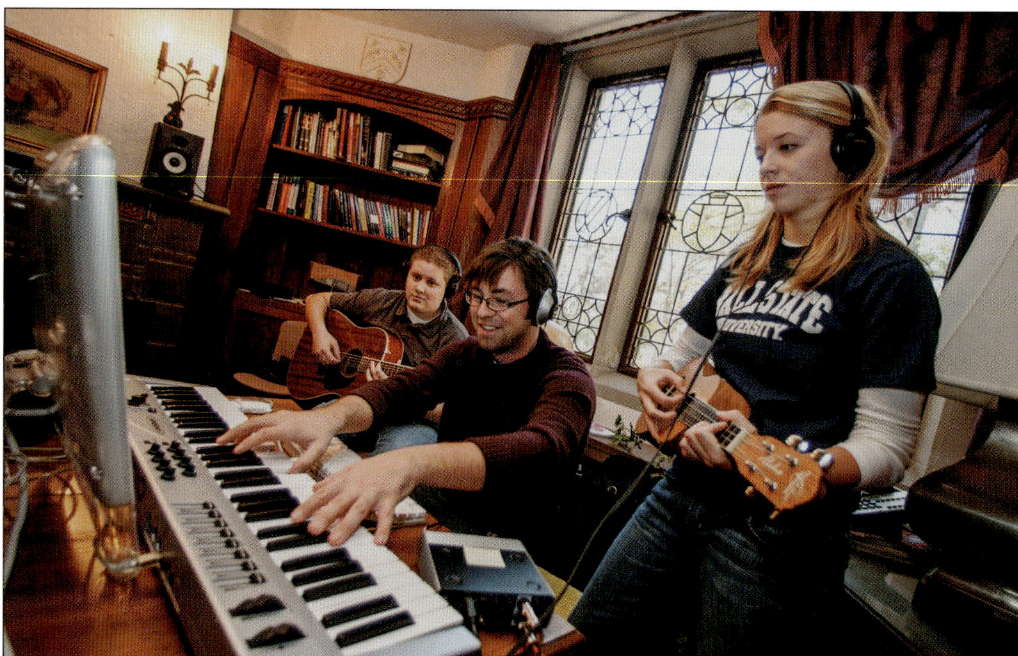

The Virginia B. Ball Center for Creative Inquiry provides semester-long fellowships to faculty members and students who collaborate on projects that have an academic and community dimension. Here, music students participate in one of the center's projects.

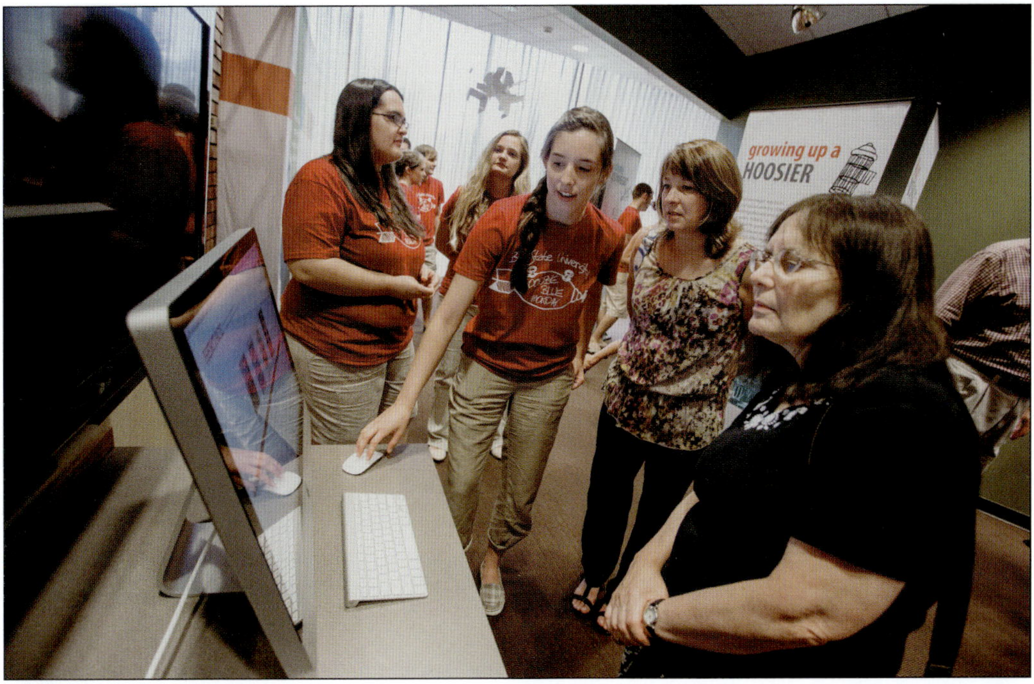

Between 2012 and 2014, a team of faculty and students, led by Rai Peterson of the English Department and Russ Wahlers of the Marketing Department, implemented an immersive learning project titled Keeping Kurt Vonnegut's Voice in Indiana. One of the main outcomes of the project was a traveling exhibit of Vonnegut's literary materials, shown here. Elizabeth Riddle, professor of English, stands at right.

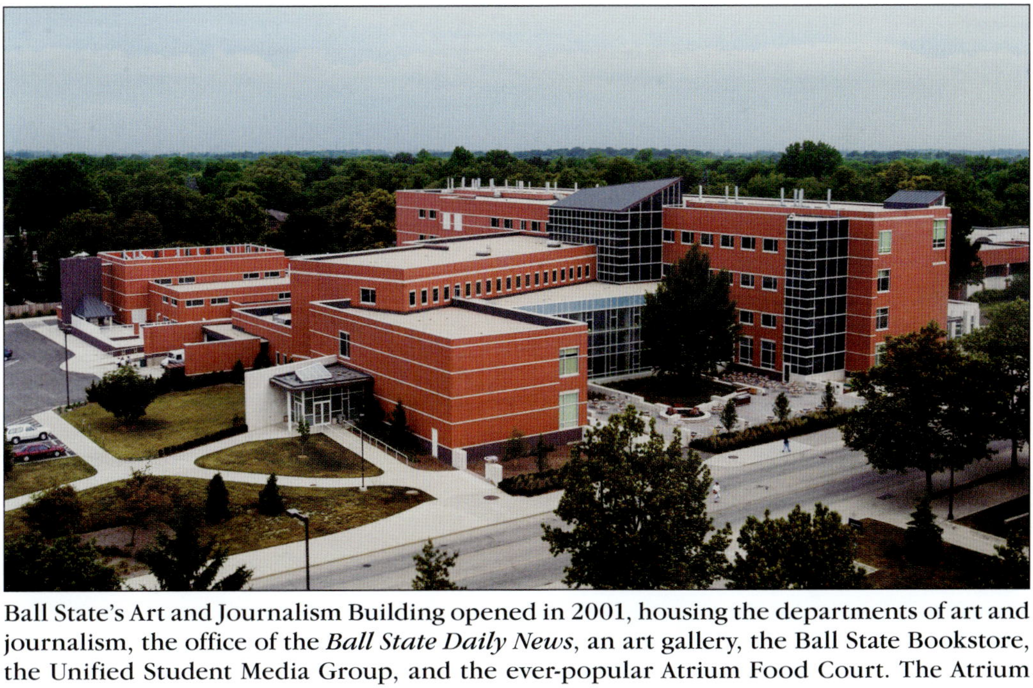

Ball State's Art and Journalism Building opened in 2001, housing the departments of art and journalism, the office of the *Ball State Daily News*, an art gallery, the Ball State Bookstore, the Unified Student Media Group, and the ever-popular Atrium Food Court. The Atrium quickly became a gathering place on campus for both students and faculty.

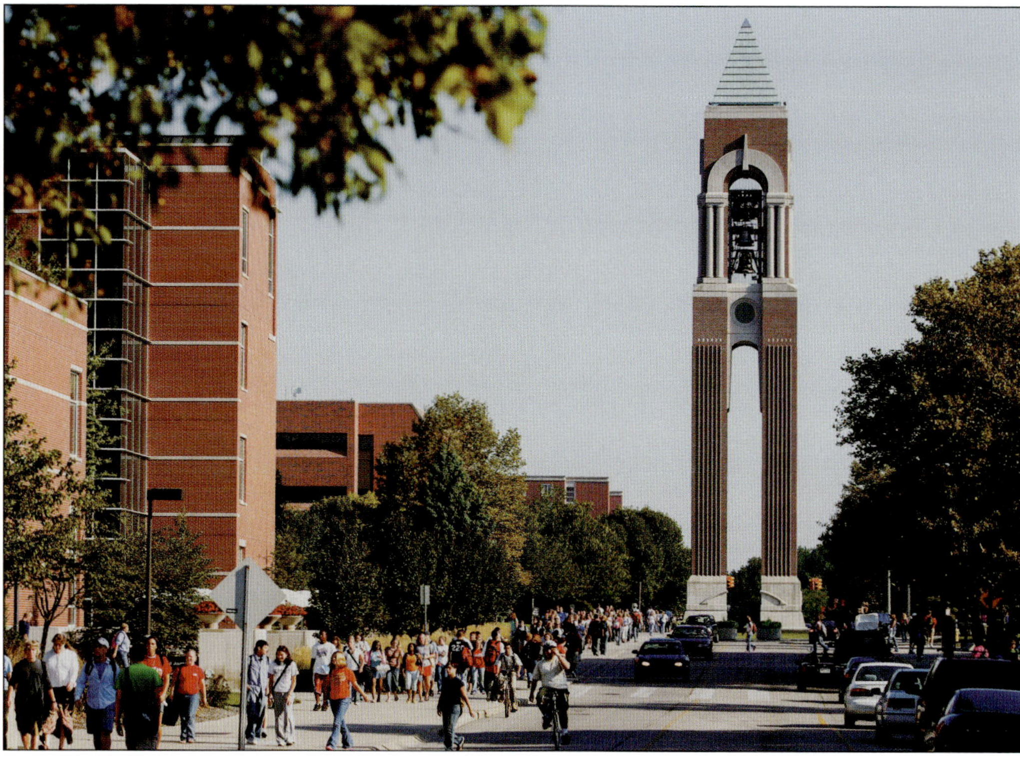

Shafer Tower on McKinley Avenue, finished in 2001, is the centerpiece of the north end of the Ball State campus. Shafer Tower is named in honor of Hamer and Phyllis Shafer, members of the Miller College of Business Hall of Fame and benefactors of Ball State and the Muncie community. The tower rises 150 feet and includes a carillon with 48 custom-made bells.

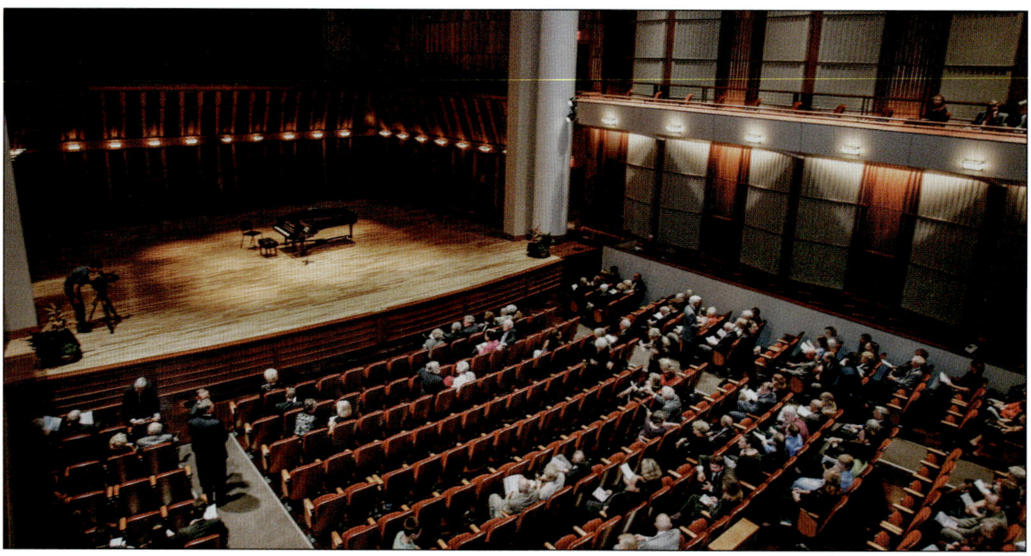

Named in honor of David Sursa, a prominent Muncie businessman, and his wife, Mary Jane, the Sursa Performance Hall in Ball State's new Music Instruction Building was completed in 2004. The auditorium featured the latest in acoustic advancements. David and Mary Jane Sursa contributed $1 million for the purchase of the 50-stop Sursa Family Concert Organ.

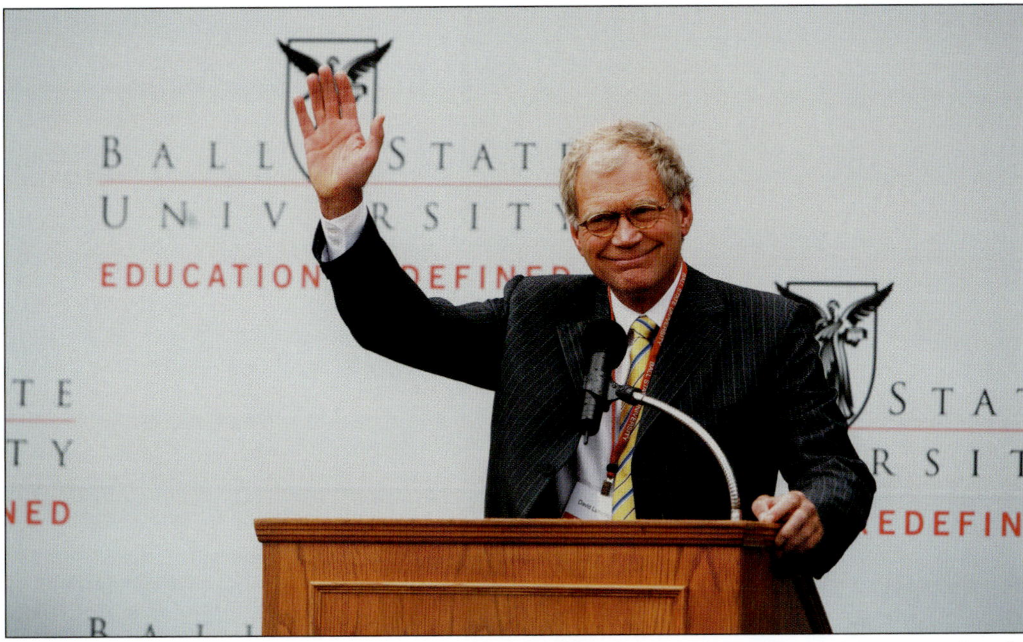

David Letterman, the well-known television celebrity and alumnus of the class of 1969, appeared on campus for the dedication of the building named in his honor in October 2007. In addition to supporting programs in telecommunications, Letterman also established a scholarship for students interested in the field. The David Letterman Building features state-of-the-art equipment for students and faculty involved in media-related projects. The Letterman Building includes two recording studios, two control rooms, two isolation rooms, and five editing suites, and its facilities compare favorably to those found in production houses and film studios in Hollywood, New York, and London.

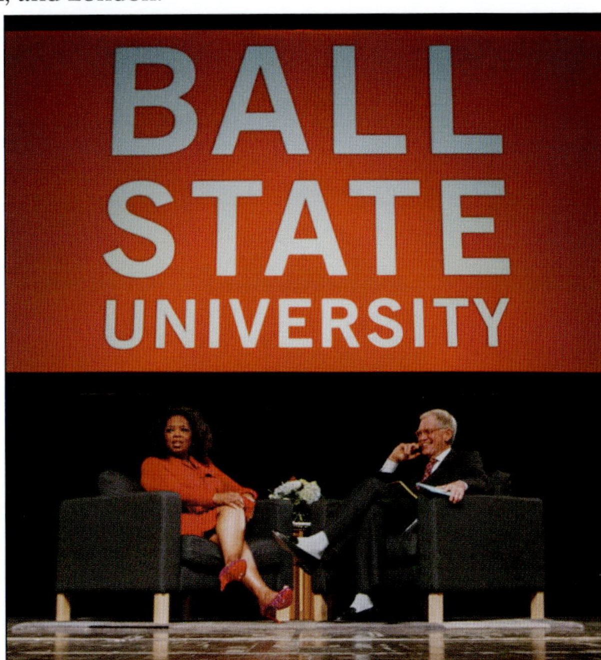

Letterman also established the David Letterman Distinguished Professional Lecture and Workshop Series, bringing technology and communication leaders to campus for the benefit of an audience of students and community members. The 2012 series featured a conversation between David Letterman and media entrepreneur and talk show host Oprah Winfrey attended by a capacity crowd at Emens Auditorium and live-streamed at Pruis Hall and the Pittenger Student Center.

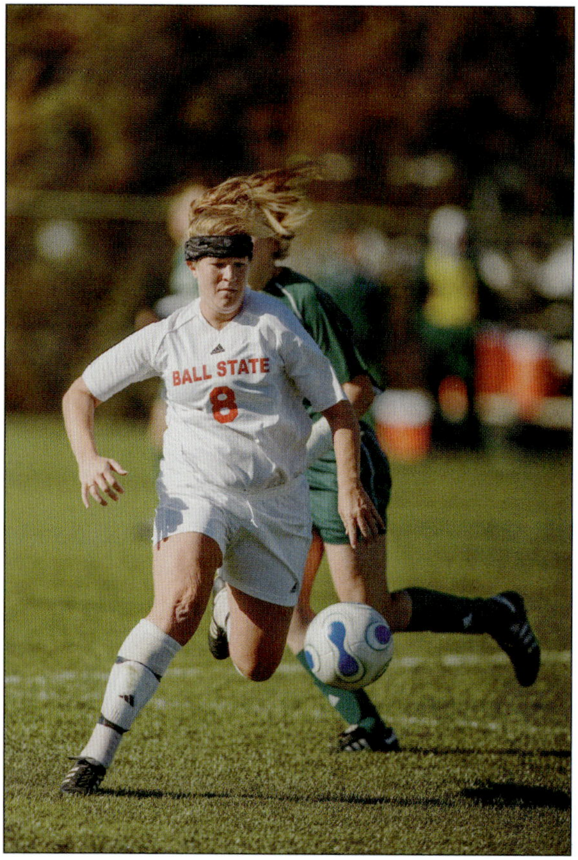

Ball State's women's soccer team won back-to-back MAC championships in 2006 and 2007. Shown are members of the 2006 team. Michele Salmon coached the teams, which were the first in program history to win MAC championships.

Formerly known as Ball State Stadium, the home to Ball State University's football team was renamed Scheumann Stadium after John and June Scheumann, Ball State alumni who made generous contributions to the football program. John Scheumann graduated from Ball State in 1971 and was a standout defensive tackle on the football team.

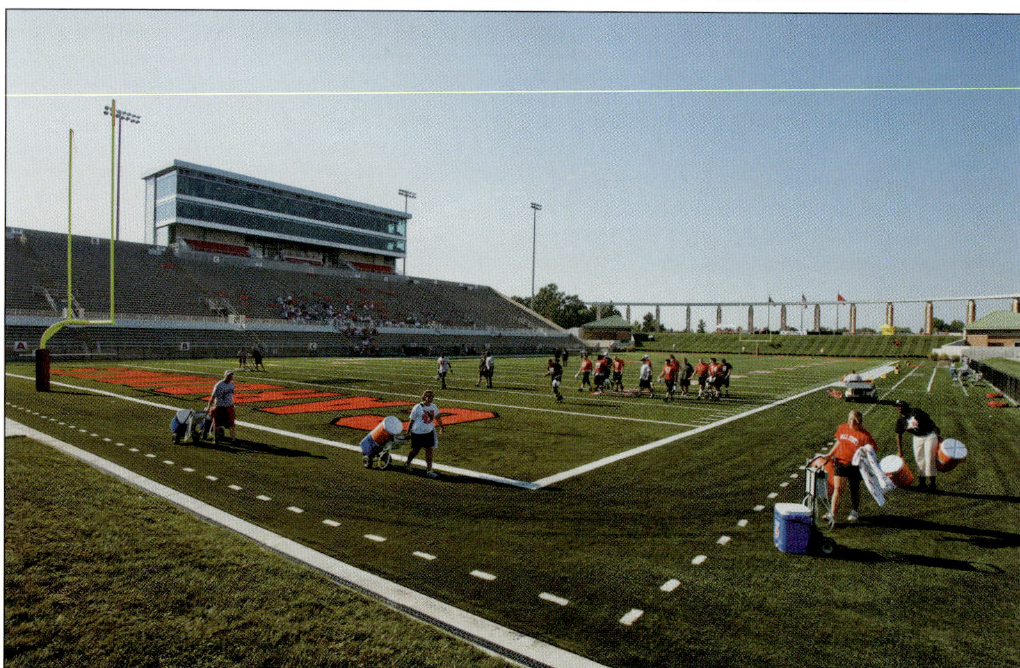

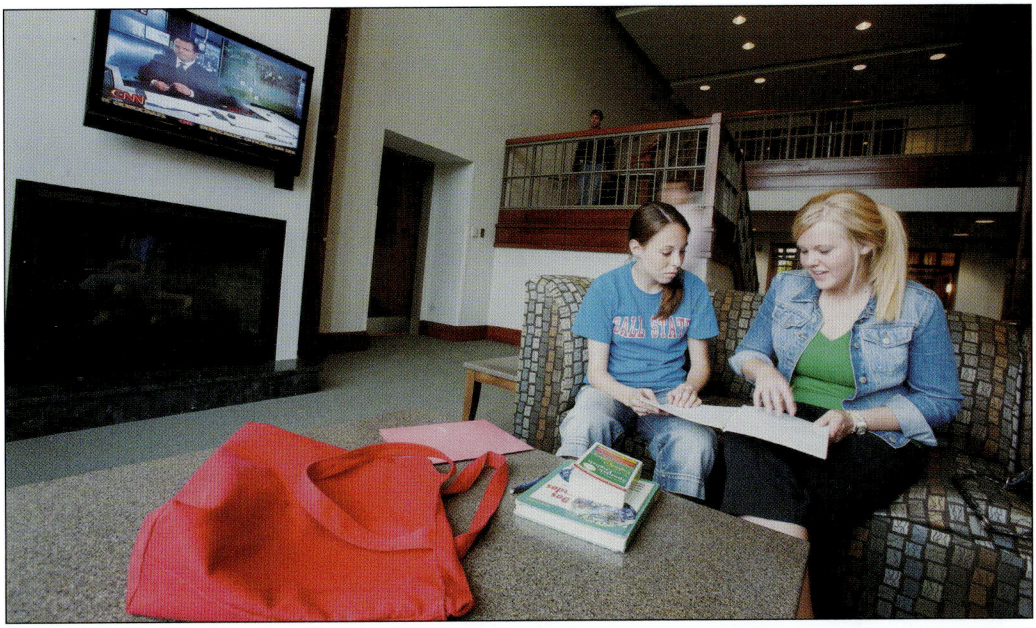

Park Hall, the first residence hall constructed at Ball State since 1969, opened in 2007. Close to several academic buildings, as well as Bracken Library and Emens Auditorium, Park Hall was named in honor of Don L. Park, a Ball State alumnus who served as vice president for university advancement from 1992 to 2007.

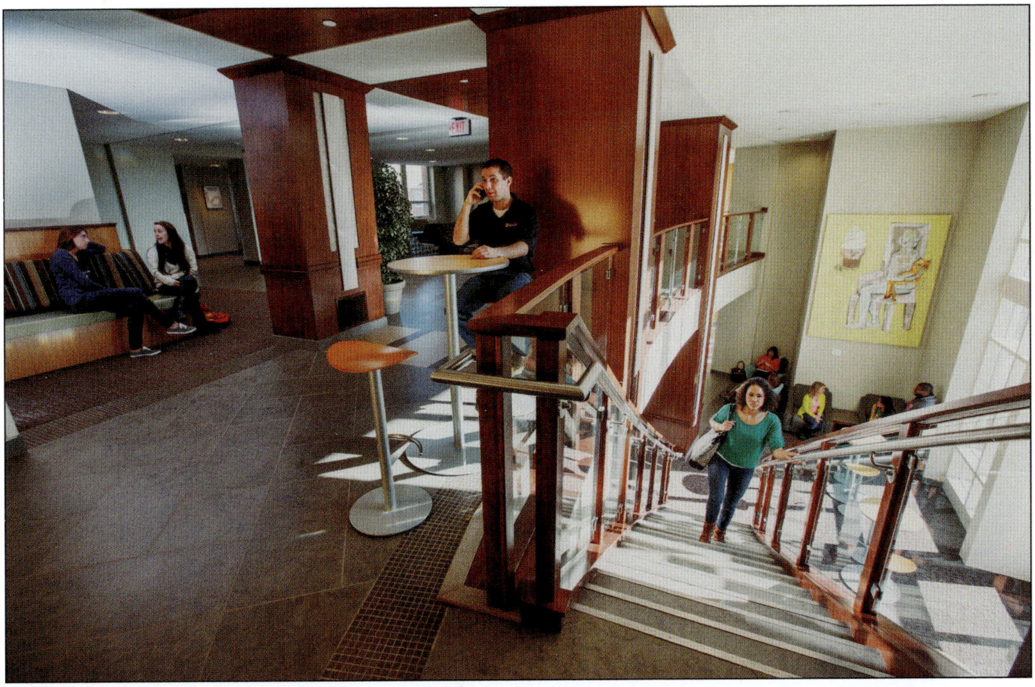

Kinghorn Hall was completed in 2010 and acknowledged for its energy efficiency, meeting certification standards for Leadership in Energy and Environmental Design (LEED). Kinghorn Hall was named in honor of Thomas J. Kinghorn, a Ball State alumnus who was vice president for business affairs and treasurer from 1980 to 2009.

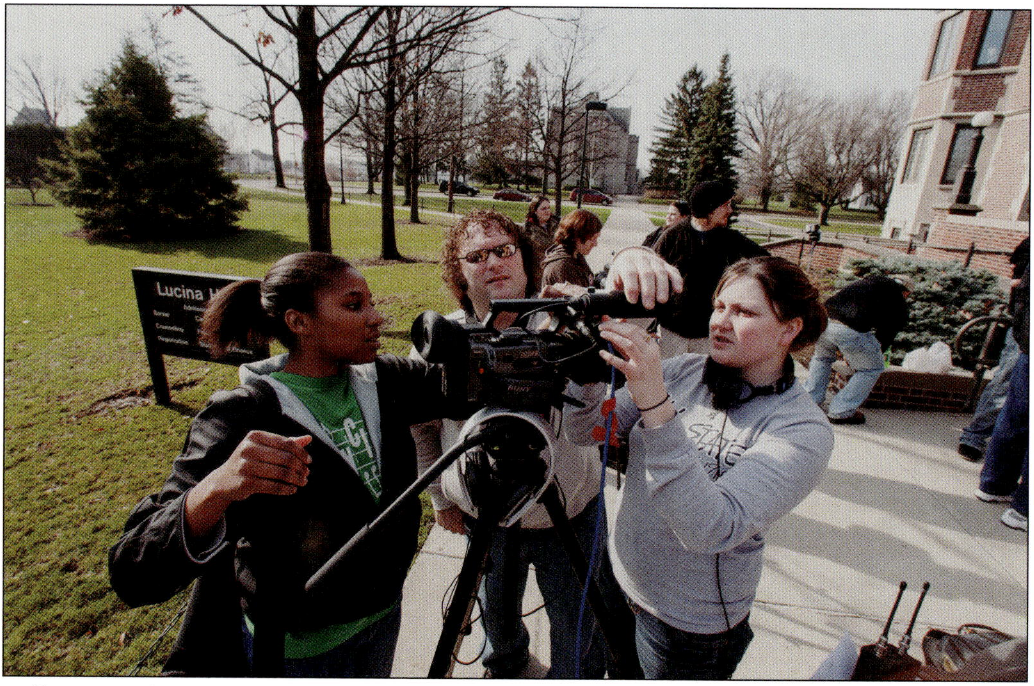

Ball State's telecommunications students gather for the filming of a project outside of Lucina Hall on campus. Telecommunications students working on their projects have become a familiar sight on campus.

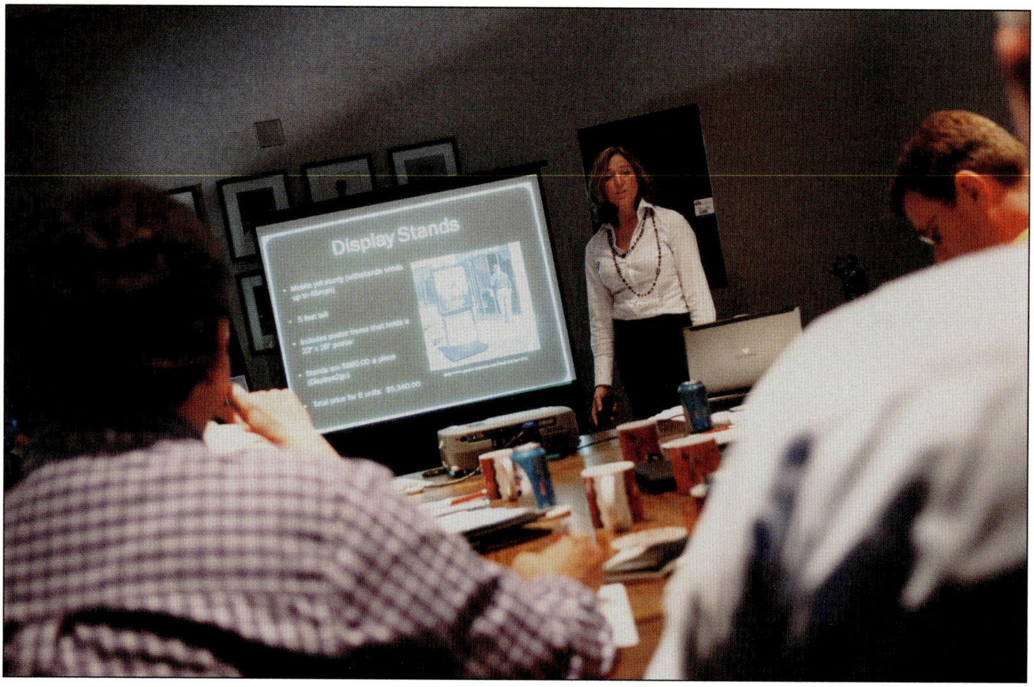

In 2008, Miller College of Business students practice delivering a presentation to pitch an entrepreneurial idea to an investor. Noted for its active and engaged student body, Miller College of Business includes over 15 sponsored student affinity groups and honorary societies.

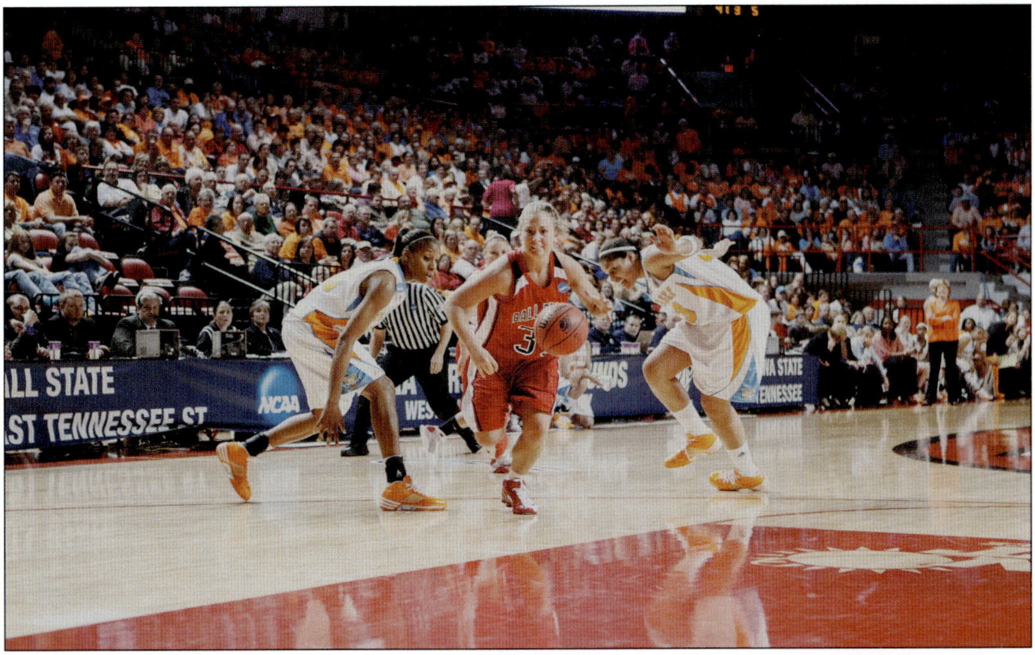

In 2009, Ball State's women's basketball team participated in its first ever NCAA Tournament. Facing off against the University of Tennessee, a perennial power, Ball State earned a stunning upset victory by the score of 71-55, marking the greatest win in program history.

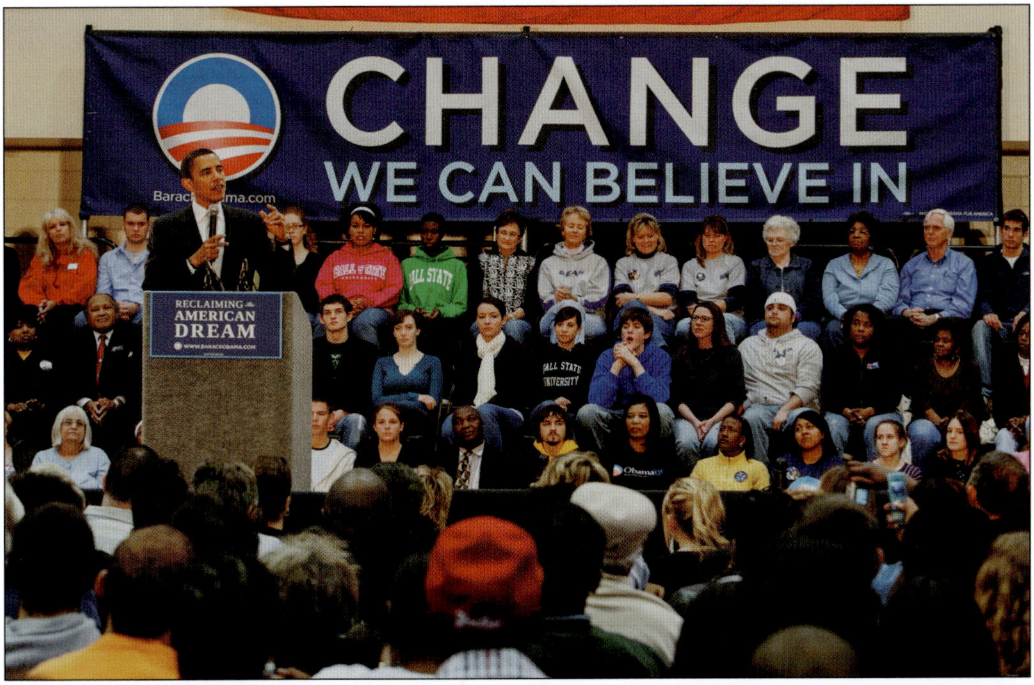

On April 12, 2008, Sen. Barack Obama brought his "Road to Change" presidential campaign to Ball State. Speaking in Irving Gymnasium, the same location where Sen. Robert F. Kennedy addressed a campaign rally in 1968, Senator Obama spoke to a crowd of 3,500 comprised of students, faculty, and members of the community.

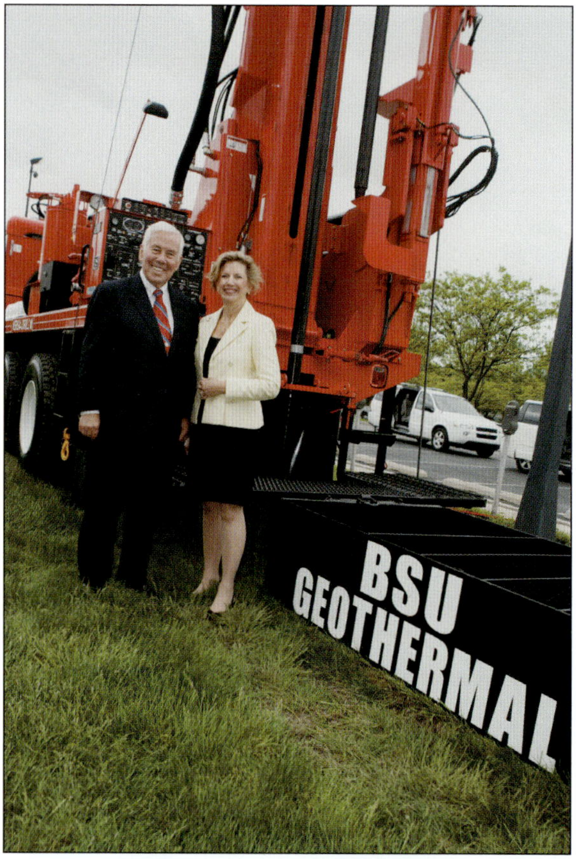

Ball State began work on its massive geothermal energy system in 2009. The system was designed to heat and cool 47 campus buildings and result in an annual cost savings of $2 million while advancing Ball State's overall goal of sustainability. Pictured are Sen. Richard G. Lugar of Indiana, a supporter of the geothermal project, and Ball State University president Jo Ann M. Gora at the ground-breaking of Ball State's geothermal infrastructure.

Angela Ahrendts is a Ball State alumna who has become a leader in the fashion and technology industries, both in the United States and in Great Britain. On May 8, 2010, she delivered the address at the spring commencement where she also received an honorary doctor of laws degree.

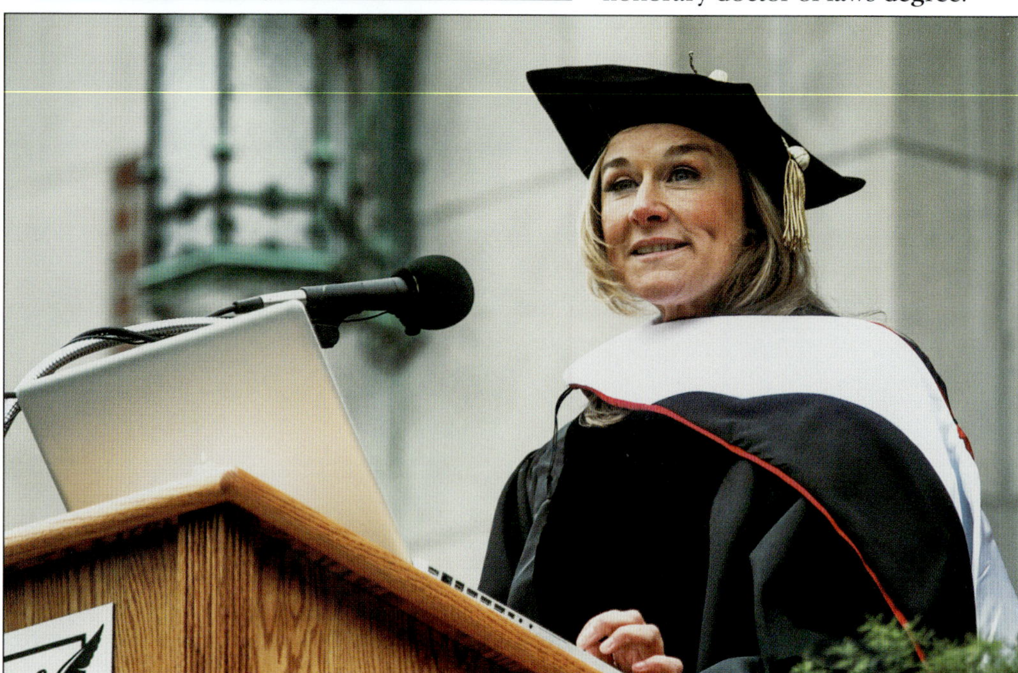

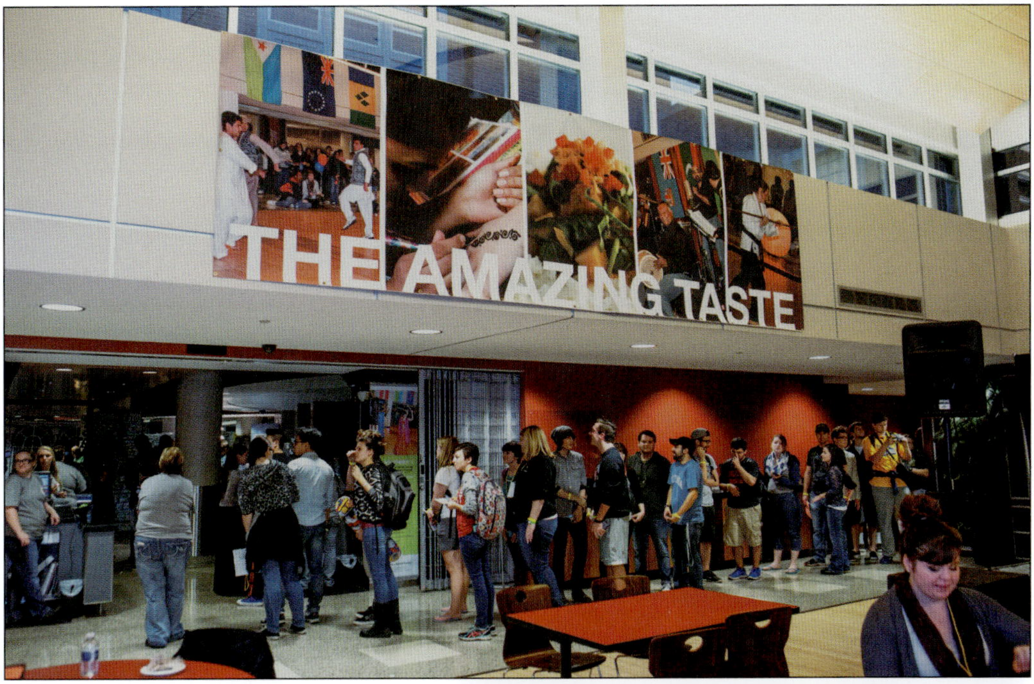

The Amazing Taste, shown here in 2015 in the Pittenger Student Center, celebrates international life on campus through cultural displays, music and dance performances, international food offerings, and a world fashion show. The 2015 event featured food from more than 18 countries as well as 15 dance and musical performances from Ball State University students.

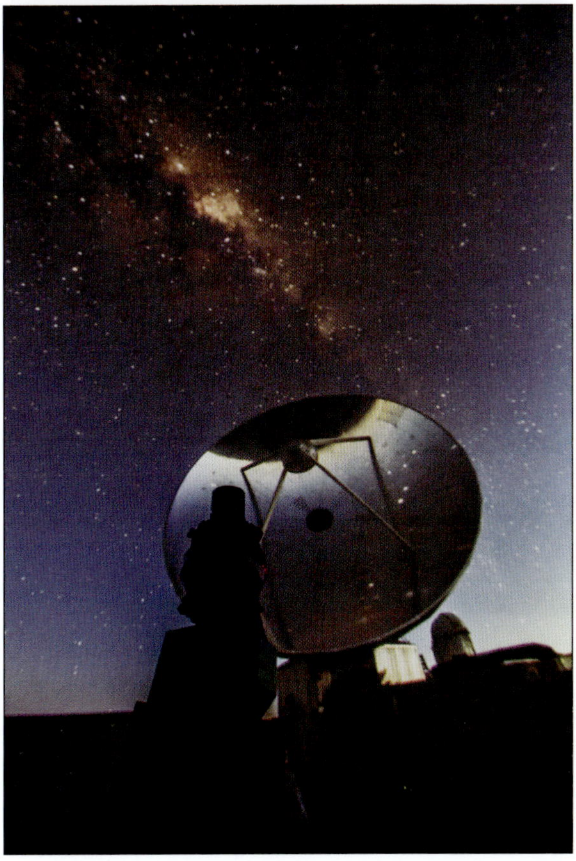

Ball State's Charles W. Brown Planetarium opened in 2014, replacing the older planetarium housed in the Cooper Science Building. The Charles W. Brown Planetarium is the largest in Indiana and has a seating capacity of 152. In its first year of operation, more than 20,500 visitors attended programs at the planetarium.

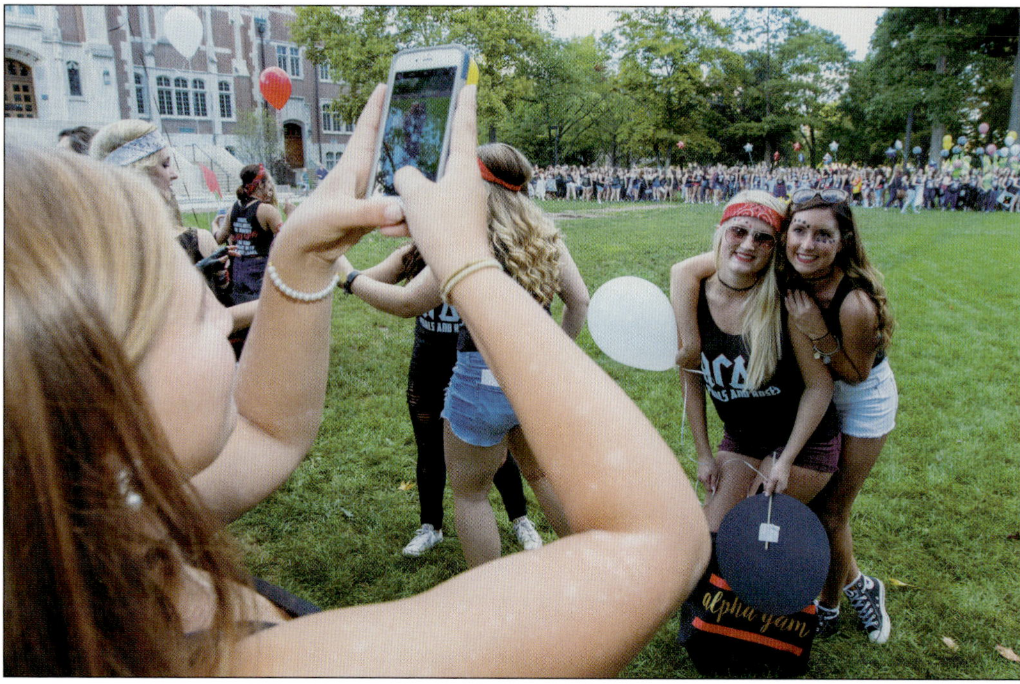

Members of Ball State's sororities gather in the Quad for Sorority Bid Day in 2016. Sorority Bid Day is historically a memorable event in Greek life at Ball State.

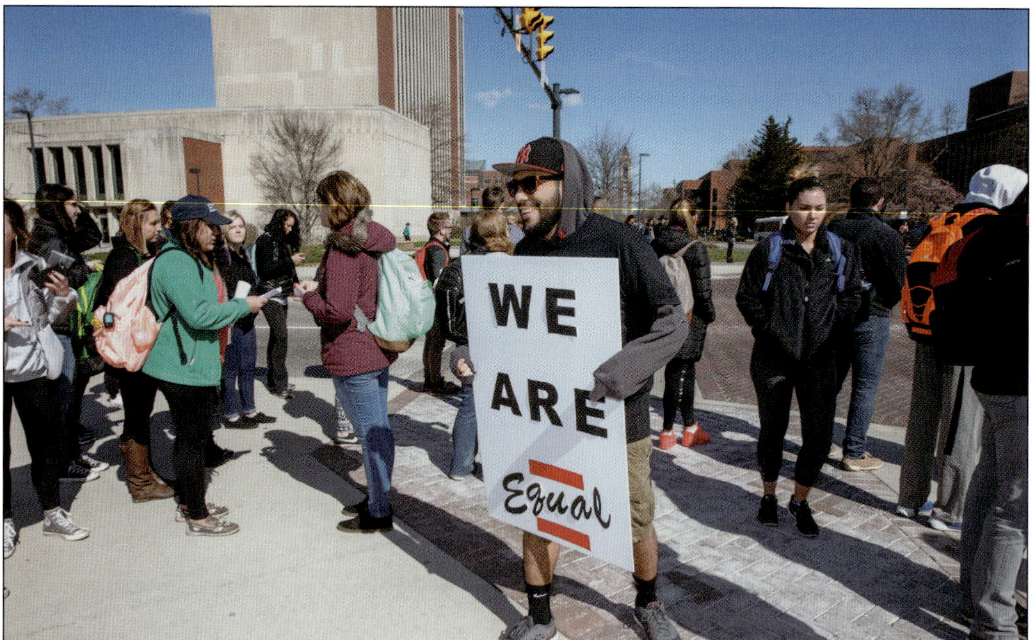

A member of the Latino Student Union participates in a "We Are Equal" march on March 24, 2016. The march from Shafer Tower to the David Owsley Museum of Art is an annual opportunity for members of the campus community to celebrate diversity and inclusion at Ball State.

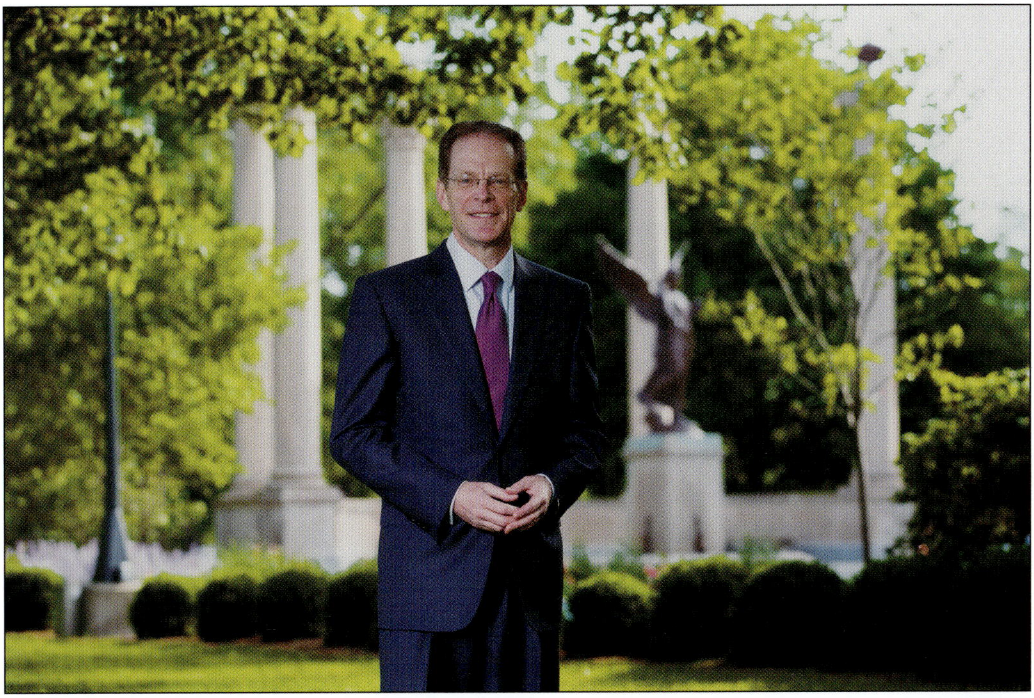

Geoffrey S. Mearns became the 17th president of Ball State University on May 15, 2017. Formerly the president of Northern Kentucky University, President Mearns holds a bachelor of arts degree in English from Yale University and a juris doctorate degree from the University of Virginia. He practiced law for 15 years with the Department of Justice before entering academic life. Prior to his presidency at Northern Kentucky University, he held senior faculty and administrative positions at the Cleveland-Marshall College of Law and served as provost and vice president for academic affairs at Cleveland State University.

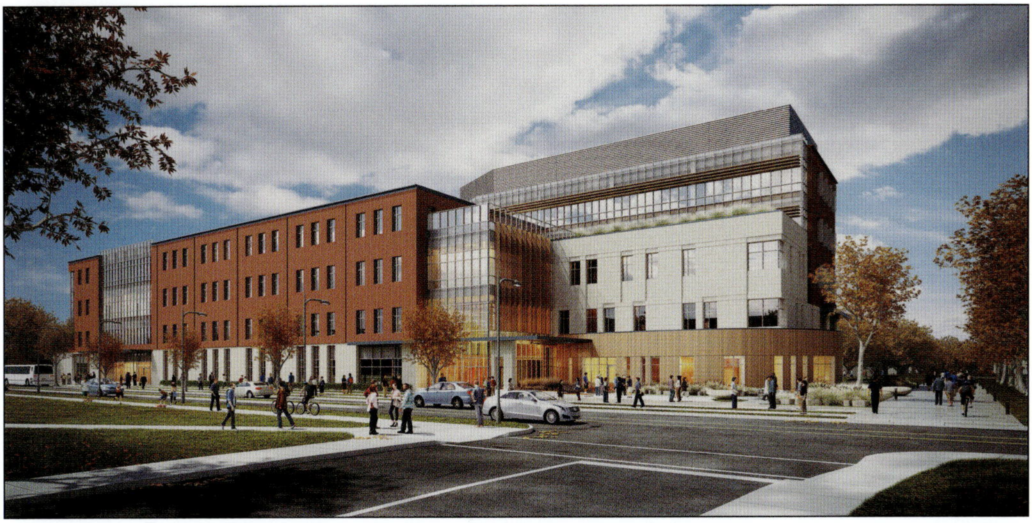

Shown here is an architect's rendering of Ball State's newest college, the College of Health Sciences, currently awaiting construction. The new building for the College of Health Sciences will enable the university to upgrade its scientific technology significantly for emerging fields in Science, Technology, Engineering, and Mathematics (STEM).